Advance Praise for *Breaking Good*

"In her inspiring and often heartbreaking memoir of addiction and recovery, *Breaking Good*, Nikki Mammano pulls readers deep into the underworld of Oahu, as she ricochets among club kids, drag queens, military men, and drug dealers. Mammano's brave and intimate story reveals the searing suffering of addiction, the painful complexity of family ties, and the extraordinary resilience and strength that people bring to recovery and healing. Nikki Mammano's wry and pointed perspective on her difficult, moving life in *Breaking Good* makes this memoir a must-read."

—**Piper Kerman,** author, *Orange Is the New Black*

breaking good

a memoir

breaking good

a memoir

nikki mammano

A REGALO PRESS BOOK
ISBN: 979-8-89565-168-1
ISBN (eBook): 979-8-89565-169-8

Breaking Good:
A Memoir

Cover design by Dan Castelli and Ora Castelli

Publishing Team:
Founder and Publisher – Gretchen Young
Managing Editor – Caitlin Burdette
Production Manager – Kate Harris
Production Editor – Rachel Paul

As part of the mission of Regalo Press, a donation is being made to Residential Youth Services and Empowerment (RYSE), as chosen by the author. Find out more about this organization at: www.rysehawaii.org.

This book, as well as any other Regalo Press publications, may be purchased in bulk quantities at a special discounted rate. Contact orders@regalopress.com for more information.

All people, locations, events, and situations are portrayed to the best of the author's memory. While all of the events described are true, many names and identifying details have been changed to protect the privacy of the people involved.

Regalo Press
New York • Nashville
regalopress.com

Published in the United States of America
Printed in Canada
1 2 3 4 5 6 7 8 9 10

For my daughters,
who healed my heart, showed me grace, and kept me in the game.
You are worth everything.

AUTHOR'S NOTE

The following is autobiographical. It is my lived experience as I remember it, and I remember it pretty damn well for someone who spent half her life on some very powerful drugs. That said, some liberties have been taken with dialogue for the sake of brevity, and some lingo might be a bit dated (for example, mainland rather than continental US, the conflation of drag queens and trans women) in the interest of reflecting the times as I and others experienced and discussed them. Some of my ideas regarding cultural identity and appropriation were similarly problematic. It was thirty years ago. I've grown.

A few "characters" are composites of different people who would have otherwise had redundant roles. I did this so that you, the reader, wouldn't have to keep track of more names than absolutely necessary. On the matter of names, most have been changed, some to protect the privacy of those I care about and others just to cover my ass. And because, while telling my truth is an essential part of my healing journey, I didn't write this book to hurt anyone, so let's all just be cool, okay? We're all works in progress.

RYSE HAWAII

Residential Youth Services & Empowerment (RYSE) is an Oahu-based non-profit organization established in 2018 that provides free resources to local youth ages fourteen to twenty-four to help them get off the streets and build safe, stable lives in which they can thrive.

Homelessness, especially among youth, is a pervasive problem in Hawaii even today, which is why an organization like RYSE is so crucial. I knew and lived among kids like these during my time on the streets of Oahu, and if not for a mix of luck and timing, I might never have made it out. Statistically, a lot of those kids didn't, but they might have if an organization like RYSE had existed back then.

In addition to an emergency shelter, RYSE offers long-term, deeply affordable housing programs, medical and mental health services, education and employment assistance, financial literacy courses, and more. The Kawailoa Access Center in Kailua is open daily, and the mobile outreach team is available 24/7 to reach youth where they are, when they need help.

I urge everyone to learn more about this amazing organization at www.rysehawaii.org. Together we can make a difference in so many lives.

CONTENTS

PROLOGUE

The mattress whined as I rolled onto my side and planted my feet on the rough carpet. As motel rooms go, it wasn't the classiest, but anything's a luxury when you spend half your nights sleeping on beaches, street corners, and the occasional fire escape. What can I say? Homelessness ain't pretty, and in my early twenties, neither was I. Sure, I had a waifish charm that, thanks to Kate Moss, was in fashion at the moment, but to anyone who had known me before my fall from grace, I'd have been a stranger.

At twenty-two I was a full-blown meth addict, though never one to pass up coke or heroin when it came my way. Living on the streets of Oahu, I did whatever it took to feed my habit. I begged, borrowed, stole… and yes, everything else you're thinking. That was how I managed to score the occasional motel room. Once a john got what he needed, he rarely stuck around, so I'd have a place to get high and crash until morning.

That night, though, I couldn't sleep. I dragged my feet across the rough, tacky carpet that no one in their right mind would run a black light over and braced myself against the dresser. I rifled through my bag, hoping desperately to find some lost stash to help me drift off, some hidden gem I'd somehow overlooked in my last dozen searches.

There was nothing.

I lifted my eyes to the mirror. The lights from outside danced across my fractured reflection, cracks in the glass spiderwebbing out from some previous impact. I was a far cry from the fresh-faced college girl who'd arrived on the island two years before, and my journey from the classroom to the gutter had been anything but a straight line.

I never officially dropped out of the University of Hawaii. I'd just been too busy discovering crystal meth in my apartment to make it to class, and once there was no money left to support myself or my habit, I turned to dealing. I was a natural, turning a larger profit every week until

I was big enough, at just twenty-one, to have people selling under me. I hadn't just made a living in the trade, I'd made a killing, and for a while, I'd lived pretty large.

The party eventually ended, of course. The life of a drug dealer, no matter how glamorous it may look on a good night, is anything but stable. Things inevitably fall through. And they had. I had been a major player in the local underworld, and now here I was, a haggard, strung-out whore lucky to be sleeping on a mattress for one night *if* I could even manage to sleep at all. How the hell I'd gotten from there to here I didn't know, and I couldn't see a way back. All I could see ahead of me was…this.

Sunken eyes and stringy hair, a tank top that had never been washed, dry skin stretched tight across my ribs, and barely enough presence of mind to be bothered by any of it. No way back, no way out, just more of this, if not worse. That was when I reached into my bag and took out the gun. It wasn't huge or impressive, but it would do.

Maybe this is better, I thought. *Before it gets any worse, before I'm too pathetic to go out on my own terms, before I choke on my vomit in an alley somewhere. Maybe this is better.*

I held the barrel to my head, daring myself over and over to just do it, just pull the trigger. It would take only a second. *She* thought it was at least a decent idea, the little girl I'd been when my innocence had been ripped away from me. It was her pain, her hundreds of untended psychic wounds, that had made me the vortex of self-destruction I'd spent most of my life becoming. And now here I was, the end result of all that dysfunction.

I leaned forward against the dresser for what felt like hours, staring at my face, red and swollen from crying, for as long as I could take before looking away. Every time I looked back up, there I was, fractured into countless pieces. There was a metaphor there, of that I was sure, but I couldn't have found it then if I'd tried.

The cool, predawn light cracked and broke as the sun came up and flared across my face. I flinched, fully depleted in every way, and dropped the gun. Miraculously enough, it didn't go off. I sank to my knees before lying down on the nasty carpet and passing out, wondering as the blackness swallowed me…

How the hell did I get here?

Part One

The Crystal Queen of Waikiki

CHAPTER 1

The Garden of Delights

I spent most of the flight gazing out the window, daydreaming about the new life that awaited me at the other end. I pictured sandy beaches, lush trees, and the sea sparkling in the sun, but when the islands came into view at last, even my vivid imagination turned out to be a poor substitute for the real thing.

The sharp tone of the Fasten Seatbelt sign shook me loose from my trance, and I jolted upright. We began our descent. I smiled at the brief bump of the wheels hitting the tarmac. It was almost real.

I stepped off the plane in Oahu, adrift in a sea of Hawaiian-print clothing, floral shirts and muumuus as far as the eye could see. The vibe was all smiles and love and leis. I could already feel the ease of the island creeping up through my toes.

Deb, an old friend from my Hudson Valley hometown, was there to greet me. I hadn't seen her since high school, but she was the same girl I'd gotten into all kinds of trouble with, minus the thick mane of 80s hair. She growled into a laugh and hugged me, then nodded over her shoulder to a tall, lanky guy with a boyish smile and a mop of curly hair.

"Nikki, this is Johnny. I've told him everything about you."

"Uh oh," I said with a grin.

Johnny rolled his eyes at Deb. "All good things. Impressive, how she tells it. Did you two really get high in a dentist's office?" As always, my reputation preceded me.

We cruised home in Deb's borrowed Jeep with the top down, stopping at a few points along the way to commemorate my arrival with some photos.

After spending a year or so in Miami, palm trees and beaches weren't new to me, but something about them was different here, serene and elemental. I felt calm and exhilarated at the same time.

Deb's place—now *our* place—was about a block from the beach, a small studio apartment on Kalakaua Avenue, Waikiki's main drag. As we pulled up, Deb informed me she had a few friends over, which was fine by me. A small, chill welcome party to kick things off sounded perfect. Johnny grabbed my duffel and carried it up for me as Deb led me inside. The place was small, enough space for a pair of twin mattresses and a coffee table, with a kitchenette and a bathroom off to the side. The room was big enough for four, maybe six people to hang out, and it was packed wall to wall with complete strangers, many of them speaking Hawaiian Pidgin, leaving me with little to no idea of what anyone was saying.

I'd thought my first night in Hawaii would be unpacking and relaxing, enjoying some local cuisine and tropical breezes. That picture had not included a full-blown party in my apartment, but there everyone was, so what choice was there but to roll with it?

I'd made a promise to myself before leaving the mainland not to party too hard. I'd been down that road before and was serious about turning over a new leaf. Deb had seemed to be on the same page when we'd discussed it, agreeing to have a little fun here and there but hold each other back from going too crazy. We were serious college students now. We had a plan to stick to if we were going to realize our dream of opening a health food store together, and for the first hour or so of the party, it really seemed like we were on track to hold to that plan. And then…the coke came out.

One minute I was bumming ever so slightly in my overcrowded apartment, the next I was hanging out the sunroof of a limo cruising down Kalakaua Avenue, drink in hand and everyone's best friend.

Most local parties aren't like that. Hawaii's wonders are mainly natural, and the locals tend to be chill, down-to-earth people. But I wasn't a local yet, and because it was my first night and I was zooted on coke, I decided to dip into some funds I'd brought with me to the island, intended for savings and careful investments, to treat my new "friends" to a night on the town.

At some point, Deb spilled that Johnny would actually be living with us, and because I was too coked up to care about much of anything, I absolutely loved the idea until I woke up and realized I'd be crammed into that tiny studio with two people rather than one. Well, too late now.

Waking up completely slammed from a night of doing blow is never easy, but once I was up and about, there was no falling back asleep. I brewed my first pot of Kona coffee and let its nutty, island aroma and the caress of an island breeze do their thing. Stepping out onto the lanai, I clutched my mug in both hands, sipping slowly as I took in the view. By the time I reached the bottom of the cup, I was fully awake, but Deb and Johnny were still out cold. Eager to explore my new neighborhood and not knowing when my guides might wake up, I grabbed my keys and a pack of smokes and ventured out into the bustle of Kalakaua Avenue.

Though part of the United States, Hawaii is separated from the mainland by almost 2,500 miles and *centuries* of history, and the native culture comes through in ways big and small. A muumuu is considered business attire, and people speak Hawaiian Pidgin on every corner. The native art and aesthetic are everywhere, and the general laid-back vibe can put even the mellowest stoners in LA to shame, but the spirit of the islands shows in the details you can only pick up on by actually slowing down, looking closely, and just living.

I walked up and down the avenue all day, ducking in and out of the little side streets where vendors haggled with tourists over trinkets off their tiki carts. Surfers—real ones who grew up in the waves—walked around with easy smiles and the ocean in their hearts. And at every turn, the music of drums or ukuleles.

And then, of course, there was my introduction to the local cuisine. Spam is a staple of any Hawaiian diet. It's everywhere. You could stop into any 7-Eleven and grab some Spam musubi, a thick slice of the stuff on a bed of rice, as commonly as you would find a hot dog or nachos on the mainland. It's gone in three bites, but it's cheap, filling, and perfect for someone who doesn't have a lot of money, which a lot of locals didn't. Two servings of that could hold someone for an entire day if they weren't accustomed to three square meals. It did the trick in a pinch, but that was not the cuisine that wowed me when I hit the strip.

People sat at small noodle shops whose counters wrapped around the front so that some were seated right off the sidewalk. The bowls smelled amazing, and I made a note to try some later, but I already had my eye on my first Hawaiian lunch. I stepped into what could have passed for any fast-food establishment and walked out savoring the freshest, most flavorful sushi I'd ever tasted—and for the cost of a dollar. I followed it up with some freshly sliced papaya that the street vendor garnished with a lemon wedge, then started back home.

Home. This was my home now, and I intended to live there as authentically as if I'd been born on the island, because I'd be damned if I was going to walk the streets looking like some *haole* tourist. Haole is what native Hawaiians call us white folks. It's not a term of endearment. With my blonde hair and blue eyes, I was about as haole as they came, and I quickly realized what that meant in terms of how I'd be regarded by the locals. It didn't really bother me. Considering white people's long, involved history of fucking the Native Hawaiians over, they could call me whatever they wanted.

I stopped in front of a head shop called Hawaii's Natural High and lingered at the window display just long enough to realize I was back on my own block. In fact, the front door to my building was just around the corner. My unintended lap around the neighborhood had been pretty good for my first time out, so I took it as a sign to call it a day. As I zipped up the stairs to our apartment, I followed a sudden, inexplicable urge to continue past my door to the deck, where I found Johnny smoking by the pool.

"Where's Deb?" I asked, sitting beside him.

"Sleeping. Have fun exploring?"

"I did, actually. Is this really, like…every day here?"

"Pretty much. You get used to it. Not like it ever stops being awesome. You just, like…learn to believe it's real. It becomes just another part of you." He took a long, slow drag. "It's a great place to be when you've, like…run out of places to be. You know?"

I did know. I'd run out of places to be a long time ago. All I'd done since then was run from one to another to another. It was nice to stop and rest a while and not have to worry so much about where I was headed next. I could hear in Johnny's voice that he understood that need for peace, and I didn't know why exactly, but it wouldn't have been hard to guess. I could smell it on him, the same ghosts I could never quite outrun, but chose not to say anything. Not yet.

Johnny turned to me, flashing that goofy smile of his, and offered me a cigarette. I figured I could use one, so we sat there and smoked, and I realized that maybe having an extra roommate might not be so bad after all.

The week leading up to New Year's Eve was packed with sightseeing. I rented a little red moped like Deb's, and we drove all over the island: to beaches, unpaved mountain trails, little hidden spots that weren't so hidden if you were anything but a tourist. She took me to campus to give me the lay of the land, and I bought myself a University of Hawaii sweatshirt and baseball cap at the bookstore. It's strange how much meaning can be sewn into a mass-produced bit of merchandise. I'd done the college thing before, but this was different. This was a real university, and I belonged here. I was going to really do it this time—become somebody and go places.

When New Year's Eve rolled around, I dipped into my funds again to spend an epic night with Deb and Johnny at a restaurant right on the beach. We ate lobster and drank champagne like we were hot shit, and of course, when midnight struck, we all did a line together to ring in 1994, because what's New Year's Eve when you're twenty without a little coke?

There were a million perfectly valid answers to that question, all of which I'd chosen to ignore. I didn't have to tell Deb that this had to be our last big hurrah before classes started in a few weeks. We were on the same page. With that line firmly drawn, I permitted myself to let go and enjoy the soft, glowing bliss of this last wild night.

As if that's how it works. As if one more dip into the kind of partying we'd done in high school would have ever been enough. There was always another reason, another occasion, another excuse. It wasn't a problem; we just got high a lot, often enough that we occasionally forgot to do things like eat or bathe or follow through with all our big plans.

Oh, there were plans. Every day we made plans, first for how we'd tackle the first day of classes, then the next semester, then by the end of the week we'd planned our entire lives out, jacked up on coke the whole time. We told ourselves every time we got high that it was the last, that we'd stop tomorrow, but we never did. The weeks before class started were like one endless, drug-fueled party, on the strip or sometimes the beach, punctuated by stretches of daylight, half of which we slept through. And the drugs were good. Really good. Even the pot I scored, Kona Gold and Maui Wowie, was top-shelf—green and gold, pungent, and clean. We were goddamn connoisseurs, which wasn't all that strange, given our side hustle.

Deb had a part-time job at Hawaii's Natural High, and it didn't take much to hook me up with one. We spent entire days at the shop, selling bongs, pipes, and trippy tie-dye tees to locals and tourists, but several times a day we'd lock the door, hang a Be Back in Ten Minutes sign, and sit on the floor behind the counter doing whippets, bong hits, and lines of coke.

When we were actually working, we made the acquaintance of countless dealers and addicts who were more than happy to barter actual drugs for drug paraphernalia. When they didn't have any to trade, they found more creative ways to pay, most of which suited us just fine. It's not like the stuff they gave us ever made it into the register.

One customer paid for some glass pipes with his pet chameleon. We definitely got the good end of that deal. Our new pet, Cool Mac, was chill, colorful, and low-maintenance. He lived free-range in the apartment and never needed to be fed. As with many homes on the island, our windows were just rows of broad glass slats, which were usually tilted open to let in the breeze as well as several species of bugs for Cool Mac to snack on. He got a full belly, and we never had to worry about massive flying cockroaches, so it worked out for everyone.

While Cool Mac's belly was always full, ours weren't. With all the coke running through our systems, we often forgot to eat until one of us was sober enough to notice we were starving, at which point we'd head on over to Sizzler, where we'd gorge ourselves for hours to make up for lost time. When you're that hungry, a cheap buffet of meat and starches, topped off with pudding and Jell-O in every color of the rainbow, is just about as good as it gets. We'd be so stuffed by the end that we could barely walk out the door, but it was totally worth it.

As the three of us walked home one night, Deb and I on either side of Johnny, he threw an arm around each of us, and much to my surprise I leaned into him. There was just this feeling of connection between the three of us. It wasn't poetic or flowery—we'd just spent the last few hours pigging out after lying around high on cocaine for several days—but in its own patchwork, graceless way, it was real. At least it *felt* real.

"Hey, ladies," Johnny said, slipping inside the apartment, wearing a huge grin. "Who's down for some fun?"

"You're in a good mood," I said.

"That I am. One might say *ecstatic.*" He produced a tiny baggie containing three speckled pills. I'd done a lot of drugs in my time, and psychedelics were nothing new, but I'd never gotten around to ecstasy. Neither had Deb. We didn't take much convincing. A quick look at one another, and we were good to go. "It doesn't kick in right away, but when it does, we'll be rollin'. Yo, let's go down to the beach. Nighttime on the beach will be perfect for this." We each took a pill, and after that it was just a matter of time.

Kalakaua was bustling when we hit the strip, all lights and tourists and action, and we ran into a few local kids we knew. We got so sidetracked having a moment with our friends that I forgot about my impending high until it hit me. A tingle in my head started to work its way down my spine and through my body, and suddenly I was feeling it, rolling for the first time in the middle of Waikiki's main drag, tons of people walking and talking all around me, and *what the fuck was happening?*

I had this huge smile, and my senses were dialed up to eleven. Every sensation vibed through me like an earthquake. When a breeze whistled through, the warmest, most beautiful feeling rose up in my skin and gave me chills. Someone brushed up against me as they passed by, and I got goose bumps. The lights were brighter than I'd ever seen. I turned to Deb to find her smiling back at me. A warm, euphoric rush of affection crashed over us like a wave, and we were pulled to one another by some strange gravity. We embraced there in the street, grinning so hard our teeth were glowing in the dark, and I couldn't make out a word of what anyone was saying. And I didn't need to.

Out of nowhere, I felt a powerful urge to get to the beach, as though the tide had washed all the way up to the sidewalk and found my feet, coaxing them back to the shore. I'm not sure whether I actually beckoned Deb and Johnny to follow or just thought it when I looked at them, but I grabbed Deb's hand and pulled her along. I couldn't even feel the sand giving way beneath our feet. As far as I could tell, we were just floating along without touching the ground, the lights from the street growing smaller behind us as we neared the surf. At some point between the street and the water, we'd left our clothes behind, and the three of us were frolicking in the waves, innocent as children…or as close to innocent as one can be, high on designer drugs.

Every touch, every smell—the salt of the ocean, the fizz of sea-foam lapping against our bodies, the light caress of our drenched hair sweeping across our skin—was an explosion of sensation. It was just us, a found family of three, children in Eden, free and perfect and alive. What came after that I don't remember. I can't recall much of that night, just the moments scattered across it where my life was finally perfect. My past was so far behind me, I was certain if I could just keep up this pace, I could outrun it forever.

There was still plenty of money left over from the nest egg I'd brought to Oahu, and sharing that tiny studio with Deb and Johnny, living on Pop-Tarts and ramen, the temptation to splurge on fun stuff was too strong to resist. If we felt a whim to island-hop to Maui at thirty bucks a head, there was nothing stopping us. We could be back on Oahu in a matter of hours or we could spend a day or two (or three), getting a small motel room or even sleeping on the beach, and we did. One morning, we just woke up, decided "fuck it," and off we were.

We hit a supermarket for provisions before we even paid for our motel room, picking up all the staples for a night of rolling on ecstasy. We mixed Cocoa Puffs and Rice Krispies Treats cereal into a delicious, sugary chocolate milk soup we could have lived on. There were donuts, both of the chocolate-frosted and powdered-sugar variety, the latter ripe for cocaine humor. And, of course, whipped cream for spraying directly into our mouths or onto white chocolate macadamia nut cookies was a must. The way it all engages the senses when you're rolling is unreal. We even impulse-bought some glow-in-the-dark necklaces and cheap leis at the checkout counter, because why the fuck not?

By noon, the three of us were sitting on the beach, enjoying the sun and the breeze, sharing a joint. It makes no logical sense, and I can't explain why, but the sun just seemed different on the islands—softer somehow. We took our hits of ecstasy just in time to catch the sunset, the sky melting into a bright, bold gradient from gold to rose like tropical sorbet. My memory gets a little hazy after that, but I remember heading back to the motel room, having forgotten about all the snacks waiting for us there, only to be pleasantly reminded of them upon our return. Our ecstasy trip compounded by a nice sugar buzz shot us straight past giddy into mildly delirious.

I was huddled on the floor in a dark corner of the room when I noted that our glow-in-the-dark necklaces were actually glowing in the dark. Filled with a sudden, desperate need to share this revelation, I leapt up so fast I collided with the bed before hopping up onto it. When I jubilantly pointed out that our necklaces were glowing green, Johnny looked down and flashed a big, goofy smile. Deb and I grabbed the leis and threw them over our necklaces, doing our own lackluster rendition of the hula for Johnny, who clapped and whistled for us. He jumped up on the bed and joined us, and we stood in a circle, holding each other tight, giggling as we spun at what felt like light speed but was no doubt the sloppiest ring-around-the-rosy in history.

Deb was the first to pass out, while Johnny and I sat up, smoking in the tranquil blue moonlight. We talked for a while about nothing of consequence. Then, as we started to come down, a stray comment or two betrayed thoughts a little darker and deeper than either of us wanted to entertain. There was something behind Johnny's eyes, something I'd caught a glimpse of that first day by the pool, and I had an inkling of what was haunting him. People like us can smell it on each other.

"I get tired sometimes," I said. Johnny nodded, needing no elaboration. I'd worked so hard and traveled so far to find a little peace. I wasn't eager to shatter it, and it wasn't my place to rob Johnny of his. And yet, I had to ask, because I already knew some of his story without him ever saying a word. I knew it all too well. "Just once? Or was it…?"

He shrugged, taking another drag. The moonlight in his eyes began to wobble. He held it together until I touched his shoulder, then he started weeping freely. I came close to him and hugged him, and we held each other in the silence.

There are a dozen reasons why what happened next should never have happened, not the least of which were that Johnny was Deb's boyfriend and I wasn't really attracted to him, but it wasn't about lust or passion. It was a lifeline, a way back out of that conversation for both of us, and it worked. At least it felt like it did.

Afterward, as Johnny and I pulled on our shirts, the reality of what we'd done sank in. It wouldn't be repeated but it couldn't be undone, so what were we supposed to do with it?

Nothing. We did nothing. We'd reached out to each other in an unexpected surge of pain and memory. It was comfort and connection, but it was also betrayal, so we buried it deep and never spoke of it again.

A little over a week before classes started, Deb and I woke from the heavy sleep that had followed a rather intense coke binge. We were downing a fresh pot of Kona, doing our best to adjust to our unwelcome sobriety, when Johnny returned with company.

We'd seen Vic before from our lanai, loitering at the pay phone across the street a few times a week. He was hard to miss: a lanky guy with suntanned skin, long, auburn, wavy hair down his back, and a splash of freckles. Hovering behind him in the doorway were two surfer boys who looked suspiciously young, but people were always figuring me for younger than I was, so who was I to make an issue? I'd been doing lines since I was sixteen. They wanted to party? That was their business.

Johnny introduced Vic as his hookup, and I quickly put together that whenever Johnny disappeared for a few hours or days, he was probably at Vic's place. Well, if Vic was his hookup, there was no time to waste in hooking us up. Deb and I were managing our hangover as best we could, but a little hair of the dog couldn't hurt.

Vic took a seat on the floor at our coffee table, pulled out a glass pipe with a round bulb on the end, and emptied a baggy of some shiny, translucent rocks into it. Whatever this stuff was, it was something new. We were expecting to do a few lines, but okay, we could wait and see where this was going.

Vic sparked his lighter under the bulb and rolled it from side to side, then lifted the pipe to his lips and inhaled deeply. He held it for a moment before exhaling the longest stream of smoke I'd ever seen—more than a cigarette drag and a hell of a lot more than a joint. It was like the steam stack of a locomotive. I wanted to know what was in that pipe and was eager to try whatever it was until the words "crystal meth" escaped Vic's lips.

I'd heard about meth, of course. You don't run in the circles I'd run in for as long as I had without hearing a few stories, but I'd never been in the same room with it, much less been presented with the option of doing it. I could feel myself inching toward the invisible line in my head, the one I'd always promised myself I'd never cross. There were some highs that led to places I didn't want to go, and yet, there I was, considering it. I had already broken all the rules I'd set for myself about my clean slate in Hawaii by doing coke and ecstasy, and I was already pushing it. Meth was a bridge too far.

I declined, but Johnny was already taking a huge hit off the pipe, Vic's small "entourage" waiting eagerly for their turns. And suddenly all I could think about was how much I wanted to try it, to explore a brand-new high. It was obvious Deb really wanted to try it as well, but also shared my reservations, so we weighed the risks and agreed on a compromise: We would not smoke crystal meth that day—we would snort it. That would obviously be the more responsible thing to do.

Vic warned that it would sting our noses, but please. We'd put all kinds of shit up our noses. We could handle meth. No *problema*. Vic turned out to be right. The meth stung the fuck out of our noses, but it was worth it for the rush that immediately followed. I sat back and let it take me, and whatever innocence had been hanging on by a thread fell away for good and drifted off on a warm, salty island breeze.

CHAPTER 2

Up in Smoke

In my denim cutoffs, oversized tees, and flip-flops—part Gen X uniform, part island couture—my transformation from mainland transplant to island local was nearly complete, and the addition of a semi-transparent teal beeper (cell phones were still pretty scarce) to my ensemble clinched it. I set up a long-term rental for my moped, and when Deb and I weren't working at the head shop, we would cruise around the island, wind in our hair and nothing more on our minds than staying on the road.

I showed up to campus for my first day of classes in flip-flops and sunglasses, ready to take on academia like a serious college student. And I did…for about a week. After that, Deb and I started doing lines of coke to celebrate how great we were doing at the whole college thing, and it wasn't long before we were showing up to class to make a brief appearance, only to duck out as soon as attendance was taken.

One morning, only in our second week of classes, we woke up, downed some coffee, and headed to campus, convinced that since we'd abstained from coke for a few days, doing a line or two before class would be totally within bounds. I can't for the life of me remember why I'd signed up for Astronomy, but there I sat at the back of the lecture hall, trying and failing to be present and take notes, already dying to do another line. Deb was holding the last of our most recently purchased supply, which we had agreed to do together between classes, but I couldn't wait that long. I packed up my books, quietly slipped out, and headed straight for the nearest pay phone to page Deb. Before I even reached it, my own pager went off and I smiled. We were more in sync than I'd realized.

"That's not going to do it," Deb said, her voice echoing in the fluorescent-tinged restroom. It was a ridiculous statement coming from someone still wiping the excess powder off her nose, but I couldn't disagree. The high had already hit, the initial rush still surging through us, but we were already thinking about what would come next. Then a light came into Deb's eyes. "What about Vic?"

"What about him?" I said, knowing full well what she was implying. Was crystal meth really on the menu right now? Coke and ecstasy, sure, whippets when the mood struck, and pot all the time, but we only ever did meth when it came our way, whenever Vic stopped by. He'd given us his number the first night we'd met him, but we'd never used it until now. Every second dragged as we lingered by the pay phone, waiting for Vic to answer our page. When it rang, I yanked the receiver off the hook with a manic tension, and Vic gave me his address. *It feels kind of wrong to be doing this without Johnny*, I thought on our way over. But not wrong enough.

By the time we got to Vic's place, I was zooming through a train of coke-charged thought: What would a meth dealer's place look like? Would there be people there? Were we playing it cool enough? Didn't want to spook anyone or harsh the vibe. Vic was our hookup and such an easy one. We couldn't risk burning that bridge.

Anxiety began to crackle through my nerves when Vic answered the door with a mellow smile and welcomed us inside. Two of his boys hung back on the couch, already tweaking, so Deb and I popped a squat on the floor, and Vic handed us the pipe. We'd never actually *smoked* meth before, working under the addict logic that snorting it wasn't as bad, but there's a first time for everything.

"Go ahead. It's so much better," Vic said. He helped me light the pipe and held my hand to twist it from side to side, making the smoke swirl around in the bulb as I inhaled. It was smooth and deep, and when he told me to hold it in my lungs, I did. When I exhaled, the trail was thick and long, and the rush that quickly followed was fucking insane. Deb followed suit, and as the rush hit her, she turned to me. The look we shared, one we recognized immediately in each other from years of partying together, said one thing and one thing only: We were home.

We went back to campus for our next day of classes, but we didn't last the full day or the one after that. By the end of the following week, we weren't even showing up anymore. My run at the University of Hawaii hadn't even lasted a month.

By then, Deb and I were done with coke and all the other stuff. Why even bother when you had meth? Coke may have technically been a better high, more intense and euphoric, but the comedown was way too harsh, even painful, for a high that didn't last very long. Meth was just smoother sailing. You partied for days, tweaking nonstop until you passed out for twelve to fifteen hours. There was no comedown, no pain. It was barely even a choice. We still did a little tripping with X or psychedelics for variety here and there, but the meth was constant, and I was paying for everything with the funds I'd brought with me from home. Deb and Johnny were family to me, and what was mine was theirs. I was happy to share. I mean, who wants to party alone?

Our little family had become incomplete with the disappearance of Cool Mac, who vanished for several weeks, though we were so high all the time it took us a while to notice. We figured he'd taken off, back to nature. Well, if this was Cool Mac's fate, I'd miss him, but freedom was his to enjoy. Then, a few weeks later, while we were tripping balls in our apartment, he fell out of the sky…or so it seemed. After weeks of not knowing where he was, he fell from the ceiling, right onto my pillow. Deb and I were tripping so hard we actually took a moment to speculate on how Cool Mac had learned to fly, but we got over it and picked him up and kissed him. I popped him right on my shoulder, welcoming him back to a home he'd never left. That was the last time we were all happy.

Johnny was the one who suggested snorting our ecstasy, but we all took to the idea equally, and we had six hits of it ready to go. That was the moment I realized that anything solid could be snorted straight to the brain for a faster high. In my twisted, fucked-up world, this was what a nice, low-key evening at home looked like: three twentysomethings sprawled on the floor of a studio apartment, fucked up out of our minds.

We pushed our beds together in the center of the room and clung to each other as our feelings started to bleed into one another, smiles plastered on our faces. We laughed dreamily and danced until at some point I found myself at our little coffee table, crushing up another pill. I saw no need to tell the others. They were busy loving up on each other, and I'd paid for the stuff anyway, so I snorted that pill. And then another. I didn't realize I'd hit the floor until I opened my eyes, staring up at the ceiling. I grabbed the leg of a chair beside me, but I couldn't pull myself up. I'd lost all muscle control.

I managed to roll over onto my side and reached for Deb and Johnny, but they couldn't even see me. They had fallen completely into each other's orbit, giggling giddily and kissing, oblivious to the fact that I was even there, much less overdosing. I tried so hard to keep my eyes open, but they just rolled back as I started to drift. I couldn't even call out for help, and even if I had, what were the odds they would have heard me? Then everything went dark.

The next thing I knew, Deb was shaking me by the shoulders, calling out my name. She relaxed considerably once I opened my eyes, and though all I wanted was to go back to sleep, I knew if I did, she would just start calling out to me again. Nearly an hour had passed before her and Johnny's high had dimmed enough for them to even notice me on the floor, passed out and drooling. When we counted out the pills remaining, it appeared I'd snorted three, which is already three times the dose any normal-sized person would need, and at five feet tall with no meat on my bones, I was far below normal-sized. By some miraculous stroke of luck, I'd survived, but I couldn't help but wonder what would have happened if Deb and Johnny hadn't come down when they did. They hadn't even noticed me collapsing right in front of them.

In a painfully sobering moment, I realized that as close as I felt to them, I would always be on the outside of whatever they had. I couldn't fault them for it. A threesome wasn't something I was looking for, but it still hurt to know that bottom line: I was alone. I could share a home with them, I could supply them with a steady stream of coke, ecstasy, meth, and whatever else they might crave, but it would always be them and me, never quite *us*.

After that night, we started to drift apart. It wasn't anyone's intention; it just happened. Given enough time, there isn't a friendship on this planet that addiction won't wear down. Deb and Johnny started going off on their own more often, leaving me free to go get high with Vic, disappearing for two, sometimes three days at a time. I didn't feel welcome with them anymore, and they resented me for pulling away, especially given who I was gravitating toward.

I arrived home one night to find Deb and Johnny waiting for me, seriously pissed that I'd been at Vic's for two days, hanging with the "big boys" without them. The simple fact was that the more I hung with Vic and the more business he got from me, the less he bothered with my roommates. In their minds, I'd usurped their hookup and blocked their access, and on top of that, I'd had the gall not to invite them along. I couldn't believe how pissed they were about how I'd let them down and ditched them, when the two of them were constantly slipping away, leaving me on my own. A sharp conversation escalated quickly into a full-blown shouting match, and I hit my limit. I stormed out and went to the beach to clear my head.

It was close to midnight when I sat down in the sand, just beyond the reach of the water. I'd been up for nearly three days, meth-addled to the point where I could feel my heart in its resting state. The home I'd made with Deb and Johnny had fractured, and the fragments were drifting. There was nothing I could do to fix it, and I wasn't even sure I wanted to.

The distant sound of drumming broke my trance, and when I looked up in its direction, I saw a bonfire a ways down the beach. It called to me, soothing and inviting, and in my sadness and loneliness it was exactly what I needed. It seemed to waver like a heat haze, making me wonder if it was really there or just a hallucination born of some lingering trace of meth mingled with serious sleep deprivation.

As I neared the bonfire, the shapes around it came into focus, a handful of native Islanders sitting around the blaze, drumming and singing. I couldn't understand a word of their language, but their song was one of the most beautiful things I'd ever heard. One of them looked up at me, never ceasing his drumming, and the others looked up in response. I froze, certain I'd intruded upon something sacred, something not meant for some ultra-white haole who didn't know when to mind her own business and stay on her end of the beach. But then he smiled at me and nodded to the sand at my feet. I sat down and listened as their songs filled me with peace and comfort, and I eventually fell asleep.

When I woke up under the rosy dawn, the only sound around me was the waves crashing on the shore. I sat up, sand in my hair and on my face, and looked around, letting the haze of my post-meth sleep roll off me like mist. It was a new day, and I knew one thing with perfect clarity. I was on my own.

Shortly after that, I moved out of our apartment and into Vic's second bedroom. I'd been spending so much time there and was such a reliable customer that he'd offered. All in all, he was a pretty good roommate. Sure, there were always customers dropping by, and Vic's boys always seemed to linger, but I was fine with that. I had my own bedroom and meth whenever I needed it…for a price, of course. The only trade-off was the frequency with which I might walk out into the living room to find Vic working on his "art."

Vic's art. Okay.

So, one thing about meth is it's a completely unique experience. I've gotten high in a lot of ways, each with its own quirks, but tweaking on meth is a whole different animal. Everything, and I mean *everything*, is kicked into overdrive. The simplest task becomes an obsession. You see a spot on the kitchen floor, grab a paper towel to rub it out, and next thing you know, the roll is down to three sheets because you've just spent the last three hours scouring the entire kitchen until every last square inch shines. The whim strikes you to do some laundry? Suddenly you're a laundry specialist. Every single item of clothing you own will be washed, dried, meticulously folded, and sorted by color, size, and whatever other category your methed-up brain can conjure. That term paper you've been avoiding? No problem. A hundred words fly right by. Two hundred? A thousand? Ten thousand? Doesn't matter. Consider it done.

Of course, despite even the most mundane task being imbued with meaning, you never seem to notice how rapidly its importance fades in favor of the next shiny thing. You start out stripping and rebuilding a car, building a deck, or laying down new carpet, but before you know it you're sitting at your coffee table for days at a time, painstakingly constructing a house out of playing cards and popsicle sticks, attention focused to a razor's edge to ensure those toothpick stairs are *perfecto.*

Meth can inspire all kinds of activities or hobbies. Vic blew glass.

I'd pass through the living room on my way in or out, and half the time there he'd be, sweaty and shirtless, melting down glass with a blowtorch and using every bit of lung power he had to reshape it. The kitchen counter and the floor would be littered with empty cans of Hawaiian Sun, some of them only half empty and abandoned for a different flavor, a fresh craving Vic had pursued before even satisfying the first. He would roll the glass this way and that, holding it close enough that he would blow a bulb onto the end of it. He made vessels, drinkware, sculptures, and figurines, filling every corner of the apartment with them. It was his pride. It was his joy. It was his art. And he did it all the damn time.

The fact that he could have burned the whole building down at any moment didn't occur to me then, but he could have. A blowtorch in the living room? I mean…what the fuck? But I was so deep into my little meth world that walking through my living room to find a shirtless six-foot tweaker *working a fucking blowtorch* was completely normal.

Vic's hobby was weird, sure, but it was a negligible drawback as far as I was concerned. Overall, life was pretty good—good enough I didn't notice how rapidly my checking account was emptying out. One day I was tweaking on the couch with Jackie Boy and Kai, two of Vic's boys, when my beeper went off. When I returned the page, a clerk answered, announcing the name of a check-cashing center.

"Hello? I was paged from this number?"

The clerk told me to hold and passed the phone to a cop.

"Ms. Mammano, my name is Officer Parks, Honolulu PD. We got your pager number when we contacted the bank. We received a call a little while ago from this location. It appears a couple of kids have been cashing checks in your name for thousands of dollars each. They weren't too smart about it, going around to several places like this one within a very short time frame, but long story short? They're being detained on site."

I was floored. Who could have…oh…of course. I realized three things immediately. One, that I hadn't used my checkbook in weeks, because—two—I'd left it in the kitchen drawer of my old apartment, which meant—three—Deb and Johnny had been stealing from me. It was insane for me to go anywhere near the cops as I was still very high, but righteous fury overrode common sense, and twenty or so minutes later, I arrived at the check-cashing place, where Deb and Johnny were being held, wrists cuffed behind their backs. At the sight of them, my body seized up with rage. I wasn't completely innocent. The Maui incident was proof of that, but that had been a foolish impulse, a one-time lapse in judgment that Johnny and I had had the decency to regret. Stealing from me, on the other hand, was a choice Deb and Johnny had made several times over, so fuck them both. I was done.

I agreed to come down to the station to give an official statement but hesitated before calling a cab. An addict walking right into a police station? Even as the victim in this scenario, it was a questionable move. As I lingered on the curb outside, I wondered if I should just get back in the cab and hightail it, but I'd already agreed to make a statement and didn't want the cops paging me again, much less tracking me down to Vic's meth den.

I don't recall actually taking the first step forward; my feet just sort of carried me along through the glass doors. To this day, I can't believe I willingly walked into the Honolulu Police Department, tweaking on meth, to give my statement to the police. I kept looking over my shoulder the whole time, hoping it didn't look too suspicious. It was probably for the best that I didn't see Deb or Johnny while I was there. Anger might have made me lose control or reveal something best kept to myself.

Afterward, Officer Parks offered to drive me home, but I didn't want him anywhere near Vic's, so I had him drive me back to Deb and Johnny's to pick up anything else I might have left behind. It's not like they'd be there to stop me.

"It's a real problem here on the island, you know," Parks said as we idled out front. "My daughter, she got caught up in it. I don't even know where she is these days. Your friends, I could see it in their eyes. Maybe they're beyond help, maybe they're not. I'd like to think they're not." He looked at me. He had to know. If he could see it in their eyes, he could see it in mine. Before he could say another word, I thanked him for the ride and got the hell out of the car. I'd gotten the message. I didn't need to hear any more and didn't care to.

I entered the apartment to find it empty. Anything I might have forgotten was already gone. Deb and Johnny had stripped the place bare and sold everything. Even the lighting fixtures were missing. I stood there in the dark, mourning the memory of what we'd shared, and then I left it behind. I didn't even lock up. Why bother? There was nothing left for anyone to steal.

I spent that night thinking about Deb and Johhny, what they'd done to me, how they could have done it, and how much it hurt. Well, I had the upper hand now. All I had to do was nothing, and they'd go to trial with no case for a public defender to work with, and that would be it. Prison. For how long, I didn't know, but prison nonetheless. The sting of disappointment and betrayal nearly convinced me to let them twist in the wind, but then a wave of sadness doused that flame, and all I was left with was ashes. How much better than them was I, really? Another roll of the dice, maybe I'd have done the same. And I could try to downplay it however I wanted, but I had fucked my best friend's boyfriend, so maybe the moral high ground was not mine to claim, at least as far as Deb was concerned. Maybe the best thing to do was just call it even and call it a day.

I called the station the next day and told Parks to let Deb and Johnny go. I'd be dropping the charges. He met my decision with disbelief and disappointment, but a bust slipping through a cop's fingers was not my cross to bear.

There wasn't much left of the money I'd brought to Hawaii and there wasn't any more coming in, so when Vic offered to give me a cut of the profits if I sold some of his meth for him, it wasn't even a question.

I started small, getting a sixteenth of an ounce, maybe even as much as an eighth, and selling to the locals he'd point me in the direction of. It didn't take long, though, for me to branch out to the "friends" I'd acquired over the past few months living on Kalakaua Avenue. Those friends had their own friends who had their own friends, and pretty soon I was Vic's trusty lieutenant, doing half his dealing for him. The arrangement worked out pretty well for both of us. I moved whatever he gave me without fail, usually within hours, so the profits were steady and I always had enough of a stash to keep me going.

I usually went out on my own, taking care of business on my own schedule, but once in a while I'd tag along with Vic, sometimes for business, sometimes pleasure. He dealt mainly at the club across the street from my old place and a couple other hot spots, but on occasion he'd hit an after-hours club located in this warehouse. During the day it was the empty, dormant outlier to the dozen active warehouses on the street, but deep into the night, long after those businesses had shut their doors, it came alive, not that you would know it from more than half a block away. This underground club was, by design, one of Waikiki's best-kept secrets.

Vic was perfectly at home amidst the pulsing, sweaty crowd. When he was dancing, he was in his own world, barely aware anyone else was even in the room. It was just him, the beat, and the meth coursing through his bloodstream. When he came back down to earth long enough to make some connections and sell, he did all right for himself, but as those occasions grew fewer and further between, I stepped in. I'd always been a girl who knew an opportunity when I spotted one, and over the course of a few nights in that warehouse, my little business under Vic blew up. I started learning names and passing out my beeper number while Vic let the music carry him away in a manic strobe of flashing colors.

I had my first big night dealing at that club, unloading more product than I ever had in one place at one time. Everyone got to know the new "it girl," and they introduced me to their friends and their friends' friends. The chain reaction was uncontrollable. And there I was, this little thing, wading through the crowd, selling to anyone and everyone who was buying, and turning a decent profit. I was still working off whatever Vic passed along to me, essentially his runner…for a while, anyway.

I came home one day and made a beeline to the fridge for a can of Hawaiian Sun, only a few gulps in before I realized Vic was sitting on the couch, looking sketchy as fuck, as he so often did, with a beautiful girl who looked about my age. She had dark hair and bright green eyes in which I could see, even from that distance, the slightest simmer of annoyance.

"Hey," I said, raising my can as I passed by. The girl smiled back, her irritation vanishing just long enough to nod a silent "what's up" to me before returning her attention to Vic.

Whatever. I had my own problems without stopping to think about why he might be taking shit from some chick. He was gayer than a rainbow flag, so it wasn't an angry girlfriend, an ex, or anything like that. She was probably a customer pissed off at him for being out of meth when she'd come calling, which wouldn't have surprised me. Vic always seemed to be running out faster and faster.

"A customer?" he said to me later that night, then scoffed. "That wasn't no customer. That's Keilani. She's the boss." He cracked open a Hawaiian Sun with a grunt. "And she wants to meet you. Like, for real."

A few days later, Vic took me with him to Keilani's apartment, which was a stark reminder of my place in the grand scheme of things. Vic's apartment was definitely a step up from the studio I'd shared with Deb and Johnny. It had multiple rooms, for one thing, a bedroom for each of us and an actual kitchen off the living/dining area. But Keilani's place… Keilani was *living.* She had nice furniture and appliances, a huge TV, and art that hadn't been welded together in a meth-fueled fantasia. It was a *real* apartment, a *real* home. Her business must have been phenomenal.

"So, Vic tells me you're moving product under him?" Keilani said as we gathered around her coffee table.

"Here and there. I do okay."

"More than okay from what I can tell." She grinned faintly as she sized me up with the ease of someone who holds all the cards and knows it. "Seems to me it'll be more convenient for all three of us to just cut out the middleman. Vic won't have to give any of his supply to you, so he'll have it on hand to sell himself, and you'll pick up directly from me. You know, like, on a trial basis, just to see how it works. Sound good to you?"

It took a second to register. "Uh…yeah. Sure."

What was I going to say? No?

CHAPTER 3

Between the Devil and the Deep Blue Sea

I stood at the pay phone around the corner from my apartment, tapping my foot, debating whether or not to page Keilani again. It wasn't even 6 a.m., so I considered the possibility she might just be sleeping, but it was starting not to matter. My customers were setting off my beeper like crazy. Tweakers can (and often do) go all night, only to come down from a high in the early morning, so these were perfectly normal business hours, and Keilani knew it. Even so, I didn't want to piss her off. Finding yourself on the bad side of someone with hired muscle, however charming she may be, is never a great idea.

The phone rang, and the sudden rush of adrenaline made me a little dizzy. When you're suddenly one step closer to getting a fix, your whole body knows it, and a ringing phone is as good as Pavlov's bell. This was business, sure, but it was also how I would replenish my own stash and ensure my next high. I yanked the receiver off the hook so hard I nearly fumbled it.

"Hey, Keilani." I managed to keep my voice more or less steady, playing it as cool as I could, considering it was my first official page and pickup from a big-time supplier. "Sorry about the time, but I've got customers. If I can get an eight ball, it'll be sold in, like, an hour." Still new to the trade, I took my cues from Vic, who never carried much more than an eight ball (an eighth of an ounce) at a time. I read this as experience and good judgment on his part but would soon realize an eight ball was the most Keilani could trust him with at a time. He didn't move a lot of product at the clubs, often partying more than selling. Keilani had already been looking to replace him for a while before the happy accident of meeting me.

On Keilani's word, I headed over to her apartment. She led me back to her bedroom and invited me to pop a squat on the floor while looking down at me from her bed like some kind of queen holding court. She filled her pipe with meth and smoked with me while she portioned out the eight ball I'd asked for, my supply for the day…or so we thought.

I left Keilani's at around 8:30 a.m. By 10:00, I was on the phone with her again, sold out and in need of more product. "Okay," she said, considering her next move. "So, look, I can't do this all day. Get back here pronto." So, I went, and Keilani re-upped me not with another eight ball, but an entire ounce. I was completely floored. I'd never held that much meth in my hand. I'd barely held a fraction of that much. Reading me easily, Keilani just smiled and assured me I'd need it. And I did. By the end of the day I'd sold the whole thing.

Dealing came naturally to me. Nine times out of ten it all came down to knowing how to talk to people, and if there was one skill I'd cultivated over the years, it was how to be and say whatever people needed, if only for five minutes. I was also the safest person on the scene to buy from, because being seen with me wasn't likely to raise any red flags. All the other dealers were rugged-looking or burned-out guys, and almost always native Islanders or of Asian descent. That's who the police profiled, not tiny blonde girls.

I'd wander Waikiki all night, sell to some kid from the university who, another toss of the dice, could have been a classmate. Then I'd make a customer out of his friend who spent his nights barely working at a poorly lit gas station on some side street. Back then I'd give my beeper number out to just about anyone, and there were plenty of people to take it.

I'd barely eaten breakfast one evening when I was paged down to the beach off the main strip. The sky at twilight was a cool indigo that heated up to pink at the horizon, the kind of sky better suited to romance-novel covers than illicit drug deals. The pay phone to which I'd been paged stood just in view of the Waikiki Pier. As I neared it, a slouching silhouette perked up. It was a kid about my age.

"Hey," I said with a casual nod. He looked me up and down, stuck his hands in his pockets, and shuffled over. "You're not from around here, are you?" I said, failing to conceal my smirk. I couldn't help it. He stuck out like a badly hammered nail.

"I'm on vacay with my folks," he said. "Already used up my stash." He'd spent the afternoon asking around for an easy, discreet hookup, and the haole girl had come highly recommended. We did business, and then a few nights later we did business again.

Dealing only got easier as I learned to navigate the scene with relative ease. It helped that the image Nancy Reagan and D.A.R.E. had drilled into my head of drug dealers and their clientele—grimy alleys and trench coats—couldn't be further from what I'd encountered. Palm trees and salty ocean breezes painted a very different picture. Sure, my clients weren't always the classiest folks Oahu had to offer, and I got a peek at more than a little meth mouth, but by and large I was just another local, enjoying the island life day by day and making a living like everyone else.

Okay, not exactly like everyone else.

I wasn't clueless, nor completely without conscience. I knew on some level what I was doing was wrong, but you can justify just about anything to yourself under the right (or, I suppose, wrong) circumstances. Yeah, meth was a powerful high and potentially dangerous, but it was just another product, and people were going to find a way to get what they wanted whether or not I had anything to do with it, so I might as well turn a profit. It was a hard world I was finding my place in, and a certain moral flexibility was simply a necessity, but I wasn't made of stone. I still had a beating heart under my thickening skin.

I sold what I got from Keilani at a considerable profit, leaving me plenty of wiggle room to take payment in trade, which I often did. If customers wanted to pay me in brand-name sunglasses, designer clothes, and purses by Gucci and Louis Vuitton, I accepted them, no questions asked, no sleep lost, provided they'd been stolen from shops and boutiques. But on one occasion when a customer handed over his mother's engagement ring, I felt like utter shit taking it and couldn't hold on to it for more than a day before insisting he take it back. Whether he returned it or kept it to buy drugs off someone else I don't know, but I knew I couldn't keep it. I didn't have much of a code, but at least I had that.

There were other trades, all kinds of practical arrangements like food carts and restaurants where, as long as I kept my customers there supplied, I ate for free whenever I wanted…at least until those customers got caught by their bosses. I traded ridiculously small amounts of meth for mopeds and cars, and found myself driving around the island in an exquisitely tacky purple Jeep that I made no apologies for. Clients even leased apartments in their own names, which was how Keilani always managed to keep a low profile: minimizing her own liability by never leaving a paper trail. In just weeks I'd gone from another broke college dropout to someone who walked tall at five-foot-nothing because of the clothes I wore, the car I drove, and the sway I held. I was a tiny, blue-eyed mainlander who grown men called "boss" without irony.

As for my roommate, Vic kept on selling small-time, but no longer to me; I'd become *his* hookup. He made little attempt to conceal his resentment, but it wasn't enough to keep him from buying what he needed. He grew weirder and more reclusive, doing what he wanted in the little meth world he'd created for himself, and I was happy to let him. I'd since found a far more kindred spirit.

Keilani and I had vibed with each other from day one, but in our line of work actual friends were hard to come by. Even then friendship didn't guarantee trust, so we took a while to feel each other out. We kept things friendly but professional at first, then after a while I started lingering at her place after our business was concluded. We'd tweak and talk and watch the day bleed away into night, laughing over stupid shit. She taught me about the business and about protecting myself. When faced with the choice of fight or flight, I was, as I always had been, a runner. Keilani was not. We were the same age, but she'd been in this underworld from the business side a lot longer and had developed the kind of backbone and savvy you need to thrive in it. That and a ton of "fuck you" money to ensure she could move loads of product, stay high, and never take shit from anyone. No one could get the better of her. Or so she thought.

Keilani's ever-present strong-arms, these mountainous Samoan guys who were part bodyguard, part errand boy, and all muscle, were paid well enough to ensure their loyalty. But there's always someone with a better offer.

The day came that Keilani was beckoned to her front door by an unscheduled knock, and checked the peephole to find one of her strong-arms waiting outside. What she couldn't see was a guy she didn't know at all standing off to the side with a gun he promptly shoved in her face the second she opened the door. The strong-arm and his coconspirator backed Keilani into the apartment, duct-taped her mouth and arms, and robbed her blind. Money, drugs, jewelry; they cleaned her out.

She managed to free herself some time after they left and was twice shy about answering the door for anyone, but when I swung by later that day for a routine check-in, she let me in. Shaken and humiliated, with no product to give me, and none left even for herself, I got her high with some crystal I had on me. It was the least I could do. I knew that she'd be able to build herself back up sooner or later, but I wasn't about to let her twist in the wind. It wouldn't be good for business, true, but she'd become a real friend, and that meant something to me, now more than ever.

I'd built up a sizable stash of my own of cash and jewelry, enough to spare Keilani a little start-up capital to keep good faith with her connections. Within a few hours, I returned to her place with a Domino's box in hand, announcing myself as pizza delivery.

Once she vetted me through the peephole, pulled me inside, and locked the door behind us, she opened the box to find no pizza inside. However hungry she might have been, her disappointment was curbed by the $25,000 in cash where a medium ham and pineapple was supposed to be. Keilani was one tough bitch—it was part of why I liked her—but at that moment I saw nothing but relief and gratitude in her eyes. She was able to pay me back within a day or two, and once she did, there were no further questions of trust for either of us.

While it's not an absolute, where there are drugs, there are often hookers, and plenty of them had my pager number. One of them, a woman named Juliet, mentioned a friend of hers in need of a new connection.

This friend distributed coke, meth, and whatever else there was demand for to all the clubs in Waikiki, which meant a ton of business for anyone selling to them, so I agreed to meet with this mass distributor at their temporary home, a pay-by-the-day hotel suite on Kalakaua. I knocked on the door, expecting some surly thug or over-the-top pimp type to answer. What I was *not* expecting was the most majestic drag queen I'd ever seen in my life.

Tall and fabulous, Roxanne—Roxy to her intimates—moved with an effortless grace that could put royalty to shame. Next to her, most drag queens were merely drag commoners.

"Get you a drink, honey?" she said in a deep but feminine voice. I demurred, still trying to keep it professional. Roxy sized me up with her slim Islander eyes, then shot me a look that said "suit yourself" before drawing me further into her makeshift boudoir. Gowns and wigs hung off chairs, and an extensive array of eyeshadows, lipsticks, and nail polish crowded the vanity to the very edge of clutter.

Roxy took a sip of a cocktail I couldn't identify and casually asked me to front her an entire ounce as though it were a stick of gum, assuring me that by daybreak she'd deliver the cash. It wasn't a leap of faith I'd typically make for a first-time customer, but there was something about her I knew I could trust, if only her desire for a solid business relationship. And worst-case scenario, I could just hustle twice as hard for a day or two to make up the difference, so I said fuck it. I picked up two ounces from Keilani, delivering one to Roxy and selling the other myself, and by morning I'd flipped them both. Roxy had sold her supply at enough of a profit to reimburse me in full and have plenty left over for herself. A score like that was definitely worth a second go.

I arrived at Roxy's place a little earlier the following evening to find a small army of club kids and drag queens in various stages of prep. It looked like some backstage dressing room, clothes and shoes everywhere, people bustling around, getting ready. On Roxy's cue, I got her guests high as they adjusted their wigs, applied their makeup, and zipped up their stunning gowns. They welcomed me to their little pre-party, entreating me to laugh along with them like I'd known them for years. And as I saw them smile with and defer to Roxy, I realized she was much more than their host. She was the fierce, witty den mother to this little tribe of proud freaks who spent their days sleeping and their nights ruling the underground nightlife of Waikiki. They all loved her, and it wasn't hard to see why.

It became my nightly ritual to show up at Roxy's to drop off her supply, and after the first few days I took the offered drink and the approving smile that came with it. Music would play, and we'd all dance and get high as they prepared for a night of clubbing and dealing. It was a good system, better than I'd hoped. One ounce turned into two (not counting the ounce I hit the streets with myself), and before I knew it, every morning between 4 and 6 a.m. my beeper would go off, and I'd head over to meet Roxy and one or two of her runners on the strip, where they'd hand me thin stacks of nine hundreds wrapped in a tenth, totaling thousands in nightly profits. I'd load it into my backpack, head to Keilani's to get more meth, go home to sleep for a few hours, and repeat.

Though I'd usually leave Roxy and her entourage to take care of the clubs while I sold elsewhere, I still had to check up on my business every so often, and I was more than happy to. The clubs were always a crazy good time. I would tag along to whichever one they were hitting and have myself a drink and a dance but spend most of my time sitting at a table in the corner, taking in the scene and watching Roxy's runners make me money.

Techno beats would thump through the floor and up our bodies, and lights spun above us, wild and chaotic, streaking our skin in pink, blue, and green as the night thickened around us. In between techno beats and vogue trances, money changed hands, and the wild masses scored my product amidst the musky scent of sweat and poppers, paying no mind whatsoever to the petite blonde in the corner. Everyone wanted to hang with Roxy and her runners. If they'd only known I was the source of their tweaking, I'd have been mobbed, but I was able to enjoy the anonymity provided by my go-betweens. I could join and leave the party as I wished, and I always had options.

Though their clientele didn't know me from Eve, the club owners were well aware of who I was and were more than happy to host me in their back rooms, where we could watch the frenzy on the dance floor.

The club owners loved giving dealers the royal treatment, because we got them high for free. By that point, tales of the haole with the good shit had gotten around, so these owners thought it was a big deal to party with me, and I was fine to let them think that. There was nothing to be gained by tipping my hand and letting them realize that *I* was the one on a wild ride, touring this adrenaline-charged, neon-lit bacchanal.

Those post-clubbing sunrises were something else. A Hawaiian dawn is always a guaranteed beauty, but those early mornings on the strip, that low crackle in the air of fading highs and a night properly conquered—there's nothing like it.

One of my favorite club kids, Jeremiah, would refuse to let the night die without a fight. Even as we walked on from the club, Jeremiah would give his best sashay, stopping every few yards to vogue. And just when you thought he'd delivered his big finish, he would climb a lamppost, wrap his leg around it, and dip, striking one last pose, earning our cheers and applause.

Club kids are known for their artistry with hair, makeup, and clothes, but Jeremiah was in a class by himself. His makeup was to die for, often a huge star around his eye in pink or yellow, contrasting perfectly with his lipstick. Most nights he ended up with enough glitter in his hair to frost it silver, and he'd wink at us, then shake it off like pixie dust.

I sometimes wonder what became of him. We called them club *kids*, and not club *dads*, for a reason. Whether by an overdose, an act of violence, or a disease, many never made it very far past their Neverland days, and I know Jeremiah most likely didn't, but I like to think he's somewhere right now pushing fifty and telling the hot little twink he keeps on the side about his tiny pixie of a dealer from the mainland who always loved to watch him dance.

The income from the clubs was sizable and steady, but I didn't have enough big dealers under me to keep me from dealing directly on the street and making my nightly haul one meth head at a time. When you're an accidental prodigy in the criminal underworld, opportunity just sort of finds you, and it wasn't long before one literally appeared on my doorstep.

I was heading home around noon, ridden down by more daylight than I'd become accustomed to. The dark circles under my eyes could not have been flattering, but I was too focused on stumbling through my front door to care. I reached my building and turned a sharp corner, nearly colliding with this jacked mountain of a guy, veins popping on his muscles and everything. He was handsome, clean-cut in a way that screamed military. I apologized, chuckling, and started up the stairs to my apartment. He followed.

"You just move in?" I probed, keeping one eye on him.

"Visiting a friend." Though it rolled off the tongue naturally enough that I could believe it, I knew he was lying, and he could tell I knew. "Sort of," he admitted. Through a crack in his stony, military exterior, I could see a hint of something self-conscious, even a little paranoid.

Ah. He was a user.

My suspicion was confirmed when he followed me the rest of the way to my door, and I turned to him, now perfectly at ease. "I'm not sure Vic's home." Total lie. Vic was almost always home, but it couldn't hurt to get a little more confirmation of my suspicions.

"If he's home, let him know Lucas is here."

Sure. Why not? I went inside, where Vic was sitting in the kitchen, announced Lucas, and went to my room to sleep.

A couple of days later, I passed through the living room to find Lucas visiting again, this time with a similarly built guy sporting a crew cut, blue eyes, and a sunbaked tan. Vic called me over and introduced me to his customers. I was right about Lucas being military. He was a naval officer stationed at Pearl Harbor Navy Base. The other guy, Max, was in the service as well, but he was army, stationed at Schofield. Both used the meth they bought from Vic to supply their respective bases, where there was plenty of demand. I don't know what the scene looks like at present, but in those days the number of Oahu military personnel hooked on meth was staggering.

I'd been living with Vic for a little over two months at that point but had never seen Lucas or Max come by to do business. Of course, now that I'd actually met them, they kept turning up. They would come by, sometimes together, sometimes alone, to get high and buy off Vic. Sometimes I'd join them. No reason to be anti-social.

Then one day, Lucas showed up, and Vic just didn't have anything for him, having likely smoked half of what he'd been carrying. He apologized to Lucas, who was very not cool with it, then ambled over to the couch to not give a shit. He was tweaking out so hard, he probably forgot Lucas was there the second his ass hit the cushions.

"I can hook you up," I said with a shrug, which was exactly what Lucas wanted to hear. I used my dealings with Roxy as a template and made a similar arrangement with Lucas: an advance of product in larger quantity than he'd normally receive (a full ounce), with the promise of reimbursement. That worked out for both of us just fine.

The next time Lucas came around, Vic happened to be out and about, so we just repeated our deal. A few days later, Max showed up, seeking the same arrangement. Vic didn't look too happy about it, but I didn't have it in me to care. From that point on, Lucas and Max were buying directly from me, and once again Vic became a casualty of the free market.

Lucas and Max found a far more reliable supplier in me than Vic had ever been, and by coming to see me once or twice a week, their business grew. In turn, my business grew while my liability diminished. I was making a lot more money moving a lot more product without ever having to leave my apartment. I was now the supplier for two military bases and the entire club scene. Not even six months into the trade, and I'd become the fucking Crystal Queen of Waikiki.

I now had a lot more free time to myself to chill or even sleep if I was sober enough to be physically capable of it. The more influence and cash I acquired, the more I understood Keilani's desire to retreat into her own space, and I found myself spending a lot of my time at my apartment, to the point where the occasional "getaway" became a necessity. With the cash I was pulling in every night, a few nights here or there in a deluxe hotel suite on the strip was well within my price range, especially on the occasions I didn't have to pay at all; I had customers everywhere. Considering how fast everything was changing and how much stress I was taking on, a few nights in a king-size bed with all the room service I could ask for was totally worth it. Plus…it put some distance between me and Vic. With everything that had passed between us in such a short time, our friendship was all but over. Nevertheless, I still had a few reasons to hang around that funky two-bedroom apartment.

There was a small pack of teenage boys who were constantly hanging around, often staying the night. They were all either street kids or may as well have been, considering their total lack of parental care and supervision, but all of them sought Vic's like a sanctuary where they could forget their troubles, and he was happy to have them. He was no saint, I had no illusions about that, but I thought he must have seen something of himself in those lost boys. At the very least he saw a craving for meth, because he was Johnny-on-the-spot when it came to hooking them up with some.

Vic's boys—Kai, Jackie Boy, and Zeke—were always around, and I was usually happy to see them. They were charming in their way. I'd cook for them, or we'd order pizza. We'd play video games, watch movies, get high, and laugh about stupid shit. Sometimes we'd just go for walks, talking for hours. It wasn't lost on me that they were only a few years older than my brother Michael, who I hadn't spoken to since I'd fallen off the grid. I must have really missed being someone's big sister, because I fell back into that role all too easily.

Hanging with the boys in my downtime was oddly comforting. Beyond the little brother factor, being with them was a tiny bit of peace in this new life I'd been swept up into, one that was wild and exciting but could also be insanely scary if I slowed down long enough to really think about it. But I was making it work somehow. Scared shitless and high as fuck more often than not—but surviving. I'd found my new rhythm and a modicum of peace to keep me going.

And then I learned just why Vic was getting those boys high.

CHAPTER 4

Vic's Boys

I didn't recognize the number on my beeper, but when I made the call, the voice on the line was unmistakable. Less than a sentence in, I knew where the conversation was going. We'd done this dance before.

"Just sit tight, okay? I'll be right there." There was no use giving him any shit. Not until later, at least. I stepped out into the living room, where Kai and Jackie Boy were hanging out on the couch. "Hey, dude, could I get a ride?" I asked, and Kai jumped up immediately, ready to serve, eyes wide and mouth twitching. From the look of him, he'd hit some meth only a few minutes ago, but a free ride was a free ride. I turned back and asked Jackie Boy if he'd be okay until we got back. He just nodded feverishly, munching on some Cap'n Crunch, his arm in the box almost up to the elbow.

Kai was waiting for me downstairs in front of the beat-up old station wagon that doubled as his home whenever Vic and all other couch-surfing options were unavailable. He opened the passenger-side door for me and helped me in, ever the perfect gentlemen where I was concerned.

"How's your mom doing?" I asked, my best attempt at conversation, given how tired I was. Kai shrugged and stared ahead as we cruised down the street. I didn't press him. I knew how his mom was doing, probably the same as the last time he visited the shitty room she rented, infested with so many roaches the walls looked like they were moving. I couldn't blame her, and I don't think he did either. She hadn't asked for mental illness so debilitating that she couldn't take care of herself, much less raise a kid, any more than she'd asked for the poverty that barred her from seeking the treatment she desperately needed. And Kai? He was just a kid. He couldn't save her. All he could do was get out of there and dull the pain the best way he knew how.

When we arrived at our destination, I told him to wait in the car. The last thing I needed was a methed-up minor following me into a police station. I went around the side of the building, up the ramp that led to the plain steel door through which I'd find a desk sergeant who looked about as pleased to be there as I was. I gave him a name, forked over a few hundred bucks, and took a seat while I waited. Forty-five minutes later, a tall, well-built eighteen-year-old—white but born and raised on the island—was escorted over by an officer and released into my custody.

"Thanks," he murmured.

"How many fucking times, Zeke?" I just shook my head and headed for the door, beckoning him to follow.

"Shit, man," Kai said as Zeke slipped into the backseat, light cuts and bruises all over his face. I felt for the kid. It had to hurt, but if he was going to start some macho shit like he always did, this was going to be the result. It wasn't my problem, and yet paying hundreds of dollars to bail him out every time was rapidly becoming just that.

"Last time, dude," I said. "I am not doing this again."

"I know."

"No, I don't think you do. Seriously. Last time." Zeke nodded. I leaned against the window, smudging it. Kai didn't care. I sighed out the last of my frustration. "You hungry?"

"Yes," they both said, and a tiny pulse of laughter escaped me. We made sure to bring enough home for Jackie Boy, but he was gone when we returned to the apartment. I asked Kai where he might be, but all I got from him was a shrug. Jackie Boy was Kai's cousin and the youngest of the three, fifteen at best. His dad had split a long time ago, his mom was in jail, and without anywhere else to go, he just floated on the streets, barely a teenager and already hooked on meth. How he could be so damaged so young and still have a smile that could light up the world I will never know. I hated to think he was out there somewhere begging for enough change to afford a Spam sandwich when I'd just brought home a Big Mac for him, but there was nothing I could do about it, so I stuck it in the fridge and went to bed.

Living with Vic had grown awkward. The fact that I'd surpassed him as a dealer in just a matter of weeks had become this elephant in the room that neither one of us really wanted to acknowledge. Thankfully, we never really had to. He was methed up pretty much all the time and getting sloppier with his business every day. I'm sure he was less than thrilled to be losing customers, but it beat losing his own hookup. He grew more and more content to just hole up in his room and tweak out to his vintage vinyl collection for hours and hours. Far be it from me to stop him unless I actually needed something.

I woke up the morning after I'd picked Zeke up from the police station, needing to talk with Vic about something. What it was I don't remember, but it was apparently important enough that I knocked on his door. When I didn't get an answer, I knocked again, and then retreated into my room. When I tried *yet again* half an hour later and still got no response, I began to lose my patience. I knew he wasn't sleeping. I could hear movement, and his music was loud enough to wake the dead. Why the fuck couldn't he just come to the door? The conversation would take a minute, maybe two. And then, out of some dark, hidden corner of my mind, a thought emerged.

A chill seized me, my whole body rattling as I connected the dots. The way the boys looked at him with a blend of need and disgust, and the way he looked at them, like game in his crosshairs. Why would a pack of straight teenage boys hang around some club queen in his thirties? For the drugs, of course—more than they could get anywhere else. And how were they paying for it?

Holy shit. How could I have not seen it before?

I hammered on the door with my fist, demanding that Vic open up. I had to get in. I had to stop it. If my gut was right, it would have been far from the first time, but so what? Every moment I could prevent, every bit of dignity and sanity I could keep from being sliced away from whoever was in there selling his body to Vic—every second mattered.

The door finally opened, and Vic slinked out, not even looking at me as he headed to the kitchen. It was entirely possible my knocking had had nothing to do with it. Before I could say anything, Kai wandered out into the living room, more than high enough for his mind to be anywhere but on what he'd just done to "earn" that high. I needed to act quickly, but I also needed to talk to the boys first. Vic was a big guy and dangerous, and what if—the odds were slim—but what if I was wrong? So, I showered, got ready, and went out to do some business while I worked out a plan.

Sitting on what I'd discovered took a record-breaking amount of restraint, but I managed to wait until that night. I knew once Vic had stepped out, he'd be gone for at least a few hours. He wouldn't bother leaving the apartment for anything less. Once he was gone and I was alone with the boys, I took my shot.

"Kai, man…what were you doing in Vic's room earlier?"

"What are you talking about?"

"You were in there with him for like…hours." He dodged the question a few more times, but I couldn't let it go. "Dude, it's okay. You can tell me. Kai, come on." I turned to the others, both of whom looked just as uncomfortable. Zeke sank even further into the couch somehow. Jackie Boy's eyes darted around the room as he tied his long, curly black hair into an explosive ponytail. He sat there, silent for a moment, then stood up and headed into Vic's bedroom. I entered to find him standing in front of the closet.

"Jackie Boy? What's going on?" He didn't answer. He just kept staring. Kai walked up, gently brushed Jackie Boy aside, and reached up to sweep his hand across the shelf, probing for something. He froze, then pulled it down. Shaking, he turned over a small stack of Polaroids, all of them featuring one or more of the boys naked, sometimes standing, others lying on the bed in sexual positions: Vic's stash for when the real thing was unavailable.

"They're souvenirs. That's what he calls them."

They weren't crying, not one of them, but they all had the same look on their faces: complete exhaustion, like they'd already cried all their tears out long ago and had nothing left. Even Zeke, who lingered in the doorway, arms folded, looked empty somehow. They were meth-head street kids, yes, but they had only turned to the stuff because they'd been unloved and neglected and had nothing else to ease that hurt. Vic had exploited that desperation, dangling baggies of meth in front of those boys so that he could fuck them.

"Grab your shit," I said. Easy enough; none of them had much in the way of possessions to begin with. "Anything you have here, pack it up and take it down to the car and wait for me there." Jackie Boy started to protest, but I shut him down immediately. It wasn't a conversation. "Grab your shit and go downstairs and wait for me. Don't let Vic see you when he pulls up. No matter how long it takes for me to come down, wait for me in the car and *do not leave*." I didn't know how this confrontation would play out, but I didn't want to chance leaving anything behind. I pushed a bag packed with all my drugs and money into Zeke's hands and all but shoved the boys out the door.

I waited on the couch for hours, holding those Polaroids but unable to bring myself to look at them. My anger burned in waves, stoked over and over as I clamped the evidence of Vic's sins in my fingers. I would have felt sick if I could feel anything other than rage.

It was late when Vic finally showed up. In the darkened living room, he didn't even see me as he strode toward his room.

"The fuck, Vic?" I said. He halted and turned toward me, realizing only then that I'd been sitting there. I sprang to my feet and flung the pictures at him. "What…*the fuck?!*"

Vic picked up one of the Polaroids and stared at it for a moment before lifting his feverish eyes to me. His arms shot out like lightning, and he wrapped his hands around my neck, walking me backward until he slammed me into the front door. As I gasped for air that wouldn't come, a realization hit me. *Oh…this is it. This is how it ends? Fuck!*

Vic took one hand from my neck, and I struggled to draw a breath for half a second before he clamped down harder with the other, slamming the back of my head into the door again. With his free hand, he grabbed a lamp off the end table beside him, ripping the cord from the wall, and held it up. *What will he do with me after he kills me? Where will they find my body?* I was one blunt force trauma away from…well, perhaps relief. Maybe this was where my road had always been leading me. Maybe the boys were already gone and I'd bought them the time they'd needed to get away. Well, at least there was that.

I struggled for breath against Vic's grip, my throat already sore, my windpipe moments from being crushed. I stared up at the lamp, ready for Vic to bring it down and crack my skull open—if he didn't choke me to death first. He brought it up another inch, then froze, eyes glazing over. And then he brought it down onto his own head.

He let go of me immediately, sobbing and wailing as he bled. He knew what he'd done to those boys, what it made him, and that the shame and self-hatred he was feeling was his to live with. He hit himself again and again, and when he lifted the lamp a fourth time, I grabbed at the doorknob behind me, fumbling as I unlocked it, and got the fuck out of there.

I found the boys waiting for me on the curb, in front of the car, fidgeting…and not from tweaking. They were terrified. Life on the street is anything but certain, guarantees are a joke, but this shit was next level. They looked up as they heard me approaching, scanning my face for some hint of what might come next, as if I had any fucking idea.

"Let's go," I said, and on that, Zeke and Jackie Boy hopped into the backseat. Kai, of course, opened the passenger door for me and helped me in. For the first time, I actually needed his chauffeur routine. Whatever energy I had left was bleeding away. "Hey…it's over," I said as Kai started the car. "You never have to do that ever again. Ever. Understand?" The tension on their faces cracked just enough for a little relief to seep through. I faced forward and crashed back against the headrest. Why weren't we moving yet? The trauma of nearly being murdered seized me, and I was all but paralyzed. I tried to form words several times before anything came out, and when something finally did, it wasn't much. "Punch it!" I spat before I slumped in the seat. By the time we made it to the end of the block, I had completely passed out.

The first thing I saw when I came to was Jackie Boy sitting backwards on a chair, watching over me. "She's awake!" he called over his shoulder, unnecessary as Kai and Zeke were only a few feet behind him and watching me just as intently. I sat up and looked around as I tried to orient myself.

It was a motel room, cheap and seedy enough that a kid with a handful of cash could get a room without any questions.

"How long was I out?" I croaked. My throat was a still a little raw. Nearly getting choked to death will do that. It couldn't have been too long. It was still dark out.

"We got the room last night," Zeke said, handing me a can of Hawaiian Sun sitting on the nightstand. He cracked it for me, and I chugged half of it in one go.

"As in…twenty-four hours ago?"

"Give or take."

Kai brought me a snack-sized bag of chips. From the look of it, they'd cleaned out half a vending machine to have something ready for me when I woke up. They gave me the whole story: how they'd pulled into the first motel far enough from Vic's apartment for their comfort, how they'd lifted just enough money from my bag to pay for the room, how Zeke had carried me up the back stairs, careful not to be seen, since the last thing any of us needed was for someone to call the cops on three boys carrying an unconscious girl into a motel room…and how they'd waited there, watching over me until I woke up.

"So…what do we do now?" Jackie Boy asked. I had no idea. I was in uncharted waters. It had been a long time since I'd had to worry about anyone but myself, and never to this degree. Did I owe these boys who weren't much younger than me anything at all? Probably not. Even so… as fucked up as their arrangement with Vic had been, it had meant a roof over their heads that they no longer had. I didn't regret for a second ending that abuse, but I couldn't just walk away and leave them treading water. I was involved now, up to my neck, and now that I'd stepped in, I had to step up.

"We figure it out," I assured Jackie Boy, then looked up at the others, making sure they knew I meant all of us.

On the table across the room was the small mountain of vending machine snacks, tasty and good enough to get us through the wee hours if necessary, but not a meal. First things first, I ordered us pizza, and after we ate, the planning began. I'd nearly been killed only twenty-four hours ago and had nothing but the clothes I was wearing, one bag full of drugs and cash, and another with my ID and a few other personal items, but in a clutch you work with what you've got to keep on moving.

Forward. Always forward.

A few days later I found us an apartment: nothing fancy, but a two-bedroom with enough space for us to live comfortably. Furnishing the place was both quick and simple. I was not looking to flex whatever interior design instincts I may have had. I just got us some mattresses, a couch, and a couple of tables to set things on, most of it in trade. I didn't have many customers left who paid by barter—I was too big at that point—but I'd kept a few around who I had a soft spot for, enough to get some merchandise slipped out into the alley behind a furniture store.

I'd been in touch with Keilani and Roxy throughout all of this. I couldn't just go missing for a few days. Too much business depended on me, and Roxy had already wondered where the hell I'd been the night I'd slept away in the motel room, blowing up my beeper the entire time. In all the hustle and bustle, there had been no time for anything but shop talk, but once I'd gotten myself and the boys settled, I went straight to Keilani's to give her the full story.

"I knew Vic was a sick fuck," she said, shaking her head. "Maybe not *that* sick, but I always knew there was something off about him." If Keilani had been looking for a reason to finally cut Vic off completely, I'd given it to her. Just like that, it was done.

Vic disappeared into the life of a street user not too long after that. I never spoke to him after the night I escaped with the boys, and I only ever saw him from afar, skulking down the street, looking strung out and defeated. From what the people at the clubs where he used to deal told me, he more or less vanished from the scene. I heard he even wound up in jail.

I can't say I feel sorry for him—not then, not now.

"Can't forget the essentials," Zeke deadpanned as Jackie Boy tossed a box of Lucky Charms into the shopping cart. Kai was several aisles over, picking up a dozen or so bricks of ramen, and would meet up with us in the checkout line.

I was keeping one eye on the time and the other on my beeper. I never knew when "work" might call, but shopping had to get done. And while I loved the boys, I wasn't about to leave that kind of money with a trio of addicts. It would never make it to the supermarket.

"Nikki, call it." Jackie Boy held up a box of strawberry Pop-Tarts. Zeke held up cherry. Both had sullen eyes trained on me. Clearly, I was to be the arbiter of this crucial conflict.

"Guys, seriously?" I said, plucking both boxes from their hands and dropping them into the cart. "I know we don't live in a palace, but we can manage."

Our little family shopping trips had become routine. The boys wanted to make sure I picked up what they wanted and, if it was out of stock, select their own acceptable substitutes, and I wanted to make sure they didn't blow whatever money I gave them entirely on junk food. I wanted them to be kids and enjoy a bowl of sweetened oat shapes and dehydrated marshmallows, but I tried to make sure some occasional nutrition made it in there somewhere. A microwave burrito may not be gourmet, but it's protein.

I didn't have many rules, having never been fond of them myself. Life in the home we'd made was pretty much a free-for-all. I had no interest in being their mother. I wasn't there to mold them into fine, upstanding citizens, as if I knew how to be one. I let them get high. Sometimes I'd get them high myself. If they wanted to disappear for a few days, that was their call. I encouraged Jackie Boy to go back to school, which he did—I even helped him with his homework when he needed it—but if he slacked off or had decided not to go at all, I ultimately couldn't make him. I could lean on him to make an effort, but what else was I going to do? Ground him? He didn't have much to lose and if he just took off rather than put up with my nagging, he could end up back at Vic's or worse, so no. If there was one thing I made sure the boys knew, it was that they had a place to crash, food to eat, and no need to sell their bodies to have a home. The rest was negotiable.

We ate dinner when we were hungry, sometimes at nine or ten o'clock. You did your homework at three in the morning if that's what worked for you. Sleep when you want, where you want: on the couch or one of the mattresses in the second bedroom, take your pick. We didn't have much, but it was a serviceable home, and we had become our own bizarre little family. My main rule was that they be kids while they still could. Watch cartoons, get cranked up on sugar cereal, hang around and listen to music…just have that freedom, that simplicity, for whatever time you can. The world outside would close in on them again soon enough. At least I could give them something to look back on and hold on to when it did.

"I'm not saying it's not a sweet thing you're doing," Keilani told me as she portioned out my supply. "But you gotta let those kids go. They're just going to bring you down." It wasn't the first time she'd shared this prediction, and I was getting tired of hearing it.

"They're kids, Kei."

"They're a liability. Your business is good, growing steady." She was right. It was. I hadn't been dealing at the street level for a while. Outside of a few chronics I had a fondness for, my game was much, much bigger. "You have to be careful who you let into your world—and into your home, for that matter. These boys, they're users. And they may be sweet to your face, they might even mean it, but they're still street kids, with all the baggage that comes with it. You can't trust them."

I grabbed my goods and shook my head. "Well, that's my problem, then," I said. I couldn't let it get to me. I wasn't mad at Keilani. She meant well and often had solid advice, but I knew my boys. I loved them, and they needed me. In a way, I needed them too.

My apartment with the boys was the first home in Hawaii that had been entirely mine. As a dealer, I was still getting on my feet, at least compared to Keilani, and I didn't have the setup she had, but it was home. I'd been careful not to lease it in my own name. The first thing Keilani had taught me was to never put anything—an apartment, a car, *anything*—in your own name.

There are ways to get around these things. Running off Keilani's example, I kept a safe in my bedroom closet where I stored several ounces of meth for both business and pleasure, thousands of dollars, some important personal papers, a shit ton of diamonds and assorted jewelry I'd taken as payment, and a few sundry items of sentimental value. My safe wasn't heavy iron, but it was solid enough and padlocked, a secure home for all my valuables. I had that shit locked up, but I should have also locked it down, bolted to the floor like Keilani's.

Just a few months after Keilani and I had had our little conversation, I stood in front of my closet, where my safe very much wasn't. For a brief moment, all kinds of ridiculous thoughts ran through my head, like where I might have misplaced it. *Where did you leave the safe, Nikki? You must have moved it at some point. Where did you put it?* But then, of course, the only viable possibility dawned on me. Keilani had been right all along. It had taken some time, but what she'd warned me would happen had happened. My boys had ripped me off.

On some level, I'd always known it was possible. I'd wanted so badly to believe I could give them a new beginning, something better than the road they were headed down, but it takes more than some hot meals and clean sheets to heal the kind of damage they'd suffered. Live long enough by the rules they'd had to live by, and it changes you. In their world, nothing good lasted. There was no sense getting comfortable anywhere. You watch your own back and do what you have to do to survive.

I could have told them a million times that I'd never turn my back on them or hang them out to dry. I could have showed it in a million ways. It wouldn't have made a difference. They wouldn't have been able to see it.

Losing the drugs and the money was a tough hit, but they could be replaced. My personal effects…they were gone. And it was bad enough that I'd been ripped off, that I'd lost the last few shreds of my identity from before all this had been stolen from me, but knowing that the boys had been behind it cut even deeper.

An "I told you so" would have been well within Keilani's rights. I wouldn't have held it against her. But when I sat there in her living room, telling her what had happened, she just let me talk and work it out in real time. The boys had cleaned me out. All I had was the money in my pocket, and it wasn't much. I needed a leg up to get back on my feet, and when I asked Keilani for a loan just to make it into the black, I was fully prepared for her to roll her eyes and tell me I'd made my own bed, but she didn't.

"It wasn't that long ago you helped me out of a pretty tight spot. I got you."

"Thanks, Kei. Thank you so…"

"Under one condition." I felt my skin prickle. I knew what was coming. "The boys. You gotta cut 'em loose. And you can't take 'em back…*if* they come back. You wanna keep working for me, no liabilities. I need my people smart."

What could I say to that? She had a point. She'd had one from the beginning. I agreed, took a sizable chunk of change as well as some meth to sell, and headed home, planning to sleep with it all under my pillow if I had to.

The apartment felt so empty when I got there. Every trace of the boys was gone. For weeks, I went about my business, going through the motions, hurting at having lost another family. And then one day, Kai and Jackie Boy showed up on my doorstep, looking like a couple of dogs that had spent an afternoon being kicked. It had been a few weeks, and I guess the money and drugs had run out. I thought twice about letting them inside, but it was just them. Steal from me? Maybe. Be a danger to me? Never.

They apologized again and again, and I believe they actually meant it. "If you were sorry, you wouldn't have done it" is some bullshit parent logic that's never made sense. You can't regret a mistake you haven't made. You can't learn from one either, and I could see in the boys' bloodshot eyes how sorry they were.

"Is there anything left? The money and the meth…whatever. But I mean my stuff?"

Kai shook his head. Jackie Boy's lip trembled, and he told me how they'd tossed it into some garbage pit. My whole life had rolled away, down a mountain, and there was no retrieving it. With tears in their eyes, they apologized again, on Zeke's behalf as well as their own, but it didn't change anything.

“We’ll never do it again. We promise,” Jackie Boy said. I wanted so badly to believe him, but I knew what he was asking, and there was only one answer.

“I love you guys. And I forgive you…but you can’t stay with me anymore.” Jackie Boy began to protest, but I just shook my head, and they knew. They’d backed me into the situation I was in, and there were terms I had to operate under. Keilani’s ultimatum did not, however, say anything about cutting off all contact. “If you ever need anything—*ever*—you just have to find me, and I’ll be there. No matter when, no matter what. Understand?” They nodded and hugged me, then they left.

The boys kept my number and would call me occasionally, sometimes just to check in. I loved those calls. They made my day. I’d stop whatever I was doing to hang on the line for a few minutes, half an hour, whatever. I even gave them money from time to time, but my number and my address eventually changed, as dealers’ often do, and once they did, that was it. I kept on moving forward, growing in Keilani’s shadow and living by her example, doing what I had to do to survive.

CHAPTER 5

It's All Fun and Games

A chronic, in a non-weed context, is what we dealers would call a street user who would do anything for a high. My circle of customers had shrunk to a rather small, elite group, but I kept a few chronics around who had a hookup in some fancy hotel or restaurant, a knack for stealing good shit to trade, or even just a handy pair of eyes and ears.

"Shit," a scratchy voice muttered over the phone. "Cops are pulling up!"

I burst into the bathroom and started dumping my supply in the toilet. I probably could have dumped even more before the first flush, but I couldn't risk a clog. I didn't have that kind of time. Sure, I was literally flushing thousands of dollars' worth of cocaine and meth down the toilet, but when one of your regulars calls from downstairs to warn you the cops are entering your building, you take no chances.

I wedged the phone between my face and my shoulder, putting a nice kink in my neck, to keep up with the play-by-play while I disposed of as much evidence as I could. After I'd already flushed a couple of ounces, he said, "Never mind. Here they come. Not for you." I didn't quite relax, but it was enough that I stopped dumping my stash.

Still, the amount of coke remaining would not be enough to do business that night. I'd have to swing by Keilani's place for more, and after that it would take hours to cook up another batch of sufficient size. But I had time, and it had to be just right. I'd built a reputation for myself on the quality of my product—one I had to maintain.

I'd gotten really good at cooking pure cocaine cut with nothing but baking soda (unlike street crack, which has all kinds of other shit in it), good enough that I could eyeball everything—how much water to fill the test tube with, the perfect ratio of coke to baking soda, and how long to hold the bottom of the tube over my butane lighter. I would take it off the flame once the powder turned to goo, which began to harden immediately after removed from the heat. I'd then spin the test tube in wide circles by hand, a combination of skill and centrifugal force shaping the mass into a near-perfect sphere.

That smooth shape became my trademark, one I was known in the clubs for, and I had to stay on brand. People who saw that ball, anywhere from the size of a blueberry to a large grape, knew exactly what kind of high they were buying, and I always delivered on that promise.

I was at a club one night, talking shop with Roxy, while James, a loyal customer I'd met while shadowing Vic, hovered nearby with his boyfriend, Steven. Their appearance and vibe were abnormally low-key for the venue, but I got the sense that their own campier club kid days were behind them.

"You all right, dude?" I asked James as he pitched forward for a second.

He smiled, waving away my concern. "Long day," he said, then turned to Steven. "I think I should just go home. You can stay." But Steven wouldn't have it and insisted they leave together.

"Night, beautiful," James said, kissing my cheek, and I waved as he and Steven left.

"Hope he's all right," I said to Roxy once they were gone.

"For now," she said. I shrugged, not getting it. "You can't tell from his face? He's got it, baby." It took me a second to take her meaning. This was the gay 90s, and AIDS was everywhere in the circles we ran in, ravaging the community. Between the club scene, the gay scene, and the drug scene, I knew plenty of people who, for any number of reasons, might one day simply not be there anymore. James wasn't the first person with HIV I'd encountered or even done regular business with, but he was the first I'd really gotten to know. And from the look of him, he was living with full-blown AIDS, a pretty advanced case of it at that. Roxanne's implication was clear: James was on borrowed time. How much he had left was uncertain, but it wasn't much.

It killed my mood, and I didn't really feel like hanging at the club after that, so I headed home, willing to do business but not much else. I got a call from one of my chronics, a local who absolutely *loved* a cocaine high more than just about any other.

"How much you need, Mana?"

"Just a little. I can pay tomorrow."

"Then you can pick it up tomorrow."

"But, Nikki, come on…"

"You know the rules. Cash or trade. No freebies." There was a long pause. I could hear her grumbling on the other end of the line. "You're not going to have the money tomorrow, are you?"

"I—I can bring you a new customer," Mana whined.

I wasn't thrilled with the idea of having some random guy come to my home for a drug sale. I was opportunistic, not reckless. "I don't think so."

"Come on, I've known the guy a while. He's solid. And he moves a lot of product, 'kay? Like, a *lot*. It'll be worth your while."

That got my attention. Just how much was a lot? Enough to be worth an intro? I would have to size him up in person to get a vibe off him, and I could definitely cover my ass while I sniffed him out, just in case he was undercover.

"Fine, whatever. See you tomorrow." And then I hung up and called it a night.

When Mana came by my apartment the next day, she had a tall, burly guy with her. He looked very calm—a little *too* calm.

"This is Oscar," Mana gestured to her friend. "He's looking to do some business. It's a good hookup, enough to buy me a decent stash."

I gestured to the couch, and we all had a seat. Oscar told me how much he moved, which was admittedly impressive, but his supplier had grown unreliable. He was looking for someone a little more stable and accessible, and I'd come highly recommended.

"We can deal," I said, ready to talk numbers. "What's your turf?"

"O-Triple-C," he said, and I froze. Oahu Community Correctional Center. He was a fucking prison guard, and Mana had walked him right into my apartment. "It's all good," he assured me. "I keep people in once they're in. I got no interest in putting them there. We're cool."

I shouldn't have been so easily convinced, but it was a lot of money, and he had a point. If his goal had been to report me, meeting me wouldn't have been necessary. He'd already learned more than enough about me from Mana to report to his friends in law enforcement. He was there to benefit from my business, not shut it down. How Oscar knew Mana was a mystery to me. Prison guards don't generally socialize with street junkies, but it wasn't a far leap to assume she'd spent some time on the inside and met him there.

By this point, my circle of clients was down to Lucas and Max, who supplied their respective military bases; Roxy, who covered the clubs; and a handful of friends and chronics. And now, through Oscar, I had a hold on the local prison. Bringing in that kind of business made me Keilani's top earner. I had become her right hand, her protégé, and not too surprisingly at that point, her best friend.

Keilani had no complaints about our profit margin and had grown pretty fond of me, so I ended up spending a lot of time at her place. It beat stewing in an empty apartment that had gotten way too quiet since I'd cut the boys loose. Keilani's paranoia and agoraphobia had gotten so intense that she barely left her bedroom and didn't leave her apartment at all, so she had come to appreciate the value of company. As a girl her age who she could actually trust, my company was ideal. So, there we were, two badass bitches running a decent chunk of the drug trade on Oahu. Behind the scenes, though, we were just two girls who had grown up too fast, recapturing whatever simple joys we could.

We played a lot of video games. Keilani, of course, had the sickest system at the time. When we weren't in the mood for that, it wasn't uncommon for us to entertain ourselves late into the night, trying to best each other on her electric dartboard, breaking only to make grilled cheese or ramen. It was a side of her she didn't show to just anybody, a side I suspected only a few before me had ever seen.

Keilani was every bit the hardened dealer her reputation suggested. That side of her wasn't a lie; it just wasn't the whole story. Like me, sometimes she just wanted to spend a few hours talking shit over a pint of Ben & Jerry's, and why not? I'm pretty sure that's what everyone needs from time to time, whether they'd admit it or not. We were so "on" when we were doing business, commanding the fear and respect of our dealers and customers, that no one ever questioned it. No one suspected that two of the most hardcore meth dealers on the island devolved into a couple of playful girls behind closed doors, laughing and hanging out all night, binging on milk and cookies. It was like a never-ending slumber party occasionally punctuated by illicit underworld dealings.

Hawaii hadn't exactly lived up to the fantasy I'd arrived there with. It was beautiful and soothing in many ways, but I'd strayed pretty far from the plans I'd made. Everyone I'd connected with—Deb and Johnny, Vic, the boys—had all betrayed me on some level or another. Everyone except Roxy and Keilani.

One night, after a delivery, Keilani had fallen asleep with all her shit still out. I could have taken some and probably even gotten away with it, but I just put all the product and money away for her, tucked her in, and went out to the couch to watch TV until I passed out. I didn't take a single rock, not even a single hit, that wasn't mine. We'd been through so much by that point, having each other's backs and helping each other out of some tight spots, and what had grown between us was not the kind of trust I was willing to throw away.

James looked better than the last time I'd seen him, still a little gaunt but smiling and lively enough to mask just how far his disease had already progressed. We were sitting in my living room, in the middle of a routine sale. He'd left Steven at home but had brought a friend with him, which was fine. James wasn't just another customer. He was a friend, and for friends, I could relax my normally heightened sense of caution.

Bella was dark-haired with steely-grey eyes and a sly grin that never seemed to disappear. "I'm still working on the fact that you're like…the big boss around here," she said. "You look like you're twelve." I didn't take offense. I did look younger than I was, helped in large part by my small stature and youthful face. Looking like some helpless teenager was great camouflage in the line of work I was in. "Sorry," Bella said. I didn't mean…"

"No, it's cool. There are plenty of advantages to being that tiny, blonde New Yorker."

"You're from New York. No shit, where?"

"Upstate. Rockland County."

Bella rolled her eyes. "Jesus…Rockland is *not* upstate. That's Manhattan brainwashing." She jabbed at her chest with her thumb. "Utica. *That's* upstate." I nodded, conceding the point, and accepted a light shove.

"If you two are done bonding," James cut in, holding up his meth pipe. Neither Bella nor I were inclined to object. James took his hit and passed the pipe to Bella, who flicked the lighter under the bulb, filled her lungs, and then…didn't exhale. I reached for the pipe, but she pulled it away and set it down. She beckoned me toward her with a subtle flick of her fingers, and I hesitantly leaned in. She parted her lips, silky smoke curling out, and lightly pressed them to mine, shotgunning the smoke directly into my mouth. I let it fill my lungs to get myself high, but the meth was all but redundant in that regard. Something had come over me when she'd taken my face in her hands, a heady rush unlike any high I'd ever experienced—and I'd experienced a wide variety.

James's taunting whistle broke the spell, and I pulled away to the back of the couch. Bella just leaned back, grinning like a cat.

"Well, I'm getting hungry," I said. "I thought I'd order a pizza or something."

"Thanks, but I gotta go," James said, rising and stretching. "Plans with the boyfriend."

"I could eat," Bella said.

James just nodded, smiling. "Good night, beautiful," he said with a wink, then left.

Bella stayed for another few hours, and as we talked and got high, my apartment saw more laughter than it had in months. I gave her my number before she left and told her to call me anytime to buy off me or just to hang out. She assured me she would but didn't specify which.

I didn't know what to make of her. She was cool and witty, not sophisticated like Keilani, but then again, neither was I. And as much as I loved our slumber parties, that was just two girls being kids together. It was never anything like…well, what *had* my evening with Bella been, exactly?

Looking back, it hadn't been my first clue regarding where my tastes laid, but it was certainly the first to catch my attention. Guys had always been there, a part of my life like any other girl's, just muted in a way. I liked the company, but the passion I was supposed to feel, I never did. Once I started to believe I simply wasn't capable of love, I stopped searching for it, and on the rare occasion I even thought to look, I had been looking in the wrong direction.

Well…how about that?

Bella became something of a regular fixture around my apartment—there to get high, sure, but who wasn't? No one else hung around for hours to talk, listen to music, or just share the space with me, and it was nice having someone around again. The silence in my home had become deafening. There was a reason I'd spent so much time hanging at Keilani's place.

But Bella was great company, and helpful as well. She'd do the dishes and tidy up here and there. She cooked when we remembered to eat. And in the span of about a week, it was just understood that she could come by whenever she liked, stay for as long as she liked, and go. We didn't *need* each other, but we enjoyed having each other. By the time Bella finally kissed me, I let her, and suddenly it was like someone cranked the color on the TV of my mind all the way up. Everything was blazing to life. The picture that had been so flat up until now was glowing hot, and all I could think of was kissing her again.

Ohhhh, I thought as it all fell into place. *Okay.*

This one chronic, Wally, paid me in diamond jewelry and Louis Vuitton so often that even when he didn't, I'd take whatever he had to offer. It wouldn't buy as much as, say, some designer shades would, but enough to get him through the night. With the money I was raking in daily, I could afford such a negligible loss. Wally always had a big smile for me. In my position, people were usually too leery to show any warmth at all. He didn't have that problem.

He called me one night with an address and asked me to meet him there, assuring me he had something huge for me. Twenty minutes later, I arrived at a fairly upscale house, not huge but really nice. Wally greeted me and pulled me inside, throwing open his arms and presenting the foyer in a way that said, *Good shit, am I right?* It was.

"So, how much of it do you want?" he asked.

"What is this place? I know it's not yours." It couldn't have been. No way he'd be scrounging the way he did if he'd had a resource like this to trade all along.

"It's my parents' house. They're out of town." He stepped back, getting squirrelly and scratching his head. "Some meth…or some heroin. I just need…" He waved at some art pieces on display in the living room. "Take it. All of it."

I didn't know what kind of relationship Wally had with his parents. If it was a good one, this would ruin it, and if it was already in the shitter, there would be very little chance of reconciliation after using all their stuff to buy drugs. I couldn't. I'd crossed a lot of lines in the past year, a few I wasn't too proud of, but this would be a step too far.

"No. No way, dude."

"What? Come on! This is good shit!"

"I'm not cleaning out your parents."

"Nikki," he whined, "Please! I need…I need *something*." He fidgeted, pouting, waiting for my answer.

"Did you give it to him?" Bella asked me as I relayed the story an hour later.

"After making it clear that he can't ever offer me his parents' entire estate again…yeah. I gave him a little something."

Bella stopped stirring the soup she was heating up, turned off the burner, and served dinner. "That's one bleeding heart you got there," she said, not quite criticizing me for it, but about as disapproving of it as Keilani would have been. I let the comment pass so we could eat in peace. I'd finally gotten used to a sit-down meal in my apartment being a regular thing, and I'd been enjoying that trend way too much to ruin it. Besides, I didn't mind so much what Bella said when she smiled at me like that.

Not a week later, Wally showed up on my doorstep, shaking and begging me for some heroin. From the look of him, he hadn't had any in just long enough to start detoxing. I was all out of heroin. I only ever had it on hand when Keilani had some she needed to unload or a chronic made a special request, but I could ease Wally through the withdrawal as best I could. I helped him inside and saw him to the couch, where he'd spend the next few days riding it out.

For the better part of a week, I helped Wally to and from the bathroom, patted him down with cool washcloths when he got the sweats, and got him to eat whatever he could keep down. After his detox was more or less done, I went down to the nearest ABC Store, a place in Hawaii where you can buy just about anything—clothes, shoes, food, you name it—and went on a little shopping spree. I got Wally a toothbrush and toiletries, a clean set of clothes, and a pair of flip-flops. He'd been barefoot when he'd shown up at my door, and not by choice.

Back at my place, he woke up to find my "care package" waiting for him beside the couch. He showered and changed into his new clothes, then he took his toiletries and a little bag of food I'd culled from my kitchen, gave me a smile, and walked off.

I don't know what happened to Wally after that. I go out of my way not to think much about it. A happy ending wasn't very likely. I knew what the world saw: a dirty, homeless addict. And he was, but he was also more than that. We're all more than the worst people see of us, and he deserved to know that in some small way. If he could see who I was beneath the face I showed the world, I could do him the same kindness.

Keilani had me to trust and rely on, which was a good thing for her, because she sure as hell didn't trust anyone else, especially not after the incident when her strong-arm had sold her out. There was no such thing as being too careful.

All the big dealers at Keilani's level tended to leave each other alone, content to carve the island up amongst themselves. Their turf wasn't necessarily geographical. The clubs, for instance, were Keilani's domain through me and Roxy, and no one really stepped on her toes, the same way she knew not to step on theirs. The big dealers all kept tabs on each other and were well aware of who worked for who.

The fact that I was Keilani's number one dealer was common knowledge in that circle, but not just among the dealers themselves; their strong-arms knew, and that included Aleki, the guy who had turned on Keilani and held her up at her old apartment. Now living in a gated apartment complex and having a short list of about five people she let anywhere near her home, there was really only one way to get to Keilani: me. And they got to me through one of my chronics, some girl they knew would sell me out for a bag of dope. When I showed up to her place, there they were: Aleki and two other strong-arms I'd seen around fairly often. One of them, who was holding a machete, I'd even moved some pounds of meth to safehouses with.

Aleki's friend drove his machete into the coffee table and said, "Nikki, come sit down with us," and I knew I was in fucking trouble. I walked over and sat down, my bag in my lap. I figured they were just going to rip me off, so you could imagine my surprise when they completely ignored my bag full of drugs and cash and instead told me I was going to bring them to Keilani. I was to show them where she lived, then call up from the gate to be buzzed in. It was not a request or a negotiation. If I sold Keilani out, I got to walk away with my life; that was the deal.

But how could I? I was hardly an idealist. I lived a hard, dangerous life with little room for loyalty. You did what you had to do to see another day and didn't owe a damn soul an apology for that. Even so…

"All right," I muttered. "I'll take you there, but first I need to use the bathroom."

They looked at each other, then back at me, and nodded toward the bathroom. They probably wouldn't have just let me walk in there with my bag if they'd known I had a cell phone in there. They were still rare enough that few people would have even considered the possibility. I made sure to turn on the fan, locked the door behind me, and dialed up Keilani.

"Bitch, pick up," I whispered after the third ring, my whole body shaking.

"Hello?"

"Kei, I'm coming over in a bit. *Do not* buzz me in. Don't open your door for anyone, even me." I hung up, hoping it had been enough, flushed the toilet to complete my ruse, and walked back out into the living room with my best poker face. The machete guy pulled his machete from the table, looked at it, then at me, and said, "We go." And we went.

Aleki rode shotgun, while I directed the driver to Keilani's place from the backseat, Machete Guy eyeing me the whole time. What if my plan didn't work, and Keilani let us in? What would happen to her? And what would happen to me if Aleki and his boys *didn't* get what they came for?

Keilani's apartment complex was up by Nuuanu-Punchbowl, one of Honolulu's more upscale areas. They parked and walked me to the gate, where I punched Keilani's code into the call-up phone, and we waited. It rang and rang with no response, but Aleki insisted I call up again. Once again, there was no answer. Aleki and his friends were not happy, but they'd come this far, and I suppose killing me would have been a waste since they were already so close.

"We wait," Machete Guy said, and we did until someone came along and got buzzed in. This guy didn't even question why some terrified-looking girl and three huge, sketchy-looking guys were loitering outside the gate. He just let us slip on in behind him. The one time a fine, upstanding citizen's paranoia would have served me, and he just looked the other way.

The complex was like a maze, glass corridors connecting several buildings, really upscale shit. It was normally a lovely walk, the green and the sky all around you, but at the moment, I didn't notice. Every step was torture. If I stalled or led them the wrong way, they could very well kill me, and if I led them to Keilani's door, *she* could be killed. I was sweating, on the edge of hyperventilating and bracing for the worst.

When we reached Keilani's door, Aleki prompted me to knock several times. Keilani never answered. The guys were pissed, and I was scared, but what else could I do? I was relieved on Keilani's behalf, but what about me? What would they do with me now? People in my situation could end up in pieces scattered in a pineapple field if they didn't play their cards right.

After a very long, tension-filled ride, they brought me back to where they'd taken me, and after I surrendered all the product I had, they let me go. As I stepped out of the car, Aleki said, "Tomorrow, we go again." It wasn't a request, and I knew that any time they decided to try this again, they would find me. I also knew if I kept going along with them, sooner or later they would do something to make me get Keilani to open the door. I had to disappear for a while, and I had to do it immediately.

Keilani's place was probably the safest place for me, and I had to tell her what was going on. I don't know what made her pick up the phone when I called again. Chance? Intuition? I don't know. But I got her on the line and assured her I was now alone and it would be safe to let me in. I would be a while, though.

Erring on the side of caution, I took three different cabs to get back to her complex just to make sure I wasn't followed. Even then, I was a raw nerve, allowing for the possibility that they could have followed me anyway or doubled back to hide in the bushes and jump me when I returned. Every step from the cab to the gate to Keilani's front door was a risk. There was always a chance someone would be watching and waiting in the shadows to jump me, but nothing happened. I got to Keilani's door, she let me in, and I immediately turned around, slammed it shut, and turned every lock. Then and only then could I release a heavy sigh and breathe deeply as my heartbeat slowed to normal.

"They're going to come back for me," I said, gasping over a glass of water. "They're going to keep coming until they get in. Aleki's not dropping this, even if they can't get to you through me. They know where you live now. I'm sorry. I—"

"No. I know you did what you could do. But we need a plan."

"We" was right. Neither one of us was safe to leave, and we were in it together. So, in all our wisdom, we decided to do a bunch of meth and stay up all night, for days if we had to. At that point, there was no such thing as too much vigilance. Keilani retrieved two guns from her safe and handed one to me, and we stood there—methed the fuck out—for hours, guns trained on the front door. We eventually had to sit down, but we barely moved from our spots. We slid down the walls of the entry hall and sat, guns in our laps, never taking our eyes off the door.

After a brief rest we decided to resume, taking turns so that there wouldn't be another lapse in security. We took turns resting for at least two days, always ready for Aleki and his friends to return. Eventually, they did.

They tried to force their way in, but couldn't make it past the deadbolt. When they finally gave up and left, I was just about ready to pass out from the stress. And from tweaking on meth for several consecutive days.

See, strong-arms didn't live with their employers. They came along for big deals or would sometimes stop by to hang out or make a delivery, then we paid them in meth and cut them loose to go enjoy it or do whatever the hell they did on their own time. Keilani put in a call to one of her most reliable (and trustworthy, as strong-arms go) guys, a thick Samoan named Tāne, and he showed up the next day to escort me home. But first we took a detour to a secluded field, where he pulled out a small Beretta.

"You should have this now," he said, handing it to me. He pointed out a secret place on the top of the gun for one bullet, away from where the other bullets loaded in. "Most people wouldn't know there's an extra bullet. Don't forget it's there." He gave me a brief tutorial on how to properly hold and fire a gun. He showed me how to plant my feet and stand so I could brace for the recoil—and reminded me more than once that if I ever found myself in a situation where I was forced to empty my clip, I always had that one hidden bullet left. "If they tell you to drop your gun, just stare them down and lower it slow. When you get it to waist height, point and shoot. They'll never see it coming."

"I...I don't know if I can..." I really didn't. Living in the fast lane was one thing. I'd been doing it my whole life to some degree, and a little reckless endangerment or the risk of an overdose came with the territory, but hurting someone? Actually shooting them? That had never been on the table before, and I didn't want it there. I didn't want it on the table, in the room, anywhere near me. I was suddenly aware I was crying. I couldn't say for how long.

"Hey, it's them or you. Who's it going to be?" Tāne said in a steady voice.

I'd just been getting high, moving a little product, having fun. How the fuck had it come to this? *Them or you. Who's it going to be? Them or you. Who's it going to be?* It became a mantra, echoing in my head over and over, until it became the basis of every decision that followed.

"It's not going to be me," I whimpered, planting my feet.

"Who's it going to be?"

"It's not going to be me," I repeated, this time stronger.

"Who?"

"It's not going to be me!" I barked. I fired. Tāne nodded approvingly, but I didn't feel proud. I didn't feel like I'd accomplished anything but sinking further down.

God, I thought as I lowered the gun, *who even am I anymore?*

Bella came around my place later, but it didn't do much to improve my mood. It had been a few days since I'd seen her, and she'd missed *a lot.*

"Hey. I'm starvin'. You want some mac and cheese?" she said, already taking a box from the cabinet.

"No."

"You sure?"

"I can't really think about fuckin' food right now, okay?!"

She froze there for a second. I was ready for her to throw the box across the room, but all she did was set it down and sit across from me.

"What happened?" It wasn't an accusation. She wasn't demanding an explanation for why I'd just shouted at her; she was just asking.

"Let's see. One of my chronics sold me out. I've been threatened, kidnapped at knife-point so I could sell out Keliani, which I didn't do, so now I'm probably on someone's shit list. I just got through lessons on how to shoot a gun in a high-pressure scenario, because I carry one now and it's something I just might have to deal with, and *where the fuck* have you been?"

I pitched forward, cradling my head in my hands, and Bella just popped over to my side and held me.

"I'm sorry," she said.

I let her hold me and caught my breath, and it was a little better. "Bella?"

"Yeah?"

"Some mac and cheese would be kind of great." She laughed and held me for a minute before she made us some dinner.

James had been thin for as long as I'd known him, but in the past few weeks he'd grown gaunt and pale, and it didn't take a genius to work out what it meant. If he hadn't been dying before, he was now. Before the advent of antiretrovirals, all anyone with AIDS could do was get sicker, maybe slow the roll a bit with some AZT, and wait to die. James was on the way out, and none of us could ignore it anymore.

"The tumors are everywhere now," he said. The light I'd always seen in his eyes, all that jovial charm, had bled almost completely away. Even the smile he managed was faint. "Some days I'm barely even me; dementia. It just comes and goes. I'm not gonna get better. I have weeks left, maybe days, and it doesn't look good. It's already not good."

"What do you need?" I asked, dropping some meth on the table, as well as a bump of the heroin I'd started keeping around for his pain relief. He was new to the stuff, but under the circumstances it had become increasingly necessary.

"Just a little more. You know, to take the edge off."

It was a reasonable enough request. He was in pain. This was palliative, and I knew it. I couldn't do much for him, but if I knew anything, it was pain and the value of relief. I added some more heroin to his haul. I wasn't even going to charge him extra, but he insisted on paying, then he smiled at me, and the light danced in his eyes.

"Good night, beautiful," he said, giving me a long hug, then he went to the door, blew me a kiss, and left.

At around 2 p.m. the next day, I was snoozing on the couch when I was woken by a knock at the door.

"Nikki, it's Steven."

I opened the door to find Steven there, looking completely gutted, and I knew James was gone. I would have made him some coffee or tea, but I didn't have those things. A glass of water was the best I could do. He thanked me and then told me everything: how they'd lit candles and put on music, how they'd pumped James with so much meth and heroin he barely knew what was going on, how he was at least lucid enough to know that Steven was with him. Steven had helped him get high and sang along with him to the songs on the stereo, and when the rush really started to hit James, Steven made love to him.

Just *kissing* on heroin is a warm, squishy bliss unlike any other, so heroin sex is pretty much off the charts. Heroin sex with someone you love has got to be a high unlike any other, and that's how James left this world, euphoria coursing through him, chemicals in his veins and Steven in his arms.

Steven and I cried and talked for hours about life and death, love and courage, how painful the world is and how beautiful parts of it remain anyway. And we talked about James and how, even if he hadn't really gotten the life he'd wanted, it had been *his* life, and he'd ended it on his terms. There was some comfort in that, but not enough.

I held it together pretty well until Steven left, and then it hit me: the loss of my friends, of the boys, of any sense of trust I'd ever had. Even Keilani, who I knew had my back…there were limits. I hadn't reached them yet, but I knew they were there. I was an addict and a dealer, packing heat for protection and looking over my shoulder all the time, constantly surprised by the pit in my stomach from forgetting to eat. And it all came rushing forth at once.

I was sobbing when Bella showed up. Who knows how long I'd been at it? I told her what had happened, and she took me to my room, got in bed with me, and held me.

CHAPTER 6

Heat

My social life was pretty much limited to Keilani, Roxy, and Bella. Even the customers I got high with weren't really friends, and I hadn't been eager to make any since James had died, but there were a few people I met through "work" I'd chill with on occasion.

Bobby was a lot of things, not the least of which was one of the big dealers on the island. A scrawny guy in his mid-to-late fifties, his greying hair was surprisingly thick and came down to his shoulders. He was notably eccentric, his shirts loud even by Hawaiian standards, and an ardent karaoke enthusiast. He was also an informant who played both sides against the middle, left alone by the authorities to conduct his own business because of all the people he turned over to them. Never me, though. He might have, given enough incentive, but he liked me and knew my value, and you don't burn an asset like me unless the price is really right.

I'd hang with Bobby from time to time for a few reasons. First, because there weren't many dealers at our level, and having someone who got me and got my life, who I could sit down with to smoke and shoot the shit without having to look over my shoulder the whole time, was a commodity I was savvy enough to recognize. And second, Bobby's role as an informant went both ways. He always seemed to have inside information on what was going down. There was a line where our world and the cop world brushed up against each other. Bobby was that line and a valuable resource to have in my pocket. It made his regular attempts to woo me worth the trouble…but just barely.

Bobby would kneel in front of me, karaoke machine in hand as he wrapped his off-key, thickly accented voice around "I Get a Kick Out of You" as best he could, looking deep into my eyes like some lothario just a few lyrics away from winning me over. But Sinatra has never been my jam, especially coming from a man—a man old enough to be my father, no less—and I was only smiling from holding back a fit of laughter.

No matter how often Bobby hit on me, I never felt I was in any danger. Personal space aside, he never overstepped, and he never lost his fondness for me, no matter how many times I rebuffed his advances. He was genuinely nuts and genuinely funny, and the laughs and inside info were worth the occasional cringeworthy serenade.

The human mind is a truly amazing thing, more resilient than I think we give it credit for. Do something long enough and it just becomes your routine. For me, over the past several months, sleeping with a gun under my pillow and a woman beside me was just my new normal. Having Bella around full-time was new to me in a lot of ways. I'd never cohabitated with someone I was romantically involved with, much less a *woman* I was involved with, but there I was, waking up every day next to my live-in girlfriend.

The situation with Keilani and the strong-arms had cooled down, but dropping my guard was what had gotten me into hot water in the first place, so I always kept my back to the wall and an eye on the door. That was just how I operated now. It wasn't so bad.

"So, how is living in sin with Miss Bella going?" Roxy asked me one morning as she slapped the night's profits down into my hand. The street would be coming to life with commuters any minute now, and Jeremiah was half a block down, sliding his back up and down a Walk/Don't Walk sign to the catcalls and applause of half a dozen club kids.

"It's good. It's…comfortable."

Roxy mimed wiping a tear. "Aww, my little baby dyke's growing up."

"Come on, Ma," I groaned, smiling as she swept a lock of hair back behind my ear. It had started as a joke, but the truth was that over the past year, it had been Roxy I always seemed to turn to for guidance and comfort, even an education in certain areas. If that doesn't make a mom, what does?

We strolled down the sidewalk, wrangling Jeremiah and the others as we passed them. It occurred to me that I'd been under complete radio silence with my family for the better part of a year. Everything before Hawaii seemed like some kind of dream or parallel universe that faded into memory a little bit each day. But I wasn't homesick. I didn't ache with longing for my family or my old life. The new life I'd created was as complete and real to me as anything ever had been.

My trance was broken as a sour-faced passerby shoulder-checked Roxy. "Māhū," he muttered without looking back.

"The fuck is your problem, asshole?" I called over my shoulder. He didn't even slow down. "Fuck you!" I turned to Roxy to ask her if she could believe that guy's attitude but paused at the look on her face. She didn't look scared or hurt, just tired. Worn down. I'd heard the term before, but I'd never seen its effect.

Pre-colonization, the māhū were Hawaii's third gender and played a role in traditional Hawaiian society as teachers and healers, taking the female role in religious ceremonies in spaces off-limits to women. Post-colonization, however, the term had been twisted into a slur hurled at gender-nonconforming men and trans women.

The conflation of drag queens and trans women was very much a product of the time. If the vocabulary that we have now had been more commonplace, Roxy probably would have identified as a trans woman, but she called herself a drag queen, so we followed her lead. In any event, she most definitely checked the māhū box, and while she'd grown a thick skin, it wasn't bulletproof. Even *dyke*, spoken by Roxy with the deepest affection, still pierced my armor a bit, and that term was far newer to me than māhū was to her.

I looped my arm around the crook of her elbow and leaned my head on her shoulder as we walked on. I didn't have a trace of shared blood anywhere on the island, but I wasn't without family, and you take care of your own.

Having my found family was all well and good, but I couldn't help wondering about the one I'd left behind. I didn't know where I'd even begin, what I would possibly say if I did reach out, but it kept nagging at me, so one day I picked up the phone and dialed my parents' house. When my mom answered, I froze. Would I get a tearful reception? A harsh tongue-lashing? A guilt trip? I wasn't really prepared for any of those options, so I hung up and tried again the next day with the same degree of success. I called a few times, getting either my mom or my stepdad, neither of whom I was eager to speak with. Then, on the fifth or sixth try…

"Yello?" I didn't recognize the voice. It wasn't deep enough to be my stepdad's but definitely male. Oh…damn…. How long had it been since my kid brother and I had spoken? Long enough for his voice to drop an octave, apparently.

"Mike?"

There was long pause, and then? "Nikki? Holy shit! What—where have you been? Are you okay?"

"Relax, dude. I'm fine." It was the kindest lie I could tell in the moment.

"We've been worried. Like, *really* worried!"

"I know. I'm sorry. Look, is anyone else around?"

After Michael assured me I'd hit the sweet spot in the afternoon when he had the house to himself, I brought him up to speed with a sanitized version of the truth. I told him that college hadn't worked out, that I had a job and my own apartment, and that I'd fallen off the grid because I didn't want to catch shit for my choices from anyone, especially our mom. That much he understood well enough to take my explanation at face value, and after he needled an apology out of me for ghosting him along with our parents, he quickly forgave me and caught me up on his life—how he was navigating his freshman year of high school and didn't appreciate all the parental suspicion aimed at him now that he was a teenager. I suppose that was on me to some degree. I'd set quite a precedent when I was his age. Even hearing him bitch made me smile.

We'd been talking for an hour when he mentioned that our stepdad was pulling into the driveway. I told him to take the phone into his room and close the door. After making him promise not to share it or even let anyone know he had it, I gave him my pager number. He could tell our mom and dad (and stepdad) that I'd called, so they'd know I was okay, but that was it. I made it clear that if he broke this condition, I'd just change my number and disappear again.

The idea didn't sit well with him—keeping secrets had never been his strength—but he managed to keep my number to himself, so every once in a while we got to talk, and I was someone's big sister again.

I filled a fresh pipe with some meth, took a hit, and passed it to Lucas, who had swung by while off-duty to pick up his usual. His physique aside, there was very little navy about him in his off hours. He was casually dressed, and his easy demeanor would have camouflaged him as just another customer to anyone who didn't know better.

We passed the pipe back and forth, just shooting the shit, our business already concluded. I'd learned this little ritual from Keilani and adopted it myself. In my ever-increasing isolation I'd come to appreciate the value of socializing. Besides, small talk is a great way to sniff out any problems a customer might be having—problems that could come back to bite you.

Lucas had always been good for conversation, but that day he wasn't saying much. He just seemed to stew in some kind of funk.

"What's up, dude? You all right?"

He shrugged, slouching in his seat as something overwhelmed him. He finally leaned forward and covered his eyes with his hand, and I knew what it was. He'd mentioned his mom's health in passing here and there, and never in an optimistic light.

"What is it?"

"Cancer."

"Bad?"

He nodded and let one sob slip out before pulling his game face back on; good old military training.

"She's dying, and I don't know what to do for her. Even if I could get the time off, I wouldn't know how to take care of her. And a nurse…I don't have that kind of money." He sighed, shaking his head. "Sometimes you're just fucked."

Ain't that the truth? Sometimes you were just fucked, and what you needed was for someone to give you a break. I retreated into my bedroom and returned with some extra product.

"I can't afford any more."

"Just take it." He hesitated, trying to read me to figure out what the catch might be. This business wasn't exactly known for favoring charity. I slapped it into his hand. "Sell it and go home. Take care of your mom." His brow relaxed, and he nodded. Then he thanked me and left.

Lucas called me a few days later to tell me he was leaving to take care of his mom, directly implying the end (or at least suspension) of our business relationship. But he didn't want to leave me high and dry, and *someone* had to supply all his customers on the base, so he offered to hook me up with someone who could replace him. He told me she'd been helping him move the product and was good to take over if I was willing to do business with her directly. Lucas had always been solid, but I hadn't come as far as I had without taking precautions.

The first few times Tina bought from me I sent a runner to handle the transaction. I needed time to feel her out, to see if I got a sketchy vibe from any of it. After a few weeks of routine sales, I finally agreed to meet with her for our first big deal. Tina was a fish out of water on the island, a haole like me, but taller by about a foot. Regardless, she looked every bit the part of a navy transplant from the mainland, so I let my guard down, and we started to deal.

I shouldn't have let my guard down.

Tāne showed up at my door one day, his face as unreadable as ever, and I invited him right in. I even offered him something to drink. I hadn't seen much of him after our little gun tutorial, but he was still Keilani's number one strong-arm, so there was no reason to be rude. He declined my hospitality. All business, then.

"You're hot," he said in a flat voice.

"Uh…thanks, but—"

"People asking about you. Someone's building a case."

"Who?"

"Dunno. Cops? Doesn't matter. It's trouble."

Bobby wasn't the only person with eyes and ears on the inside. Keilani had her sources as well. She wasn't a narc, but she could have been with all the info that came her way. All she was interested in, though, was self-preservation. And fond of me as she was, she wasn't about to get dragged down by anyone.

Tāne made the situation very clear. The authorities were coming for me. It was just a matter of time before I went down, and when I did I had one choice in regard to spilling anything on Keilani: don't.

I wasn't oblivious. There was a reason she sent Tāne to deliver this message, rather than inviting me over to tell me herself. On the off-chance the subtlety of the message might be lost on me, Tāne made a not-so-veiled threat about the consequences of implicating Keilani. Then he sat down and smoked with me in one of the most surreal and uncomfortable shared highs I'd ever experienced before leaving my place with a smile. Not a sweet, friendly smile—an "I don't give a fuck about you, I am loyal to the hand that feeds me, so do the right thing or else" smile. It's a very distinct look.

Tāne had come to deliver a message, and I'd gotten it. I was going to get caught, I was probably going to do time, and if I wanted to live long enough to make it out, it meant keeping my mouth shut. And on top of that, Keilani was cutting me off. With the authorities on my tail, I was too much of a risk to keep doing business with. I wish I could say I didn't get how she could just hang me out to dry like that, but I knew how the game worked, and fucking up by trusting the wrong person—whoever it was—had been my own damn fault, so there it was. Along with her message, Keilani had given Tāne a huge load of product to deliver as a sort of severance package. After that, I'd be on my own.

So, who had it been? Who had turned on me? It could have been any one of my people, but in my gut I knew that Tina was involved. I didn't want her to know that I knew, but mitigating the damage as best I could meant cutting her off immediately. Maybe if I did that and laid low for a while, I'd eventually just slip past their radar and be okay. When Tina started blowing up my phone, I knew she'd been my Judas.

I laid low as best I could, and for a while things actually seemed to go back to normal. It was about a week after my little visit from Tāne that

I was walking down Kuhio Avenue, allowing myself to actually enjoy the day, when my cell phone rang.

"Hey, Bobby. What's up?"

"The feds have landed."

I halted. I couldn't have heard him right. "I'm sorry, what?"

"They're looking for you. Get the fuck off the island."

I didn't need to be told twice. I was just a dealer—a good one, yeah, but I assumed that the authorities I'd been dodging for the past month had been local police. But federal agents? That was some shit I had not seen coming.

I needed somewhere to take a breath and figure out my next move, and Jeremiah's place was close by. Given the hour, he was probably still sleeping off last night's clubbing, but pleasantries would have to take a backseat. Besides, he owed me. On some level, every club kid on the island did, and if ever there was a time to call in a favor…

Jeremiah's little room for rent wasn't terribly impressive, but it was four walls and a door that locked, and that was enough. I gave him some cash and sent him out to pick up a few things.

"I don't know, Nikki. I'm not a stylist." I shot Jeremiah a weary, don't-fuck-with-me look. He pursed his lips and flinched with ten times the necessary drama. "Oh, what? Every faggot can do a girl's hair?"

"Well, I can't do it myself, so you're going to have to do."

I should have listened to him, because I walked into that place with my natural long blonde tresses and walked out again a few hours later, wearing some short, feathered, pale maroon disaster. With sloppy bangs. Well, lesson learned: When someone tells you they don't cut hair, believe them.

I hit the pavement in a completely different outfit and the most identity-concealing sunglasses Jeremiah could find, breezing down the street in an earnest effort to appear as casual as possible, just in case anyone was watching.

When I made it to the hotel where Roxy was currently nesting, she let me in and assured me I could stay for a little while at least; there was no telling when she'd have to move on. She was happy to host me, but her style would not be cramped. She still hit the scene every night with her entourage, while I stayed behind in her room, watching TV into the wee hours. After she came home, she would sleep for a few hours, and when she woke up we'd spend the day hanging out. It was the only sliver of normalcy I had left, and I savored it as best I could.

"I don't know what I'm going to do," I said to Roxy as we sat at her dinette. She'd so deftly talked me into eating some Spam and eggs that I hadn't even noticed.

"That's all you have?" she asked. "You've run completely dry?"

"I've got more cash and product at my place, but I can't go back there."

Roxy shook her head. "No, too risky." She took my hand. "I don't know how much longer I'm going to be here, but wherever I go…"

"I'll be fine," I said, waving her away. I had no such confidence. This was it. Could I have hidden in hotel rooms for the rest of my life? Not even if I had the money, which at that point, I didn't. I was just running down the clock, bracing for the inevitable.

I had reached out to Bella on my second day at Roxy's to tell her where I was and what was going on. Wouldn't you know it…she already had an idea. The feds had come to Bella's job looking for her, an encounter she'd only narrowly escaped. Now she had to go off the grid as well, at least for a while, and there was no way we could do it together. It would be goodbye for a little while, but we had the same haunts and would know how to find each other once it was safe. At least I hoped so.

I had ditched my cell phone right after Bobby's call. The second I knew the feds were after me, there was no question my cell would be used to track me down, so it had to go. My beeper, on the other hand, I'd always kept around. The first page I answered, knowing it was safe thanks to the codes we had for each other, was Mana. She'd never been the most stable person, but there was an extra edginess in her voice, something…sketchy.

"Nikki, where the fuck ya been? You know where Bella's at? She with you?" I explained that Bella wasn't with me but had also gone to ground and might be out of touch for a while, as would I. Mana's sigh cut the silence. "You're in trouble, aintcha?" I didn't answer. "Nikki? Come on, let me help."

There wasn't anything she could do. There wasn't much anyone could do. I was stuck on an island. I couldn't hop on the interstate and take my chances; there were only so many places I could hide, and sooner or later I was going to run out. My time at Roxy's was almost up. I was out of money and any drugs I might sell to make more. I was just tapped out. But Mana pleaded again, insisting I let her help.

"I know a guy who might be able to get you off the island. Can't promise anything, but it's worth a shot, right?"

Mana was one of those people who didn't have much in the way of money, resources, or charisma, but somehow had a "guy" for everything. It seemed unlikely for someone as scattered as she was to have that kind of talent, but when I thought about how she'd managed to secure me as her meth dealer and Oscar as an ally while in lockup, it stood to reason she'd found ways to get all kind of things she needed. So, maybe her guy could help. It was a long shot, but I needed to get off the island, and I couldn't afford to be picky with opportunities to do so.

Trusting a chronic for anything is a risk and not what anyone would call smart. In an ideal situation, I'd have never even considered it, but this situation was pretty fucking far from ideal, and Mana had come through in the past when she'd hooked me up with Oscar. If the chance she was offering was legit, it could be my only one.

"I swear to God, if you're setting me up…"

"Nikki, come on. I got you."

And just like that, I caved. I should have known better. I probably did, but I wanted so badly to trust her, and it's not like I was flush with options.

We agreed to meet at Holiday Q's, a pool hall where I knew everyone. From there, who knew where it would lead? At least I'd get to hang with some friends for a while. I left my Beretta with Roxy just in case it was a setup—the last thing I needed would be an additional charge for carrying without a permit.

I crept along the bridge that connected Roxy's hotel to the parking garage. The four-foot walls on either side hid my crouching frame. Roxy walked alongside me, assuring me every few feet that she didn't see anything that looked suspicious. She tried easing my nerves with a little chatter, which oddly enough worked; terrified as I was, it was impossible not to at least chuckle at the ridiculousness of the scenario. It also took a little of the sting out of the realization that this could be it, and we might never see each other again.

I kept low to the ground until we reached Jeremiah's car, then I crawled into the backseat. Roxy told me she'd see me later, and, hoping like hell it was true, off I went.

Jeremiah dropped me off a block or two from Holiday Q's, and I walked the rest of the way. Time seemed to warp around me and I felt a little lightheaded. I still had a vague feeling that I was walking into a trap, but it didn't stop me. Before I even crossed the threshold, I knew I'd been set up—I *knew* it—but I just kept walking. Because really, what option did I have? I couldn't run anymore. I'd been paranoid and exhausted for weeks, and when I'd slept I hadn't slept well or for very long. There was still a chance I was wrong and that this would be the first step toward getting me to safety—a slim chance, but I was willing to roll the dice on it.

The dice were not in my favor that day. The second I stepped inside, a cop came out of nowhere and arrested me. I didn't resist. I had nothing left to resist with. I'd beaten the odds for a long time, and my luck had finally run out. I accepted it. Mana had betrayed me to get a charge against her dropped. I knew it deep down. I'd known it during the call with her, but I wanted—I *needed* to believe there was a chance she was legit. So I made myself believe it and ended up in handcuffs.

And that's how, after two years of breaking the law and completely getting away with all of it, I ended up in jail. Not with a wild shoot-out or a chase down an alley with cops thundering behind me, but in semi-aware surrender, betrayed, exhausted, and unable to keep going.

When we arrived downtown, the cops brought me in through an underground garage. They marched me through, hands cuffed behind me. It was bad enough knowing what was likely ahead of me, but the smug looks on their faces only added insult to injury. When we hit the station floor, the feds were waiting for us. They had built the case against me, but it was still the Honolulu PD's jurisdiction, so they'd partnered up. After a round of handshakes, I was taken into an interrogation room to be questioned by a handful of cops and NCIS agents—Naval Criminal Investigative Service, for those unfamiliar with network procedurals.

The navy…so, it *had* been Tina. I fucking knew it.

Tina hadn't exactly turned on me; she'd been with the feds the whole time. It was Lucas, I quickly learned, who had given me up. His mother had been dying. That much was true, but in his mad dash to move the last supply I'd given him, he'd gotten caught selling on the base, and the choice between going down himself or throwing me under the bus to save his own ass had been really no choice at all.

And there it was: My bleeding fucking heart and desire to see the good in people had screwed me once again. Keilani had always warned me it was a liability, that it would get me into trouble one day. That was the thing she had that I didn't. She may have been a paranoid, strung-out mess, but she had that hard edge, the ability to cut a motherfucker off and tell them to go fuck themselves, and that quality was what ultimately saved her. When the time came, she'd even done it to me.

I sat in the interrogation room as the agents laid all the evidence out in front of me. This hadn't been a run-of-the-mill sting. NCIS had placed me under surveillance for months, watching me, following me, tapping my phone, taking pictures of everything, and they had the receipts. Records of where I was, what I was wearing—if I so much as stepped outside my apartment to have a cigarette, there was a record of it somewhere and a photo to match, and now those photos and transcribed phone calls were staring up at me from the interrogation room table. I'd had no idea how big a case they'd been building. They weren't just looking to nab a dealer. They were looking to take down my entire line.

The long game could have gone even longer; they wanted to nail me for as much as they could, but once I'd gone into hiding, it was time to pull the trigger with whatever they had, and they had more than enough. And then, for reasons I'm not entirely sure of even now, the feds just handed the case to the state. They just wiped their hands clean, walked away, and the state took the lead from that point forth.

They questioned me for hours, but remembering my little heart-to-heart with Tāne, I gave them nothing. Part of it was self-preservation, sure, but also…

True, Keilani had cut me loose. She cared about me; she was my friend. But she had that survival instinct and had made the hard call to save herself. I couldn't hate her for it, but I couldn't do the same. I just couldn't. I wasn't a lot of things I used to be. I'd fallen pretty far…but I was still loyal, so I kept my mouth shut.

Eventually, a bunch of cops came in and ordered me to submit to a strip search to make sure I wasn't holding any drugs on me. I did as I was told and endured the indignity. I couldn't give them any more ammo than they already had. Then I dressed and the they asked me even more questions, all of which I refused to answer.

After a while, the cops took me to an empty holding cell around the corner, an open cell that was all bars on two sides and probably served as a drunk tank most of the time.

"Strip," one of them said. I just looked at him, confused. "Did I fucking stutter?"

"I already did this."

"Do it again."

They made only the slightest pretense about what they were doing, and I knew that when they told to me strip, turn around, and bend over, it was for their amusement. It was the first of several unnecessary strip searches done for the sheer virtue of breaking me. I was a criminal, I was under arrest and in custody, and certain procedures needed to be observed, certain measures taken…but the gross abuse of power used against me that day was unconscionable. Only one of them refrained, a tall, burly officer, the only Black cop I'd seen since I'd entered the building. He was the only one who didn't seem to find my humiliation hilarious.

A few other people joined me in the holding cell as the hours passed, but it was a quiet night. I had plenty of time and silence to sit there and think about all the ways I'd gotten myself into this mess, what I'd have to do to get out of it, and why I couldn't. After a few hours of obsessing over it all, a cop came by, unlocked the door to the cell, and took me downstairs.

It was like a dungeon down there: a row of dark, dirty cells that stank of piss. My former accommodations were for transfers and newbies, or intoxicated offenders who needed to dry out. But down here, things got real. My tiny cell was bare cement except for a small bench and a lidless metal toilet. My mind raced as the door slammed shut. What the hell was I going to do? What was going to happen next?

I was already detoxing and in desperate need of a cigarette, but all I could do was grimace and try to ignore the jones tugging at every inch of me. My senses were on hyper-alert. Everything was too real, my nicotine craving only enhanced by the meth draining out of my system. I hadn't been between hits for this long in a good while, and the withdrawal hit me pretty badly. When you're addicted to meth, it saturates your system and takes a while to clear out, but once it does…exhaustion isn't even the word. You can't even move. And once my adrenaline levels had ebbed to what in a healthy person would be normal, there was nothing left for me to do but lie down on the cold cement bench and fall into a dead sleep.

I don't know how long I was out, but I was woken abruptly by the guards pulling me out of my cell and into another room where they sat me down, put a cigarette in my mouth, and proceeded to ask me more questions. I was dying for one of them to light that butt, but they insisted that they only would once I told them what they wanted to know. My eyes darted to the Black cop, who stood off to the side, doing everything he could not to look directly at me, not to see the tactics he had little choice but to enable. But he glanced at me despite himself, frowned faintly, and looked away again.

"If you help us, we can help you, and you can go home," one of the others said, barely concealing how much fun he was having playing this game.

At that point, my blood screaming for anything to take the edge off, even just a cigarette, I wanted to believe them. Who knows? They might have even been telling me the truth. But I was young and scared, and extra-convinced after my multiple strip searches that they could just be fucking with me, so once again I gave them nothing.

For an entire day, they jerked me around like that, pulling me in and out of the cell, moving my location, and baiting me with smokes and food until I barely knew which end was up, but I never let up. And they had to feed me—they couldn't let me starve; I wasn't going to answer any questions unconscious from a hospital bed—so at some point one of the cops served me a little can of lumpy stew on a tray they slid through the food slot at the bottom of the cell door. It was cold and slimy, but I wolfed it down. Thanks to my habit and my circumstances, I hadn't eaten well for days even *before* I'd been arrested.

The officers continued to fuck with me for days, and I was too in it at the time to understand it was because of all the power I held, even at my most vulnerable. It wasn't me they wanted. It had never been me. They wanted this investigation to go all the way up the chain, to Keilani or someone on her level—someone even higher if they could manage it. And after months of surveillance and undercover work, the buck had stopped at a tiny girl too young to even merit a bachelor's degree. Taking me down wasn't the ideal endgame, but it would do. They would fold if they had to, but they kept at it a little while longer, doing their best to break me. All except that one cop.

I never learned the Black cop's name. I could've seen it on his badge if I'd thought to look, but I couldn't think of anything. Time had been passing at a crawl, so I don't know how long I'd been in that dark little cell when someone opened the food slot and a brown hand slid a few candy bars through.

"Sugar helps with the detox," he whispered.

I suspected I was hallucinating everything, the guy's voice, the candy bars, all of it. But when I reached out and my fingers grasped one of them, it was solid. It was real! By the time it even occurred to me to thank him, he was gone, but I thanked him again and again with every bite, especially once I realized that he'd probably been the one who'd brought me that can of stew. I rationed the candy bars as best I could, so that I'd have them to treat both my hunger and my withdrawal. Even at my most sparing, they didn't last the day, but it was still something.

On my second day in the cell, the door opened and the guards said they were taking me upstairs. They shackled my hands and feet, and I shuffled along. A guard's hand clamped my arm tightly as he marched me onto the elevator, then off again, and into the courtroom. I had no idea what was going on. I was detoxing, hungry, scared, and exhausted.

When they brought me back downstairs, they stuck me in a larger cell with a bunch of other women who had been through it all before and casually informed me that if I'd already been to the courtroom for arraignment, I'd be transferred soon. As usual, they just saw some kid. They had no idea who I was or what I'd done to land myself in there, so they were kind enough to give me a crash course in prison: what to expect, how to act and what to say, and how not to fuck up. I listened intently to every word. I'd already fucked up badly enough to be heading to prison at all. The least I could do was game that experience to be as benign as I could manage.

"So, wait…" one of the women said. "How long have you been in here?"

"I don't know. I keep losing track of…I think a couple days. Why? Is that not normal?"

A few of them laughed. "They keep you a few hours, maybe till morning if they pull you in late enough at night." And true to what she said, a few hours later the cops opened the door and started taking everyone out for transfer. I cracked my back, grunted, and stood up.

"Not you," the guard said firmly, and slammed the heavy, creaking door shut. Once again, I was alone in a cell, but at least now in one four times bigger than the one I'd started in. Even the bench was bigger. Well, that would at least make napping slightly less uncomfortable.

I slept some more. I had nothing else to do with the time, and it's easier to ignore your hunger when you're unconscious. Makes for some freaky dreams, though. I slept as long as my body would let me, but after a point it wouldn't take to any more sleep, so I just sat there, alone with my thoughts. I hated being alone with my thoughts. All they ever did was turn to how fucked up everything had become even well before I'd gone on the run from the feds.

It was well after dark when a guard came in to tell me someone wanted to see me. A woman in a sharp pantsuit walked into my cell with what, at that point, looked like nothing short of a feast in my eyes: a burger, fries, and shake from McDonald's. Frankly, it could have been fished right out of the trash, and I still would have eaten it. I would have eaten anything.

"It's going to be in your best interest to talk." Oh…okay, heading straight into it. Well, at least she'd given me the food before I'd had a chance to refuse to cooperate. That was a step up. She let me wolf down a few bites before I came up for air and told her I couldn't help her. She glared at me sternly. Going by her outfit and attitude, I could tell she was probably pretty high up the chain. She had to be. They'd exhausted every other option.

"I don't think you really get the size of what it is you're stepping into," she said, giving me a long stare and pulling out my paperwork. She showed me the charges against me, where my bail was set, and the time I was facing—thirty years, too much time for me to even wrap my brain around. I couldn't process what was happening. I was too loyal, too proud, and just too damn young to fully realize the gravity of the situation. Thirty fucking years behind bars, and I wouldn't budge. I couldn't bring myself to give Keilani up. I couldn't betray her. I couldn't stop eating either, even knowing that the faster I went, the faster it would be gone.

"Sorry. I got nothing," I said, popping the last morsel into my mouth.

The woman looked at me with a cool but soft expression. She was the enemy, that much was plain, but at the same time there was something else there, something not unlike what I'd seen behind the eyes of my candy bar angel. I could see myself through her eyes, this girl who, given my size and deceptive appearance, looked about fourteen years old. She must have known my actual age, but the eyes can play tricks on the heart, so all she saw was a confused, frightened kid who had a chance to mitigate the consequences of her choices and was pissing it away. I truly think it broke her heart a little, but not enough to keep her from doing her job.

"I'm sorry to hear that," she said, her voice gentle but resigned. "Keep the rest." She handed me the grease-spotted paper bag. I opened it to find more burgers and fries inside.

"Thank you!" I called out, but the words only hit her back as she slipped out the door, leaving me alone to await whatever came next.

Still ravenous, I kept on eating, slowing down the fuller I felt. When I stopped long enough to have any thoughts at all, they turned toward a question that had been haunting me for longer than I'd realized. How? How had I gotten here? How far back did it go, the start of all this?

I wanted to blame it all on my arrival in Oahu, but I knew better. Wiping the grease from my fingers, I forced myself to confront the truth. My descent had started long ago, closer to the start of my life than I liked to admit…even to myself.

Part Two

Chasing the Dragon

CHAPTER 7

Wounded

I was always a runner. I couldn't stand in my skin for one minute, and when my feet couldn't carry me far enough, I retreated into my mind to outrun the demons that would work their way inside, given half the chance. Every kid is scared of monsters at some point. Mine just happened to be real and looked like everyone else.

I learned early on to run and keep running, but there were a few good years at the beginning when I ran from nothing, when I had no reservations, no caution. For those precious few years, I was a fearless, rough-and-tumble tomboy who planted her flag and pushed forward to the next adventure. Nothing could stop me…until, when I was about three, something did.

"Where's my mom?" I asked as Harvey towered over me.

I shouldn't have needed to ask for my mother; I knew Harvey. His wife (or girlfriend, I was never totally clear on that), Regina, was my mom's best friend. I'd been around him dozens of times. And yet this time something was different, something was just *off,* flooding my young, uncomplicated mind with dread.

His reply, only four words—"We'll see her later"—was swift, cold, and anything but comforting. In my confusion, I panicked. I scanned the room quickly, then looked up to find Harvey towering over me, eyes roaming up and down my tiny frame. After that, everything went dark.

In the decades to come I would black out plenty, often the result of heavy drinking or a bad trip, but that first time? That was all-natural, the mind's most basic defense against trauma, so instinctual, so *primal* even a child can do it.

The next thing I knew I was sitting on the counter in Harvey's funky, grimy kitchen as he buckled my Mary Janes. What he said to me I don't remember now, but I listened intently as I'd been taught to do when any adult was speaking. Once he ran out of words, he lifted me down from the counter, helped me into my coat, and off we went to meet my mom as if nothing had ever happened. Only something had, and I knew it even though I couldn't remember it and wouldn't for many years. But the experience left its mark. I was never the same. From that day forward, I would wonder what every single person I met wanted from me—and whether they would bother to ask before taking it.

In time, Harvey and his family moved into a large Victorian house in Teaneck, New Jersey, where my own family had settled in the mid-70s once my parents had outgrown Manhattan. Our house was a five-minute drive from theirs, so we were there all the time. My big brother, Paul, and I called it the "Hippie House," as it quickly became a local Mecca for leftist Baby Boomers in varying degrees of denial about how over the 60s were. They would come together in their bell bottoms and macramé shawls, strumming their acoustic guitars and planning rallies and marches for the purpose of ending all the world's suffering…which is all well and good. But frankly? All those harmonized songs of love, peace, and saving the helpless rang a little hollow when I had to hear them one room away as I was being raped in a closet by one of their own.

And where were my parents when all this was going on? They were around…ish, but completely oblivious to what was happening. Should they have known? Probably, but if I squint I can kind of see how they didn't.

My mom had always been someone who only saw what she wanted to see. Even at home, she operated as though everything were the way she envisioned it through her rose-colored glasses. She treasured many of those people as her friends, and it never occurred to her that leaving me under their supervision could be dangerous, though it should have, considering how they all came together in the first place.

See, the Hippie House gang wasn't just a bunch of random locals who found each other. Like Harvey, most were current or former patients of the same therapist: my grandmother, a woman who *needed* adoration. She craved love and respect (and let's be real, worship) and found those things in a group of misfits who had originally come to her for therapy. She encouraged them all to hang out, both with and without her, inviting them right into her life and the lives of her adult children. I probably don't need to tell you what can happen when people who desperately need love, still healing from their own traumas, become enmeshed with their therapist and each other, but trust me…a recipe for success it is not.

Within this crowd, my mother and Aunt Sally were practically celebrities, the daughters of their guru, and they became the nucleus of a more exclusive group within the group. Being close to them was a kind of status symbol that few attained, and one of these patient-groupies got even closer to them than the rest of the inner circle, a woman whose quirk and brashness matched their own. Harvey's wife, Regina, became like a third sister to Mom and Aunt Sally, making Harvey as good as their brother-in-law, so there was no conceivable reason for Mom not to leave her kids under his care while the three "sisters" grabbed coffee, went shopping, or even just hung around elsewhere in the house.

As for my dad, Hippie House had never been his scene in the first place. They were my mom's friends, and he'd never really cared for most of them, so he tended to keep his distance. What little motivation he'd had to make nice burned off when he and my mom separated, so he was never in a place, physically or mentally, to discover anything. My dad is a lot of things, but perceptive and intuitive…not so much. He pretty much takes things at face value and calls it a day, and it should surprise no one that someone with that tendency and zero education in child psychology never smelled a rat. Decades later, he would tell me how Hippie House had been a cult and he'd had to get out of there. I didn't blame him. I just didn't get how he could have left without taking us with him.

Between my mom's blind spot and my dad's overall absence, I was fair game. There were stretches of hours, sometimes entire days, when Hippie House was just a bunch of kids running around unsupervised, with adults—more than a few of them damaged and disturbed—moving in and out of the picture the whole time. And that fondue pot of dysfunction yielded trouble.

You know how old I was when I walked in on my first orgy? Four years old. Tops.

I can't recall the exact time, but the only light in the room was that "golden hour" glow that makes every shadow darker and thicker. I was in Harvey's bed, staring at him, this massive lump under the covers. I made sure he was asleep, then backed up carefully and hopped down to the floor. He didn't stir. This was good. If he kept on sleeping, I just might be safe for the rest of the day. I glided across the floor, silently as I could manage, and snuck out into the hall.

The afternoon light slanted in across the floor and halfway up the wall, dust dancing in the glow. I slid my hand along the banister, following the sound of voices to the kitchen, where I found them. I couldn't fully process what I was looking at, and I still can't picture their faces, but what I *do* remember is a cluster of naked bodies doing things I knew I shouldn't be seeing. I froze there in the doorway. It wasn't long before one of them noticed me and called me over.

I wonder now if crossing these kinds of boundaries had already become normal for me, because I walked right up to them without question. They made a circle around me, each taking their turn, and I did what I always did. I survived it. Most of me, anyway. Could I have told someone? Sure. But I never would have. Like any predators worth their salt, they protected themselves by ensuring my silence. "Never tell anyone" became my cardinal law, drilled into me until it never even occurred to me to speak up.

In time, the Hippie House gang fell away, including Harvey, who Regina eventually left. He vanished from our lives almost overnight but not before passing the torch to Regina's son, Jacob. Harvey had never been a father to Jacob, biologically or otherwise. He had molested the boy for years, and, well…Jacob had learned some very, very fucked-up lessons from it, then practiced what he'd learned on me for the next few years.

One fairly ordinary day, at an informal gathering at Regina's, all the kids were playing a game of hide-and-seek, a refreshing bit of normal I was able to enjoy for a few minutes before Jacob grabbed me from behind and pulled me into the bathroom. Maybe before he and Harvey and all the others had snuffed out my bold, defiant little spirit, I might have at least cried out or fought back, but even then, I wouldn't have gotten away. Jacob was an early bloomer, maybe fifteen but already six feet tall with the body of a man, and even for my age, I had always been small. Honestly, I didn't stand a chance.

Jacob locked the door, stripped me down, and told me to be quiet in the coldest, hardest whisper I'd ever heard as he laid me down in the tub. I took his full meaning as I'd been taught. Silence was not only expected of me but demanded. Silence was to be upheld and secrets kept, no matter how much it hurt.

As Jacob went about his business, I drifted away. The discomfort, the pain, they were old news. I tuned them out. I could barely hear the shaky sound of his breathing, only the other kids beyond the door, running around, laughing and playing, blissfully ignorant of what was happening to me. It must've been nice, having a childhood where sex was this weird, mysterious thing that adults changed the channel to shield you from.

Somewhere along the line I must have started giving off some kind of signal that only predators could see and hear, which they inevitably did. It was like I had Easy Target written in neon over my head, and people made the most of it. The really sick part was that I'd gotten so used to it I stopped being surprised. I resisted a little but not much. What was the point?

I don't remember every person who sexually abused me—because, you know, trauma—but in the end, I suffered at the hands of many perpetrators. It happened standing up, lying down, with hands clapped across my mouth. It happened as I struggled to breathe with five bodies piled on top of me. It happened on a cold cement floor that scraped and bruised the tender skin of my back, my thighs, my knees. It happened with my hands tied together. It happened in kitchens. It happened in bathrooms. It happened in basements. It happened in closets.

IT. JUST. HAPPENED.

There's this photo of me, my second-grade class picture, where I'm wearing this cute dress with a lace collar and my hair is done up in a perfect, neat little bun. But you can see from my Mona Lisa smile that the girl in that picture, the one my mom dolled up and enrolled in ballet classes, wasn't the real me. The real me never made it into class photos back then, because hand-me-down jeans, a tank top, and unisex sneakers were not acceptable attire despite being my own personal uniform.

I liked riding my bike as fast as I could, feeling the air on my skin, speeding down a hill until I felt like I was flying. I would hang with the boys, climbing trees, getting dirty, playing baseball. Most boys would try to exclude the tomboy, but few of these guys tried, and on the rare occasion they edged me out, I'd just grab a book, climb a tree, and sit there for hours. I never lived up to my potential in school despite testing very well, but on my own time you couldn't pry a book out of my hands. The escape into different worlds and different lives was too alluring. My actual life left a lot to be desired.

I wasn't completely devoid of tenderness or femininity. My nurturing side came out around my baby brother, Michael, who came late to the family when I was seven years old. My parents' marriage was already on the rocks when he was conceived, and he was one of a handful of reasons they decided to give things one last try. It didn't work. That strategy rarely does.

I loved spending time with my dad, but opportunities grew increasingly rare. The third and final time he left us, when I was eight, he found an apartment just a few blocks from our house, and yet he was as scarce as if he lived across state lines. Mom was the constant, which had its ups and downs. We could always rely on her to keep the trains running on time, to make sure our lunches were packed and our laundry was done, permission slips signed, all of that stuff—but her willful blindness to life's rougher edges made it damn near impossible to trust her emotionally. I couldn't be myself with her if I tried—and I did. I constantly showed her who I was, and she painted right over it with velveteen and bobby pins to cram her idealized version of me inside a picture frame. She didn't see me. No one did. No one looked very far beyond that forced smile.

My mornings weren't like other kids'. I didn't jump out of bed and wonder what exciting things might happen that day. I woke up wondering, *Who? How many? What would they do? Where would it happen?* I knew most mornings as I dressed that by the end of the day those clothes would be pulled off. Would my little ballet outfit be safe to wear? *Will it protect me today?* It rarely did. I remember perfectly how easily it came off, how quickly my tights were pulled down to my ankles. Nothing and nowhere was safe.

I lived with shame knotted up inside of me like the gnarled bark of an old tree. It was impossible for me not to feel it, and day after day, year after year, that shame and pain swept me away until I was a small person who looked like a child and even sounded like one but was something else, something hollowed out and numb most of the time. And I got very good at hiding it, even from myself.

Paul didn't find it so easy. He had also been abused, and it haunted him. He was losing his fight with that darkness a little each day until I found him standing on the staircase with a belt around his neck, the other end tied to the railing. Sobbing, he told me he was going to jump off the stairs and die. He was all of ten years old.

"I don't want be alive anymore," he whimpered. I knew why.

While his abuse hadn't been as varied or as frequent, he hadn't escaped Hippie House unscathed. It's hard to imagine how a grade-schooler could know enough about suicide to engineer one. I was only two years younger and didn't even know what suicide was, but I did understand death and how very, very permanent it is, and that was enough. I didn't know what I could say to turn him around. All I could do was beg him not to leave me all alone.

I needed Paul. I didn't have anyone else who understood. Who else was there? Our parents? How could I depend on them when all we'd suffered had happened right under their noses? He was the only one who understood, my only witness. It was then I realized just how much pain I'd been in. I'd been able to tune it out for a couple of years, but the thought of Paul disappearing, leaving me with nothing, made me very aware. I begged and begged until he unhooked the belt, then we sat down on the stairs together and cried. We didn't speak of that day for nearly forty years, but it stayed with us. How could it not?

The next day, things went right back to normal. I would go to school, do ballet, hang out with my cousins, maybe get molested—you know, business as usual. There's no way to know how long it would have continued on like that if it hadn't been for my cousin Emily.

Emily was Aunt Sally's daughter and, at the time, my best friend. We were only a few months apart in age, both adorable and blonde, so close we could easily be mistaken for fraternal twins. She was the girly girl to my tomboy. She made me play with Barbies, which I hated, but I did my best because I really loved her. Besides, it wasn't like she didn't try to toss the ball around for my sake. She took to it about as well as I took to the Malibu Dream House, but we found common ground elsewhere, dreaming up and acting out dramatic dance routines, talking late into the night during sleepovers, and always having each other's back in a united front against our brothers or our parents. I'd have done anything for her.

It was early evening in the Jersey suburbs, the kind of breezy twilight that summers are just made for, and all the kids were playing hide-and-seek outside Emily's house. Jacob probably hadn't found an opportunity to pull me away from the group, so I was unusually free to just be a kid, giddy to join the others as they ran around, laughing and finding places to hide amidst the trees, outdoor playsets, anywhere one could hide in plain sight. The more imaginative, the better. I was running at full stride around the house when I came upon Emily sitting all alone in the grass, looking down at the ground in front of her.

I knew right away that something was wrong. For one, she was squandering an excellent opportunity to claim any one of several premium hiding places right in front of us, but more than that, I recognized the expression on her face. It was one with which I was all too familiar, but there was only one way to be sure. I sat down beside her, and she told me that Jacob had tried, for the first time, to touch her. She'd managed to get away before he could really do anything, but she was shaken all the same. Her confusion and sadness were perfectly normal, the healthy response of a ten-year-old who *hadn't* been sexually traumatized for half her life.

I didn't get it.

"Oh, please," I scoffed. "That's nothing."

Emily was, of course, horrified by my reaction, because it wasn't nothing, but fuck if I knew that. I just tried to ease her mind by explaining that she hadn't really experienced anything that bad compared to what I had. I didn't even realize that I was recounting it out loud for the first time. I didn't realize I was bringing life as I knew it to a screeching halt. I was just trying to make my favorite person feel better. I didn't, but I made her feel something.

Emily insisted that we tell someone immediately, but I couldn't. *Never tell anyone.* It might as well have been tattooed on my heart. And yet I'd told Emily and couldn't take it back, and no matter how adamant I was, she was going to tell someone whether I was ready or not. My only choice was whether or not I had some part in the conversation.

I stood by as Emily told Aunt Sally everything, what Jacob had tried to do to her and the story I'd relayed of my own abuse. I hadn't recalled everything at the time. It would be years before the full picture of my abuse would return to me, but what I could recall was more than enough to knock the world right off its axis.

Naturally, Aunt Sally told Regina, and they both told my mom, but the story didn't stop there. Within a day, everyone knew—aunts, uncles, cousins, friends. Everyone. Up until that day, while my shame and humiliation had been eating me up for years, they had been *mine* to conceal and control, and now it was all common knowledge, shared unceremoniously without any consideration for what I needed or how I felt. No one talked *to* me, just *about* me. My involvement in it all was practically incidental. But there it was. My secret was out. And Mom, Aunt Sally, and Regina had this unspeakably ugly truth laid bare before them, something horrid and sickening that now hung over all three families, each of them staring down the chilling reality of a mother's worst nightmare.

And the next day, we all had brunch.

I sat at the long table in Regina's dining room amidst laughing adults and giggling cousins. "Pass the pancakes! Pass the orange juice!" was all I heard in my darkness as I watched everyone, even Mom, laugh and eat like nothing had ever happened. She was joyous and jolly, and I wanted to die, forgotten in an instant so she could pretend everything was fun and wholesome and beautiful. Conversations whizzed by my head, but I couldn't hear a thing. I was there but I wasn't. I couldn't believe what was happening.

What I didn't understand then and couldn't recognize for many years was that my mother had a crippling fear of exclusion. Finding herself on the outside of this elite little power trio she'd formed was just about the worst thing imaginable, so she convinced herself that what had happened to me, while unfortunate, wasn't bad enough to warrant distancing herself from Regina. It hadn't been abuse, hadn't been rape; it was just kids being kids, a narrative Regina was more than happy to adopt, because who wants to admit their teenage son could do the things Jacob had done?

But what's perhaps even more outrageous than their eagerness to minimize and shuffle past my trauma is that Aunt Sally, who had followed in my grandmother's footsteps and become a therapist herself, had cosigned on all of it. How someone so intimately acquainted with human psychology, the mother and aunt of children who had been terrorized and abused, could sanction any kind of continued relationship with their abuser or his family is absolutely, one hundred fucking percent batshit bananas. My mom's approach to the entire situation had been deeply misguided, but my aunt, a licensed mental healthcare professional, had known better on so many levels and gave everyone involved the green light to just let it slide. And they did. All of them.

No one could face the truth. No one wanted the flow of their lives interrupted by the inconvenience of my suffering, so that day I learned that I was nothing. I didn't count. I didn't matter. Emily had helped me realize that what I'd been living through the past several years *had* been a big deal, that it was terrible and wrong and needed to be stopped. But if everyone could just go on living their lives, if they could feel good and happy and truly still enjoy spending time together, well, then it must be me. If I could watch my mother hug Jacob, laugh with his mother, and carry on a conversation as if her own daughter hadn't been torn apart in every conceivable way, then the shame was mine. I was the bad one, the disgusting one. Not my abusers for demolishing me, but me for making everyone face it.

Part of me died that day. Damage had been done to that sweet, fearless girl, but up to that point she'd had a chance to recover, to heal and come back from that dark place. In the wake of this revelation, we should have huddled together, mourning the loss of my innocence and taking steps to heal my wounds and move forward together as a family. Instead, my trauma was addressed in the most cursory fashion possible and promptly buried for the sake of brunch. And so, the girl I was, the girl who still had a chance, died, and left in her place was a hardened, angry changeling who looked the same and sounded the same, but would never be the same.

For years, I sank deeper into my own darkness, praying desperately for the ground to open up and swallow me whole, but no such luck. I couldn't escape the pain by disappearing, so instead I dove headfirst into a world of self-destruction, and for nearly half my life I never looked back.

Not once.

CHAPTER 8

Little Miss Badass

I wound up in the nurse's office almost every day of first grade, claiming I had a stomachache one day, a headache the next, looking for a peaceful place to find some comfort. She was sympathetic at first, but eventually told me I couldn't just keep showing up, so I stopped. By today's standards, it would have been an obvious cry for help, one of several signs during my years of abuse that something was wrong, but it barely registered as such in the late 70s.

For years, I coped with my pain by distracting myself from it. As it turned out, being the perfect little girl was an ideal distraction. I was helpful at home and a model student at school, participating in class and volunteering to help my teachers—a winning strategy since perfection takes a lot of concentration. But once the abuse stopped, so did the need to distract myself, and a whole mess of feelings I'd been suppressing quickly surfaced.

The more I thought about what had happened during that brunch at Regina's, when every adult in my life had thoroughly betrayed me, the angrier I became. After that day, satisfied that the "ugly business" had been put to rest, the three sisters continued to gather our families, thrusting me back into spending time around Jacob on a regular basis, expecting me to laugh and play with my cousins as though I didn't have a scarlet letter blazing on my chest for everyone to see. And though every second of that charade hurt, I kept it up at home and at family gatherings. At school, however, I ceased to give every last fuck.

I became loud and disruptive, and my work, when I bothered to do it, was sloppy and half-assed. I just couldn't find it within myself to care, much less concentrate. But I could find it within myself to throw some punches, and thanks to my cousin Matt I knew how.

Matt was Emily's older brother and the oldest of my actual cousins; I'm not counting Regina's kids, and neither would Matt. He hated Jacob, and with good reason. Jacob bullied Matt mercilessly, constantly beating him up and, on one occasion, pushing his bike out into traffic with him on it. And every time Jacob pulled some shit, Matt was forced to accept his apology. That was standard procedure: Make Jacob apologize, then make whomever he'd hurt accept his apology so that the status quo could be comfortably maintained. The three sisters could *not* be separated.

Surviving Jacob toughened Matt up, probably more than it should have, and he had his own demons to deal with, but he remained protective of his siblings and cousins. For as long as I can remember he's always been in my corner. He taught me how to fight: to always keep one fist up in front of my face, to strike fast and jump back, always ready to block. With his tips and tricks, I became a confident little grade school street fighter, and after a while word got around.

At some point during fifth grade, my classmates began arranging fights with kids from other schools, and for the most part I kicked their asses. I was not a big kid; I was short and slight, and my reach wasn't long, but all that fire in my belly more than made up for it.

There was this one kid who was a few years older than me but small for his age. He was down to fight me on more than one occasion, and I was happy to meet that challenge. Just as Matt had showed me, I held one fist in front of my face protectively and, on the count of three, jabbed the kid right in the nose. One, two, *pow*...and it was over just like that.

Years of abuse had stripped away all my confidence and security. Those wounds were freshly reopened every time I was forced into Jacob's company in front of everyone who knew what had happened. They could all see it every time they looked at me, and I could feel them looking. I was powerless to stop any of it. I couldn't punish the ones who had hurt and betrayed me, but I could put up my fists in front of a captive audience and at least *play* at being powerful.

Despite my best efforts (and some modest success), I was never able to slide my brawling ways and academic slacking under the radar for very long. Trips to the principal's office, sometimes with my parents but just as often without, became a matter of course, and their disappointment and frustration with me just pissed me off even more. Who were my parents to wag their fingers in my face? *They* were the disappointments, the ones who had failed me and let me down. I owed them nothing. So, when the principal, with the best of intentions, would ask me why I was acting out, I wouldn't answer. I'd just stare him down until he started talking again. Considering all the crap I pulled, you'd think the man would have written me off as a lost cause, but he never did.

"Nikki," he said one day, pausing in the middle of his usual spiel about my potential. "Why are you doing this? You're a good kid, a smart kid. What's going on?"

I kicked the floor in front of me and, as per usual, said nothing. I didn't know what to tell him. I could see this man believed in me, but I didn't get why. Whatever he was looking for, I was who I was, the four-foot tomboy who gave boys bloody noses. It wasn't an act. The girl he expected me to be, the perfect girl he'd become so fond of? She'd been the act. She'd been a mask and shield, a product of the worst I'd ever felt in my life, and *that* was the Nikki that he wanted? Well, fuck that. So he hadn't given up on that girl. So what? I had.

The musky funk of horses was oddly comforting, the only thing at that point that could have been. I fell into a shallow trance as I brushed out JD's mane, pickling in my anger—anger at my abusers for what they'd done to me, anger at the three sisters for how they'd handled it, and anger at myself for letting all my rage and volatility follow me to my literal happy place.

Nestled in New York's Hudson Valley, Frost Valley was about two hours north of Teaneck, two hours from everyone who knew me and everyone who had hurt me. In summers past it had been the only place I'd felt some measure of safety, the only place my perfect, sweet smile had been sincere. After months of acting out, shitty academic performance, and schoolyard street fighting, I had hoped another nice, long summer at sleepaway camp would wipe the slate clean and get me back on track.

Unfortunately, with all the emotional spillover making me touchy and aggressive, I was no longer the plucky tomboy the staff had adored, the girl who had always been willing to play hard and get her hands dirty, who'd had such a gift with the horses—even a semi-wild stallion like JD. I couldn't ride him—he wouldn't let *anyone* ride him—but he let me take him on walks, and I'd talk to him, keeping one hand on his neck. We brought each other a calm neither of us found in anyone or anything else, which made perfect sense to me. I'd have taken animals over people any day. At least animals are honest.

What could have been another summer of soothing campfires and peaceful horseback riding turned out to be a total shit show. Pandora's proverbial box had been opened, all my demons had flown right out, and I carried them around with me every second of every day. The staff's sweet little barn rat had been replaced with a surly, violent little nightmare who broke rules, wandered off on her own, talked back, and even flipped the bird at a counselor or two. I was on the verge of being sent home for my trouble. I kind of deserved it, and I knew it.

"Hey, Nikki," I heard from behind me. Anyone else might have made me flinch, but Stacey? She was all right. She was one of my counselors and just about the only person at Frost Valley I could still stand. "Whatcha doing all alone in here?"

"Grooming," I grumbled, not as impatient with her as I was trying to sound.

"Cool. Mind if I hang out for a while?"

I shrugged, and Stacey pulled up a stool and chatted while I tended to the horses. Any other counselor would have preferred scrubbing toilets to dealing with me, but Stacey actually seemed to like me despite my attitude.

Stacey's low-key rehabilitation of me began with small, subtle gestures. She'd give me piggybacks across the long, open fields that connected the bunks to the lodges, and we'd be in perfect unison during the boot camp–style call-and-response chants typical of summer camps everywhere. After a while, she started dressing me like her, in college tees and boxers worn over the underwear as proper shorts, a teen look of the time that was still a few years beyond me. She called me her twin with full affection, and we both laughed about it—pretty funny, considering she was nearly twice my age, at least a foot taller than me, and Black. You'd think as prickly as I was that summer, having so much to prove, I wouldn't have taken kindly to being fashioned into some counselor's Mini-Me, but I kind of liked it, because Stacey saw me. That was all she had to do, and she did it perfectly. And for that, I loved her.

Stacey loved me too, and told me so. She told everyone around us. She managed to bring out what little sunshine was left in my soul and got me back on track. A summer that began with me on the verge of expulsion ended with me standing in front of the whole camp at the closing campfire, receiving the award for Honor Camper. I don't know what kind of strings Stacey had to pull to make that happen, but there I was, accepting that award, so stunned that I nearly lit that flimsy paper award on fire with the candle in my other hand.

That summer with Stacey was, in retrospect, probably the last chance I had to take a different path. Maybe if she'd become a more permanent fixture in my life, it would have made all the difference, but she was just a camp counselor with her own life and her own hometown, and three other seasons of the year that had nothing to do with me. I hope she remembers me. I'll always remember her.

At summer's end, I went back to my life to find all the pain and fury I'd left behind in Teaneck right there waiting. And without any comfort left for me, I quickly found new ways to take the edge off.

Middle school isn't a picnic for anybody. Puberty's a rough time even for the beautiful and popular, all the more so for an asthmatic seventh grader whose social barometer had been completely skewed by years of trauma, the language in which I was speaking while all the other tweens were communicating fluently in Kid.

I was never an outcast. I just never fit anywhere. I knew pretty much everyone and hung out on the periphery of every clique, known and not unwelcome but rarely invited. Even when I managed to fake normalcy and blend in for a few hours here and there, I never truly belonged, and the loneliness was unbearable.

My brain was full of so much trauma I had no room left for schoolwork. My report cards were covered in C's and D's, because I never studied or did the reading and just cheated or blew my work off altogether. At the time, I couldn't have processed any of those feelings if I'd tried. I was just going through the motions, barely functional. Sometimes, I wished for someone to come and pull me out of my funk. Others, all I wanted was to be left alone to self-destruct in peace.

I eventually found a kindred spirit in Elena, a girl in my class who shared my love of The Doors and was always ready to launch into an in-depth conversation about them or Bryan Adams, Madonna, or any of the other musicians we adored. We'd often make plans to fake being sick so we could stay home and talk on the phone all day. I had an easier time committing to the plan, and frequently followed through while she buckled and went to school, but I never held it against her. Someone had to toe the line, and it wasn't going to be me. My attendance was already atrocious, so why even bother? What did I have to lose?

It was during a sleepover at Elena's that I got drunk for the first time. After spending an hour on the phone dial-bombing Z100 to win concert tickets to—I don't know, Bruce Springsteen, probably, we realized her parents had long since gone to bed, so we snuck downstairs to the family room liquor cabinet. Elena looked over her shoulder in a burst of healthy paranoia, then pulled out a bottle of Blue Nun. I'd never heard of it before and had no idea what to expect, but I took a swig anyway. It was disgusting. I took another.

Within minutes, we were plastered.

"Hey, listen…" I said, my voice wavering. "I just have this feeling, you know, that Jim Morrison…"

"He's really still alive?" Elena finished for me.

"He's totally alive!" I squealed, then immediately cupped my hand over my mouth, remembering how late it was. I snorted with laughter, and Elena giggled. I shook it off. "We should find him. No, seriously, we should."

"Right on. It's—this is, like, our mission."

I nodded fervently. "We gotta start, like…tracking down…some leads…" We held on to each other and collapsed into a fit of stifled laughter, and everything after that was a blur.

I remember more bottles holding a colorful array of liquids, and I remember trying to stand up with very little success. I must have made it eventually, because I woke up the next morning in the spare twin bed in Elena's room—in a puddle of my own vomit. While I'd never known puke to smell pleasant, this post-bender booze puke was so nasty and so close that it almost brought up a second round. I glanced over at Elena, sleeping in her own unsullied bed. She hadn't thrown up at all. I guess when you aren't walking around 24/7 with a raw heart, you don't drink to black out and then puke in your sleep. Just me, then?

I went straight to the bathroom to wash my face and rinse my mouth out, utterly embarrassed and wondering how I was going to apologize for this, and yet at that moment I wouldn't have changed a thing. All I could think was how good it had felt to numb the pain, to feel something other than guilt and shame, to laugh and feel silly, loose, and free of my sad, lonely little life. I couldn't wait to do it again.

Elena and I remained friends until I moved away after middle school. We drifted apart soon after that. She went on to have a fairly normal life: college, marriage, kids—in that order, if you can believe it. Normal was just never in the cards for me. I'd like to think that we'd have stayed friends if I hadn't moved, but it's not likely. Elena was all for a bit of mischief, but I was on a road to self-destruction and had passed mischief several exits back. I'm glad she found her happiness. It took me a lot longer.

Not long after the Blue Nun incident, I started hanging around more often with a boy who we'll just call Craig. At the time, he was a skinny, wavy-haired Star Wars enthusiast—nice, funny, and cute in a slightly awkward way. We'd been in each other's orbit for most of our lives thanks to our mothers' friendship, and since we lived in different neighborhoods and went to different schools, he knew me in a completely different way from everyone else. There was a freedom in that, and a sense of security, so I ended up being the first girl he fooled around with.

It was new to him, exciting and mysterious, so I went at his pace, rounding the bases but never quite making it home. Hooking up with Craig was far from my first encounter with the male anatomy, but for it to be my decision, relatively age-appropriate, and with someone who actually cared about me was a completely new experience. I never found it all that exciting (for reasons that are now obvious), but it was…nice.

Craig and I were never official, never what even a middle schooler would consider "dating." We were just two friends who occasionally fooled around out of convenience. That ambiguity coupled with my complete lack of boundaries made it not much of a leap at all to go from hooking up with Craig to letting him and his friend Scott take turns with me one afternoon at his house.

I don't remember what was going through my head as I lay there naked under the covers, waiting for Scott to undress and take his turn, but it likely wasn't anything too profound. It wasn't a huge moment for me, just this thing that happened that we weren't ever going to talk about again. I was fine with that plan.

Then, late in the spring of 1986, came Craig's bar mitzvah.

Here's the thing. Themes and budgets may vary, music and haircuts change with the times, but generally speaking? If you've seen one bar mitzvah, you've seen them all. Some middle schooler invites half his class to watch him read from the Torah, and then everyone moves on to a venue where a sea of dressed-up tweens eat an overpriced kosher lunch before dancing the hora and then rocking out to the Top 40 as best they can in a room full of adults. All pretty standard. But Craig got a bar mitzvah he'd never forget.

I was lingering on the sidelines, watching everyone dance, when some boy with a grin set in a pimple-riddled face sidled up to me.

"You're Nikki, right? I'm Chris."

"Hi," I said.

"That's a nice dress."

"Hmm? Oh…thanks." I had to take his word for it. Dresses had never been my style, but if this one was working for me, great.

"So, uh…you want to like…go somewhere? You know, to have a little fun?"

I flinched. Was he serious? "Ew. Why would I want to…"

"I don't know. Two guys at once? You tell me." I backed away a step, horrified. Chris just rolled his eyes like I was putting on a show. "It's not like it's a secret."

I couldn't believe it. He knew…he and God knows how many other people there. How many of Craig's guests—how many of their *parents*—had gotten the memo that I was the slut who'd taken on Craig and Scott at once? I scanned the crowd, making eye contact with nearly half of them, unable to tell whether their uneasy smiles and off-put sneers were a reaction to my intensity or a sign of their disapproval, their rejection, their judgment.

The adults, of course, probably hadn't heard a thing, but in middle school you have no idea how high up the rumor mill goes. That's the power of gossip: Anyone can know everything. As far as I could tell, my shame was now common knowledge, and I was stuck there, consumed by it while they laughed and danced. I felt disgusting—raw and exposed, just like I had at that fateful brunch.

I knew in my heart it hadn't been Craig that had blabbed about our little three-way grope session. He'd never have done that. When my eyes caught a hold of Scott with his douchebag grin, any doubt I might have had vanished. The fucker.

Almost in a trance, I stepped onto the dance floor just as the hora started up and joined the circle. As the outer circle moved in one direction and the inner circle moved in the other, faces passed in front of me, one after another in my mind, all of them judging me for the seventh-grade whore I was. Most of them were probably just dancing, caught in the moment, but for me it was this frenetic blur of humiliation, and it took everything not to burst into tears. And then, when I caught a glimpse of Scott's grin, I felt a lick of hatred flicker in my heart, hot and simple, burning stronger the closer we came to one another. And then, as he danced by me, I punched him right in the gut.

Scott's eyes bugged out, his jaw hanging open as he stared at me with such delicious confusion. He hadn't seen it coming. Despite knowing what he'd done and having every reason to expect some retaliation, he hadn't expected a thing, because I was just some stupid girl. A girl who could have ruptured his small intestine if she'd tried a little harder.

What should have felt like a victory, like glorious vindication, felt only like humiliation once the rush died down and my sanity flooded back. I'd been humiliated by Scott for spinning me a new reputation as the town bicycle, and I'd humiliated myself by lashing out the way I had. Time seemed to stand still. Though the dance continued and no one but Craig had noticed what I'd done, it felt like everyone had seen. Scott, lurching forward in pain, managed to keep his feet moving and avoid eye contact when we passed each other again only seconds later. I was grateful for that as I was swept away in the dance, utterly imploding.

When it was over and everyone dispersed back to their tables, I lingered on the dance floor, eyeing Scott until he stumbled away, clutching his belly. Craig, looking at me from across the room, wore a what-the-fuck expression. I didn't know what to tell him, so I headed outside to be alone, every horrible feeling soaking through me. I don't remember if I even went back inside after that.

After Craig's bar mitzvah, what little interest I had in socializing with my peers all but evaporated, and I turned my attention to older kids who were, frankly, more fun. I was all of thirteen when I started sneaking off to hang out on Cedar Lane, Teaneck's main drag, late into the night. There was this one corner by Rocklin's, a small independent convenience store, where high school kids hung out all night in their tight jeans and feathered hair—the girls teasing it out to *Dynasty*-level volume, and the boys accessorizing their mullets with sad peach-fuzz mustaches—sneaking alcohol and smoking on the hoods of their Trans Ams.

As for me, I learned all the wrong lessons very well. All I had to do was smoke a cigarette and flirt a little with some boy, and I could score a ride in his car with the promise of a heady wine cooler buzz. I wasn't the only middle schooler amongst the high school kids, but none dared to go as far as I did. I was one of the bad girls who rode the edge, and running with them made me feel so fucking cool I couldn't even find a word for it. That summer I felt alive and free, living a life so much more vibrant and textured than what I imagined my boring classmates were living. They could call me a slut or a loser or whatever they wanted. I was having the time of my life while they were "just saying no," so fuck 'em.

The next year came and went in a haze of cigarette smoke, weed, and hairspray. The mid-80s had thoroughly consumed my appearance, and I spent most of eighth grade walking around with feathered hair, defaulting to acid wash jeans, a rock band T-shirt, and white Reebok high-tops. If Heart and The Bangles had a curvy little sister, I was it, and I was quickly learning how to work my mystique to get what I wanted, which most of the time was a decent buzz. And there wasn't much I was unwilling to do to achieve one.

A short lifetime of untended trauma had eroded pretty much any concept I may have had of boundaries, so "no" didn't really exist in my vocabulary. I never turned down a drug, a sexual proposition, a chance to do something wild and dangerous; I was game for everything, and even when I wasn't, I did it anyway.

As I walked home late one night, enjoying a warm June breeze, I relished the silence, the peace. Tipsy but able to walk straight, I realized a young, developing girl should probably be afraid, walking alone at night, but how much could anyone really do to me that hadn't already been done? And if a possible random attack was the price for finding the best parties and having my taste of the wild life, so be it. The outside world didn't scare me. My fears lived far closer to home.

CHAPTER 9

A New Family

My parents' relationship had never been ideal. In fact, it was pretty fucked up from the word go. My dad had been in therapy, working through the wreckage of a starter marriage in his twenties to a woman who, from what little I know, had been erratic and unstable. After a while, his therapist, in an act of breathtaking unprofessionalism, introduced him to her daughter, also a recent divorcée. And that's how my parents met.

Considering my dad's first wife, it's not hard to see the appeal of someone as focused and organized as my mom. And human nature being what it is, after their split, my dad was once again in the market for the complete opposite of what he'd just "escaped." And that's exactly what Christine was: copper-haired and curvy where my mom was slight and brunette, funny and carefree where my mom was straitlaced and sensible, and I'm sure the fact that she was several years younger didn't hurt her case at all.

Shortly after my dad started seeing Christine in 1984, he started bringing us to her house for our weekend visits. I suppose it made sense. There was definitely more room there than in his dinky little one-bedroom apartment, even with her kids there.

When we arrived that first night, I was struck by how unusual the house's front entrance was: a naked, railing-free staircase up to a door that faced the driveway, rather than the street. It was almost like the architect had forgotten to put in a front door and slapped one on at the last minute. It opened onto a small family room with a TV, a coffee table, and that 80s couch. You know the one—a pattern of autumnal shades printed on rough-spun upholstery. On it sat two boys, one of them eight years old, the other five, just a year older than Michael. My dad introduced them to us, then gestured to the living room beyond.

"And heeeere's Christine!" he said like some game show host, presenting his new girlfriend as she entered the room, smiling broadly and waving her hands.

That first night went pretty well. Christine cooked everyone dinner, we kids horsed around in the living room, making a mess of two sets of couch cushions. It was a good time. When it came time to go to bed, Paul and Michael paired off with Christine's boys, and at her insistence, I—being the only girl—slept downstairs, on the couch in the family room. I was the only one in the house with no door and no privacy, completely exposed. That first visit, I slept fine despite the burnt air, thick with the stink of cigarettes, but it didn't last.

Christine was always sweet during the day, doting on me as much as any of the others, busting out all my favorite things for my birthday: beef stew, Carvel ice cream cake, and purple balloons and decorations. She'd joke around with me, seeming warm and personable, but then at night, after everyone went up to bed, I'd see a different side that no one else knew about.

After ushering the boys to their rooms, my dad would turn in. Christine's room was across the house, up the stairs, and back again, so my dad would be sleeping about as far away from me as possible while Christine lingered in the kitchen, drinking into the night, stewing and somehow convincing herself that I was the cause of all her problems. When it would inevitably boil over, she'd come over to the couch and shake me awake to tell me—sometimes in a vicious whisper, sometimes a raving scream—that I was evil, disgusting, and born from a witch.

Christine hated my mom so much, but Mom wasn't there to take the heat for it, so I got to hear all the ranting about how evil she (and by proxy, I) was until I'd cry and beg Christine to stop. She'd been so kind at first, but just ended up being one more person reinforcing all the awful things I'd come to believe about myself: that I was disgusting, unlovable, bad. She ripped away the last bit of self-love that I'd been desperately trying to hold on to.

How could someone be so cruel to an eleven-year-old girl? Well, there was the displaced hatred she felt for my mom. Also, I was her man's daughter, and she was definitely jealous of me for that on some level. And then, of course, there's the fact that she was a raging alcoholic.

On several occasions, Christine would usher me into her car to go on runs for these massive jugs of wine, already drunk enough to call it a night but never willing. Who knows where my dad was? Maybe sleeping, maybe in the basement watching a football game or a boxing match while the boys were upstairs playing. On those booze runs, Christine would drive us around, talking about crazy shit, drunk off her ass. How we never crashed is beyond me.

Christine was my first real encounter not only with alcoholism but addiction in general, something that would become such a huge part of my life. You'd think, given the things I saw her do, the way I saw her behave, I'd have been scared straight, but that kind of cause and effect doesn't always process in a mind so young. If it did, my life might have gone very differently.

All I knew was that when Christine asked me to do something, I did it. It didn't matter how weird or how dangerous. Anything to keep the peace in that moment. Anything to keep the storm at bay.

"Nikki!" Christine called out one night in a boozy drawl. "Come here!" I followed her voice to the tiny bathroom off the kitchen, her perfume wafting out the way it did even when she wasn't there. She was checking herself out in the mirror, and without looking at me, she handed me a large pair of craft scissors. "Give me a haircut." I resisted, but she just shook the scissors at me. "Don't be a baby! Just give me a damn haircut!"

I reluctantly stepped up onto the closed toilet lid, waited for her to stand in front of me, facing away, and started cutting. I was terrified. There was no way this wasn't going to come back around later. I knew all too well what would happen during these drunken rages. I'd end up on the floor, in tears while Christine screamed at me, so I cut as little as I could. Hopefully, she might not even notice in the morning.

"More," she said, inspecting my work in the mirror. She said it again after I did as she asked, and again, and again until it had gone from long, mid-length waves to a pixie cut. I was sure she'd kill me.

I slipped away while she was gazing into the mirror, eyes half lidded, talking to herself. I laid down on the couch, waiting for the inevitable scream that would be followed by Christine thundering over to berate me, but it never came. I eventually went back to check on her, as I often did when I hadn't heard from her in a while. She tended to pass out at the kitchen table or on the floor, and it was hard for me to get back to sleep until I knew she was upstairs for the night. When I got to the kitchen, the bathroom door was closed, so I lowered myself to the linoleum floor, with its weird, giraffe-like pattern, got down on my belly, and peered under the door. I could see her feet planted in front of the toilet—she was sitting—with her pants around her ankles. And I could hear her snoring.

"Christine?" I called out as softly as I could, not wanting to stoke her anger if I could avoid it. "Are you okay?" No response. I watched under the door to see if she moved when I called her name, trying a few more times before opening it to find her slumped forward, completely passed out. I was able to rouse her just enough to help her to her feet and upstairs, muttering a few words with her eyes all but closed. When I opened the door to her room, my dad was sleeping like a rock. He didn't even stir when she fell into bed. I sighed and went back downstairs to catch a few hours of sleep before the boys came down to watch their cartoons.

The next morning, Christine was livid, screaming about how her hair had been destroyed. My dad was right there the whole time, so she didn't rage out on me like I'm sure she wanted to. She knew to reel it in in front of him, but she also knew how to effectively communicate to me her fury, with the implicit threat of more torment in the near future.

My dad wasn't *completely* oblivious. He saw how much hair was on the floor and how little was left on Christine's head, and he had to have some inkling of how off-the-wall she was capable of being, but he just didn't want to deal. So, he simply told her it looked good, lit a cigarette, and chilled at the dining room table, hoping she'd exhaust herself. And she eventually did, so it all worked out for him. All in all, denial and avoidance came pretty easily to him. It took a full-on attempted assault two years later for Christine's abuse to really register.

The whole "family"—Dad and Christine weren't married but had been living together for some time—had piled into a two-car caravan for a lightweight camping trip at a campground with dug-out fire pits and cinder block showers. As with everything, it started out fine. My dad grilled us up some burgers and hot dogs. Michael and our quasi-stepbrothers ran around while Paul and I sang along to the entire *Born in the U.S.A.* album several times. And Christine, well…

I hadn't really paid any attention to what she was doing. Despite sweating like a pig and getting eaten alive by mosquitos, I was having such a genuinely good time for once that Christine's constant drinking and surly disposition had completely escaped me. I was as surprised as anyone when, as we were all sitting around the campfire, she came running toward me out of nowhere, her fist cocked. The look of abject fury on her face was unforgettable. I can still see it. She could have struck me and absolutely would have if my dad hadn't pushed her back just before she reached me.

"What the hell? What's the matter with you?" he bellowed, flushed with rage. I was terrified in that moment, but some small part of me was relieved. My dad was by no means the perfect father, barely present and not terribly attentive when he was around, but right then, right there, he came through for me. He wasted no time in packing up our stuff and getting the three of us the hell out of there, leaving Christine and her boys at the campsite.

The ride home was long and deadly quiet after the first hour of my dad ranting at full volume to no one in particular. As I'd been conditioned over the years, I took everything out on myself. Sure, I'd just been sitting around a campfire, chatting innocently with my brothers when Christine had come charging at me, but we were essentially leaving because of me, so *I* had obviously ruined the trip. I couldn't see it any other way.

Within a week, my dad found an apartment and moved out of Christine's house. I was so relieved to be safe from her after two years of terror. My father didn't magically become Superdad, but at least I didn't have to contend with any raging alcoholic girlfriends. And what you need to know about my dad is that for all his flaws, he was so chill and easy when I was with him. I was able to relax, and that meant a lot to a kid who was always looking over her shoulder for the next threat.

Then, a few months later, I arrived at my dad's apartment for a scheduled visit, and he pulled out a huge tub of my favorite flavor of ice cream, chocolate marshmallow from Bischoff's, a Teaneck institution and one of the last great ice cream parlors. A jolt of pure joy ran through me, and I giggled.

"It's from Christine," he said with a hesitant smile. "She's really sorry about the camping and…here." Sure. A sugary bribe to overlook two years of abuse? Why the fuck not? Why should I have expected anything different?

I couldn't believe it. I couldn't believe he'd even consider getting back together with her. That's what he really wanted. All he needed was for me to let him off the hook, to give my blessing. I thought he would protect me.

My dad moved back in with Christine. I didn't really see him that much after that. I couldn't go there. I didn't feel safe. I hated that house. I still hate that house. And much to no one's surprise, he didn't make much of an effort to see me after that.

Around the time of the camping debacle, while my dad's relationship with Christine was on the rocks, my mom started getting serious with some guy she'd met at a singles dance. Gene was a good man. A little too amused by his own jokes, but he was kind, thoughtful, and a pretty good match for my mom. Like her, he was in education, progressive in his politics, and Jewish. Marriage was pretty much inevitable. This, of course, meant certain complications.

Gene had three kids and a home of his own, across the New York border, in the affluent suburb of New City. And while his older son was already a fully grown adult, his younger son had just started college and still needed a home base for summers and holidays, and his daughter was a high school sophomore like Paul. There was simply no way our house in Teaneck was going to accommodate all of us, and Gene's house had more square footage but not enough bedrooms. The obvious and most diplomatic solution was to find a new house for our new family, and for several reasons, New City was the most practical choice.

Gene put his house on the market. A nice house in a nice neighborhood, it was an easy sell. It just needed a little work. The wallpaper in the kitchen, for instance, needed to go, and Mom decided to hire someone to do it.

And that someone was Jacob.

I don't know how I got wrangled into accompanying them on this errand. All I remember is taking a literal backseat to one of my abusers on the drive up to New City, confused, ashamed, and unable to even understand why. Once again, when given the chance to choose me over her precious friend's precious son, she'd chosen him, doting on him with her little nicknames and fond laughter. And to make it worse, she'd dragged me along, insisting I help him do the job she was paying him to do, leaving us alone together *for hours* while she was off elsewhere in the house, working on other projects.

Un-fucking-believable.

We moved into our new house in July of 1987, and it was not the smoothest transition in the world. It took us all a while, but we found our rhythm. Not an easy one, but a rhythm. The Brady Bunch we were not, but we learned to live together…more or less.

By October, my dad had married Christine, and Paul and I had stopped going to their house altogether. Dad would come by to pick Michael up for his weekend visits, then again to drop him off, but we were rarely around, usually off hanging out with our friends, so we almost never saw him. When we did, he'd say a quick hi, maybe ask a few generic questions, then leave.

Dad's lack of effort wasn't all that surprising. We have a half-sister, Laurie, the product of a fling he'd had just out of high school. He'd fled to the army to dodge that responsibility and hadn't met Laurie until her teens, long after he'd missed his window to be a father to her. And while he was genuinely happy to get to know her and acquaint us with our sister, I don't imagine he ever lost a ton of sleep over all that lost time. Object permanence is not one of his strengths. It was pretty much out of sight, out of mind when it came to Laurie, as it eventually was with us.

Paul and I often went months to a year without seeing Dad, and he didn't really seem to care all that much, but he was still our dad, so we arranged to swing by for dinner one night. It was just one dinner, and it gave Paul an excuse to make the most of his shiny new driver's license, so why not? As we drove down in my mom's station wagon, singing along to the radio, we let our guard down, daring for just a little while to be happy.

When we arrived, Dad was glad to see us. Christine was drunk. She'd gotten worse in the interim. Time was, she waited until everyone was asleep to get plastered. That night, she'd been tossing 'em back before we even showed up, and by dinner she was completely trashed. That was the only way she could have lost enough control in front of everyone the way she did.

Dad, Paul, and I were talking in the living room when my head turned at the sound of Christine screaming as she thundered toward me. I started to shake and cry, reliving all the times she'd come at me, berated me, tortured me. I was like an animal caught in a trap, panicked and wild, and I fled to the far end of the room, but after a few steps there was nowhere left to go. As Christine neared me, I crumpled to the floor and begged her to stop.

"What the hell is this? What's going on?!" Dad yelled out as he sprang from the couch, Paul right behind him. I was relieved but also pissed. What the fuck was he asking questions for? Christine had made no secret of her feelings toward me. From the beginning she'd snapped at me constantly, picking apart everything I said, even yelling at my dad about me. Maybe he hadn't known how bad it was. Maybe he was just taken by surprise in the moment, believing the camping incident had been the last of it, but there he was, demanding an explanation.

Paul was so confused. He couldn't believe what he was seeing, but instinct must have taken over, thrusting him between me and Christine. As he helped me up, I looked my dad straight in the eye and said through my tears, in a shaky voice, "She's been doing this for years."

Dad didn't follow us out, and I never knew why. Still don't. Paul helped me into the car—I was still too shaken to move on my own, tears running down my cheeks—swung around the driver's seat, and peeled down the street. Looking straight out onto the road ahead of us, we drove in silence for a few minutes, then once we hit the highway, Paul finally spoke up.

"We're never going back there, Nik. Never again." And we never did.

At fourteen, my relationship with my dad was essentially over. I'd eventually forge a new one several years later, but it was never the same as when I was a kid. Those years are just lost, and I don't know much about his life during that time.

I know he stayed with Christine for a while, long enough to have a kid with her in 1990. Our half-brother wasn't enough to save their marriage, but the pregnancy motivated Christine to finally put the bottle down and get herself into AA, and without the alcohol—surprise, surprise—she became a very different person, working the steps and paying it forward. Too little, too late where I was concerned, but to her credit, she stuck the landing. As far as I know, she's been dry for thirty-five years. And you know what? Good for her. Sincerely.

Still…an amends would have been nice.

CHAPTER 10

Our Lady of Bennigan's

When I moved to New City in 1987, the summer before high school, I was hit with a crushing wave of culture shock. The town was effectively a John Hughes movie: an affluent suburb of McMansions, designer clothes, and kids who got shiny new Beemers for their sweet sixteens—a far cry from the rock 'n' roll, Trans Am town I'd come from.

Our new house, comfortably sized for my mom, new stepdad, and the five kids they had between them, was positively modest compared to the chic, angular, modern homes just down the block. I'd moved into a house twice as big as the one I'd left behind and was somehow still on the poor end of town. It was a good thing status had never meant that much to me.

I didn't have the easiest time adapting. I spent the first half of high school more or less invisible to my classmates, because I didn't understand their social Olympics and had no interest in learning. But I did catch one person's attention.

Joey had a cute face, a wily sense of fun, and his own car. He was mega-rich, even by New City standards, but you'd never know it by his demeanor, humble and sweet. We would skip school and take long drives down the Garden State Parkway in his Iroc-Z with the T-top open, letting the industrially tainted breeze blow through our hair. We didn't even care where we went; we'd just pick an exit and turn off to get gas and snacks before laying out on the hood, talking as we got drunk or high, often both.

One time, we skipped school and spent an entire day at the Nanuet Mall, stoned and nursing a bottle of something we'd smuggled in—whiskey or maybe bourbon—nipping just enough throughout the day to keep our buzz going. While drifting through the pet store, we decided to liberate a hamster and give it a day of adventure. Joey spent hours carrying the little guy around in his pocket, and we pretended to have conversations with him while we sat in the food court, slipping him French fries and chunks of burger buns.

Later on, as we were stepping off the elevator, Joey halted in his tracks, frantically feeling the inside of his jacket.

"He's gone," he said, his eyes wide.

"What do you mean he's gone? Where would he…"

I spotted the hamster scurrying along the metal railing inside the elevator, and dashed for the doors, but they slid closed before we could pry them back open. We bolted for the stairs, racing the elevator to the second floor, laughing hysterically the whole way up, and made it just in time for the doors to open, revealing our little friend chilling on the railing, practically waiting for us. We jumped inside and scooped him up, laughing our faces red as the doors closed again.

Once outside, at the tree line across the parking lot, we set the hamster free, convinced in our infinite teenage wisdom that we were saving his life. Then, we went off to take care of the munchies, because what else was there to do? And that was Joey and me.

I don't know if anyone has ever loved me quite the way he did, with that fearless, naked affection that comes only with youth and innocence—well, as innocent as any boy up to his eyeballs in testosterone can be. He adored me, and I loved being adored but I didn't love him, not the way I knew I was supposed to. It didn't occur to me then that I might be gay. I just figured I was so damaged that whatever I *did* feel for Joey, whatever I was capable of feeling at all, was the closest I was ever going to get to the real thing, the kind of love that all the movies and pop songs went on about. Maybe my high school romance wasn't normal, but I was sure it was better than I deserved and probably the best I was going to get in this world, so I accepted it and tried to be the best girlfriend I could.

Paul's trauma had shaped his childhood differently than mine had. The depression that had led to his suicidal thoughts had also manifested in a significant weight problem, but by the time we'd gotten to New City, he'd shed the weight and learned how to hide his pain behind a charming grin, so the charm was all the kids there knew of him. It got him friends. It got him girls. It got him a whole new life, at least on the surface. What it didn't do was heal the damage underneath, which he coped with in many of the same ways I did. His new friends didn't see his darkness, but it was something we'd always had in common and, in a way, always would.

The move had been an opportunity for Paul to reinvent himself, and he'd taken it very seriously and made the most of it. A lot of kids in his position would have cut their freshman sister loose to avoid the possible drag on their upward mobility, but he never did.

A few weeks after I turned sixteen, in the summer of '89, Paul helped score me a job as a seating hostess at Bennigan's, where he'd been waiting tables for about a year. I spotted him at the start of my first shift, hanging at the back of the restaurant by the pay phones, having a quick smoke break with another waiter, Omar, who I'd already met in passing once or twice. I caught their attention with a little wave, which they returned, then whipped around at the sound of the door to greet my first customer.

It wasn't a customer, just a waitress wandering in from the parking lot, smiling with half-lidded eyes. I didn't need to sniff the air wafting off her to know she'd just hit a joint, probably in the parking lot, and I decided right then and there that Amanda and I were going to get along just fine.

Later that week, as the two of us sat in the parking lot, getting stoned, Omar came over with a bottle of Snapple and a pack of Parliaments and tossed them to me.

"Thanks, dude," I said. "What do I owe you?"

He waved me away with a baby-faced smile. "Forget it. You're one of us now." It wasn't long before I believed him.

The next day, I was invited to a party at the home of one of the waiters, not as Paul's sister but as Nikki the seating hostess, just another friend from work. I had never in my life felt so utterly normal. It was weird—nice, but weird.

I spent that first party getting so fucked up I still don't remember it, but when I showed up to work the next day, several Polaroids from the party had been tacked up on the bulletin board in the kitchen, one of them featuring me with Mark, a skinny, curly-haired waiter I'd met the first day on the job but hadn't really talked to. He'd announced himself with the shrill sound of rubber screeching to a halt in the parking lot and breezed in as he fastened a novelty button to his loud regulation suspenders, mumbling a thoroughly unconvincing apology. In his scramble to sweep his tardiness under the rug with some performative diligence, he'd never bothered to introduce himself to the new girl, yet there I was in the photo, dead asleep on his shoulder.

"You basically introduced yourself, laughed your ass off for thirty seconds, then passed right the fuck out. Right here," Mark said, tapping his shoulder.

"Shit. I am so sorry." I looked away, embarrassed.

"Nah, it's cool," he said, smiling. He nodded to the picture again. "Totally worth it." And that's how I met one of my best friends for life.

Each shift at Bennigan's began and ended with a joint in the parking lot, most of us huddled around a white Jeep that belonged to Omar's best friend, Brandon, a kid from a few towns over who, like the rest of us, had found a place on our little Island of Misfit Toys. When a shift started, I'd be the first to go inside, the rest packed into Brandon's Jeep, obscured by a thick haze of smoke. When I sat the first table in someone's section, I'd duck out into the parking lot and call them inside, collecting the wait staff one by one until the dinner rush began. Each time, taking a toke to keep me nice and toasted.

This was simply business as usual. On any given night, every single server at the New City Bennigan's was high as a kite, the entire front end of a franchise family eatery run by a pack of stoner teens in khakis and overly decorated suspenders.

The munchies were inevitably a factor.

"Yooooooo," I said one night with a broad grin, my breath freezing in front of me. Amanda, Mark, and I were standing in the walk-in freezer, marveling at the trays of ready-to-plate Death by Chocolate desserts. We exchanged a greedy glance and in unison said, "Totally," in the Valley Girl accent everyone effected at the turn of the decade.

Mark grabbed one of the desserts and held it out to us. With the THC baking our brains, we began passing the chocolate-shelled rocky road ice cream around, cracking up as we took bite after bite.

The freezer door opened, and Paul poked his head in. "Hey, stoners, birthday at table 106. Finish up and get your shit together." He winked at us and closed the door.

The Death by Chocolate was already gone, but the evidence of it was all over our faces. We filed out of the freezer, snickering, and stopped at the slop sink to wash our hands and mouths. Less than a minute later we were blending into a cluster of servers, clapping in time as we sang Bennigan's cheesy happy birthday song. Mark and I exchanged a sideways glance, barely managing to keep it together.

The rest of the summer blew right by, most of it spent in the company of my coworkers and the other kids I met through them. I ended up with more friends from the surrounding high schools than my own.

We always had a blast together, even at work. After we closed the restaurant down at night, we'd linger in the parking lot, smoking up and playing wiffle ball. There were at least a dozen of us at any given time, and we weren't quiet, but the cops never bothered us. They knew we worked there and never got violent or destructive. We were just goofing, so they left us alone to laugh, screw around, and make runs to the gas station for whatever we needed, and we didn't need much. As long as we were stocked up with Snapple, snacks, and smokes, we were all set.

Before I knew it, I was back at school for my junior year, but it wasn't the grind it had been before. School was just a place I stopped at for a few hours every day, and I put in just enough effort not to flunk out. Beyond handing in my homework and working my shifts at Bennigan's, I had zero responsibility. I spent 99 percent of my waking hours wasted, breezing through school, having finally found my tribe. It was the best my life had ever been. Naturally, this proved the perfect time to become acquainted with psychedelics.

Up until that point, booze and pot had been the hardest I'd gone, but once mushrooms, angel dust, and all other hallucinogens showed up to the party, tripping became the new standard.

One morning, the built-in answering machine on my phone (each teen in the house had their own phone line, the only status symbol our parents could afford to give us) clicked on, waking me with my outgoing message. I was ready to fall back asleep when a low, cryptic voice said, "Nikki…get up, get up. It's time to take your acid."

I snorted with laughter, still groggy but awake enough to play along. I picked up the phone to say a quick hello, but Mark just came alive on the line and insisted I get up and head over to his house. "My folks are out of town, and it is the perfect morning for some day-tripping! Get your ass over here!"

Was it the weekend? A school day I'd failed to wake up on time for? Honestly, I don't remember now, and at the time I didn't care. I hopped out of bed, still in my PJs, brushed my teeth (but not my hair), and sped over to Mark's house in my janky, fire-engine red Volkswagen Fox, with its gray, nicotine-perfumed upholstery.

It was truly a great day, spent smoking up and tripping balls in Mark's living room. I dropped acid within minutes of arriving, and holy shit…I was in a whole new world.

Mark put on some music, oldies we'd grown up with thanks to our Boomer parents, and told me he was going to "explore," which could have meant anything, considering he was tripping out of his mind.

"Dance!" he called to me from five feet away and across the world. I looked around, and suddenly I was the only person in the room and all I could hear was the music, so I just started grooving out. Before long I was getting down to Jefferson Airplane's "White Rabbit," very aware of my body but at the same time floating in space. My eyes were closed, but I could see lights flashing all around me in time with the music of the spheres, and I just rocked out, lost in the magic of the cosmos.

And then, somehow it was several hours later, and I was late for dinner.

I walked into my house still totally fucked up, with every intention of slipping through the kitchen and down the hall to ride out the rest of the trip in my bedroom, but there my family was at the dinner table, all their eyes on me. It would look suspicious not to eat with them, and I was too out of it to come up with a decent lie, so I excused myself to wash up and disappeared into the bathroom.

I braced myself against the sink, my heart beating so hard I could feel it in my knees, but everything seemed like it was drifting somehow. I looked up and gasped.

"Holy fuck..." I whispered, fingering my cheeks and forehead. My face didn't look like my face. Whose face was it, and how would I get mine back? Because I had to; they would know. My family would notice that I wasn't wearing my own fucking face! "Okay. Okay okay, just breathe. Just play it cool, and they won't notice."

They didn't notice, at least not that my face was different, because, outside of my acid-fried brain, it wasn't. I can only imagine what I looked like as I watched the chicken cutlet on my plate moving around on its own while the cups smiled at me. All I could do was coach myself to act as normal as possible, reminding myself to cut my food into small, human bites and eat it with my fork. *With my fork*; that was very important. Smile at the family. Answer when you can.

My cup kept trying to start a conversation with me, so I told it to shut the fuck up before it blew my cover. Then I panicked, realizing I might have done just that, but no one at the table seemed to be reacting, so maybe I'd merely *thought* it, in which case, the jig wasn't up yet. I was fairly certain no one at the table could read my thoughts. Probably.

"I'll be right back!" I blurted out, playing it as cool as I could as I fled to my room. I shut the door, then flipped on the light, grabbed my notebook off my desk, and started writing myself a letter.

I am tripping the fuck out at the dinner table. And my cup is being such a bitch. Fuck! Nikki, get your shit together and get back out there!

After psyching myself up, I returned to the dining room to finish dinner with my family, and that was it. No one said a damn thing. I still can't believe I got away with it, but once I did, I knew I could do it again, and there was a dangerous freedom in knowing it.

Rather than having to constantly depend on my friends for weed whenever I wanted some, I managed an introduction to their pot dealer. I had my own income now, so why not? And whenever I had some left over, I figured hey, why not flip it for a small profit? So I did. More money meant more weed, starting the whole cycle over again, and as someone my friends and coworkers had almost constant access to, buying from me became a lot more convenient, so I found myself with a little side hustle in addition to my hostess job.

Word got around pretty quickly that the blonde girl at the greeting stand at Bennigan's was a dependable weed hookup, and it wasn't long before selling weed to the masses became a reliable source of income. I managed to run a steady business right under my boss's nose for months without him finding out. More than one steady business, actually.

I'd been the seating hostess at Bennigan's for a few months when the management decided to promote me to "host manager," a position they'd created for me to justify all the responsibilities I'd taken off their hands. At sixteen, I was still too young legally to be a waitress, but I was herding the other hosts, keeping track of and making up shift schedules for all the employees, making sure shifts were covered, and pretty much any other task the management didn't want to bother with. I didn't get paid a single extra cent for any of it, but it did allow me to schedule all my friends to work during my shifts, so I was cool with that. It also meant that since the manager could more or less remain in his office, what with me up front to deal with any seating issues that arose, I didn't have to worry about getting caught when engaging in any less-than-legit activities of my own, like selling pot or taking bribes.

That's right. Bribes.

Look, this was Bennigan's in 1990. As far as kitschy family dining went, it was the hottest spot in town, and on weekends, we got positively slammed. If a family of four showed up for dinner, they could be looking at an hour-long wait just to get the crappiest table in the house. My talents then weren't terribly varied, but if there was one thing I knew, it was how to read people and work them. I'd size someone up, feel out whether or not they'd be game, then lean in and whisper, "Okay, you're looking at a forty-five-minute wait, but for twenty bucks, I can seat you in five." The offer was almost always met with a smile and a twenty slipped stealthily into my palm.

The truth was the management had totally taken advantage of me. They'd seen a smart, capable kid who could take some work off their hands at no extra cost and exploited me. And I exploited them right back. The situation worked out for everybody. I was just the only one who knew it.

My on-the-clock efforts turned a decent profit, and made it easier to acquire weed, shrooms, even LSD when the mood struck, but if an opportunity to get high for free came along, I wasn't about to turn it down. Free is always the right price.

I had just finished my shift, sharing a joint with Amanda out in the parking lot when she had an epiphany.

"Hey, you want to do something a little stronger?"

"Like what?" I said.

"Valium?"

I laughed. "Now? Where the fuck are we going to get Valium right now?"

"From, like…my other job."

I took a moment to order my thoughts enough to remember what Amanda's other part-time job was, then I sputtered with laughter. "You want to jack a fuckin' vet's office?! Would kitty Valium even work on us?"

Amanda rolled her eyes. "It's not…there's no kitty Valium or people Valium. It's just Valium. Huge jars of it just sitting there for the taking."

We had a good chuckle, my Volkswagen venting smoke like the Mystery Machine, and got quiet. A few minutes later, on our way over to the vet's office, Amanda explained all the basics we needed to know for our little heist, and it was agreed that it was probably best that I stay with the getaway car, it being mine and all.

So I sat there in my car, at the far end of the parking lot in front of the vet's office, making my best effort to blend in and not look at all suspicious, for several minutes before a high-pitched siren wailed out, shattering the silence. Apparently, despite having been sober enough to formulate an otherwise flawless plan, Amanda hadn't been quite sober enough to remember to deactivate the security system.

"Go go go!" Amanda screamed as she came bursting out of the building, pills spilling from her fists all over the pavement. I turned the engine over as she hopped in and slammed the door, and we sped off down the street, tires screeching. She hadn't even put the lids back on the jars; she'd just busted the hell out of there.

As we cruised down the street, our faces were cast in the flashing red and blue lights of police cars sweeping past us, toward the scene of the very crime we'd just fled. Whatever mellow the pot had granted us was long gone, and we each popped a few of our newly acquired pills just to calm ourselves down.

We drove around for a bit to give the pills some time to kick in. Just as the Valium finally started to affect me, I realized I was running dangerously low on fuel, so we went straight to the gas station across from Bennigan's, because at that time, all roads led to Bennigan's.

Sky-high on pot and Valium, which had relaxed our muscles to a fraction of their use, I was having a hard time getting out of the car, so Amanda offered to pump my gas for me. She donned her rhinestone-studded Laura Biagiotti sunglasses as she stepped out of the car to avoid any suspicion, as if the cashier would've cared. After a minute, I could swear I heard a strange noise. I listened more closely and heard a faint voice whine, "Help me," a few times.

Glancing over my shoulder, I found Amanda struggling to hold the gas nozzle up to the tank, her meticulously teased and sprayed hair barely held in place by her hot pink butterfly clip, Biagiottis riding her nose. I got out of the car, barely able to walk myself, and we rallied together, summoning every precious ounce of strength and coordination we had to hold the nozzle up and fill the tank. We mustered just enough self-awareness between the two of us to recognize the sheer ridiculata of the entire evening and burst into hysterical laughter.

After that, we were spent. I couldn't even drive my car across the street to the Bennigan's lot, so I pulled it away from the pump and parked in one of the adjacent spaces before Amanda and I, still giggling, crossed the street to sober up over a plate of nachos.

We were pretty frazzled by the whole ordeal, but the gains were worth it, if only for a one-time win. And soon enough, our little heist made for a great story, but there was one person who didn't find it amusing at all: my boyfriend.

Oh, Joey…so open and adoring. All he wanted was to party with his girlfriend like normal high school kids, and while part of me craved that normalcy too, once my hardcore partying took off, there was no going back. I couldn't take him with me where I was going. He probably would have followed me eventually, but I couldn't let him. He wasn't broken like me, and he deserved better. Breaking his heart was the only way to save him, and it did. I like to think that made it worth it.

You'd think the great pet-Valium heist would be a one-of-a-kind story, but it wasn't the only time I'd gotten high by way of a professional medical establishment. The second such experience was courtesy of none other than Deb.

Long before our misadventures in Hawaii, Deb and I met through the Bennigan's crew and vibed right away. She was a wild one like me, with even less to lose. Her dad was well-connected in local circles, so we pushed our luck a lot harder than we would have otherwise. We'd get high and laugh our asses off in her room, only to have her mother barge in, flustered and scolding us for nothing more than playing our music too loud, clueless that inside the wardrobe there were lines of coke cut and ready to be snorted the second she left. It only made us laugh louder once she was gone.

Cocaine, as Rick James himself once said, is a hell of a drug. It was more expensive and a lot harder to obtain but worth the high it provided. I actually felt good about myself on coke. More importantly, I felt no pain. And Deb…well, Deb just loved to have a good time and could always afford one, so if she was offering, why not?

Like me, Deb had been coming up on her senior year of high school, but the summer had left her schedule wide open for her part-time job as a hygienist's assistant at a local dentist's office, to which she had the keys. Of all the coked-up adventures the two of us went on that summer, the night we "visited" her place of business was probably the wildest. It went a lot more smoothly than the incident with the animal hospital, mainly because Deb had the presence of mind to deactivate the alarm before it could go off.

"All right, Calamity Jane," she said, nodding to a door at the end of the hall. "Wait for me in exam room 3. I gotta go turn on the oxygen."

"What do you mean, turn it on?"

"Well, it's not on 24/7. That would be so fucking dangerous. I just turn it on, it flows into the tank and becomes the oxide in nitrous oxide, and we're good to go."

No further explanation was needed. I headed into the exam room to wait while Deb handled the mechanics, hoping somewhere at the edge of my senses that one of us would remember to turn the oxygen off again.

Deb strolled into the exam room and joined me on the floor near the tanks. She put the mask over my face and turned on the gas. I already had plenty of pot and coke in my system, so the infusion of the nitrous oxide catapulted me right into the stratosphere. I was completely gone.

I can only imagine the look on my face as I sat there, unable to move, slumped against the wall in possibly the most blissed-out, fucked-up state I've ever been in. I don't even remember Deb taking the mask off, but when I came to, it was strapped to her face, and she was gone—physically there but bombed out of her fucking mind. She started to giggle and snort, and then I giggled and snorted too. We laughed until we could hardly breathe, then tried to talk a little, then laughed even more. If laughter is contagious when you're sober…please. Everything felt so dreamy in that moment as we passed the mask back and forth, barely able to sit up straight, talking in enthusiastically slurred speech about everything and nothing.

I don't remember how we made it out of there that night, but we must have had the wherewithal to cover our tracks, because Deb's boss never mentioned a thing about it, and Deb kept that job for some time afterward. What can I say? We were good.

I no longer recognized myself in my peers, not that I ever really had to begin with, but now? While their thoughts revolved around taking their SATs, applying to colleges, and whether or not they'd be able to avoid the freshman fifteen, I had no concept of the future. All I had was the present, and presently I was barreling toward the edge of a cliff at full speed.

I felt alone and adrift all the time. My awareness of how out of control my life had become made me feel even worse. I was a lost cause.

I remember being forced to endure one of those tired *Just Say No!* assemblies that try way too hard to be hip and with it, but really just end up being so condescending and lame that kids just end up tuning them out. There was this incredibly on-the-nose skit about a group of kids faced with the option of either getting high or saying no to drugs, and *of course* one person dressed in white represented light and safety, while another in black represented drugs and darkness. So subtle.

I rolled my eyes, enduring this bullshit as best I could, watching the actor in white saving all but one of the "kids" while the actor in black claimed the last one. I laughed as they stumbled into the shadows offstage together, because I knew the script even then, and I knew that I was that last kid. I was supposed to identify with the light and the kids saved by it, but that wasn't me. I wanted to be pulled into the darkness. That was my reality, what I gravitated toward. The danger, that rush of adrenaline… *that* was me, and I knew it. Even then.

Dealing and taking bribes at the hostess station made me decent money, but it was a gig I couldn't keep up forever. A slip-up was inevitable, and when my boss found out, I considered myself lucky he didn't call the cops on me.

"It was a good run," Mark said, passing me a joint in the parking lot. "I'm honestly surprised you managed to keep it up as long as you did."

"Whatever. I'll find something else."

"Oh, yeah. No doubt," he croaked through a cloud of smoke. "I'll miss you, though."

I smirked at him sideways. "I got fired, not murdered. We'll still hang all the time."

"Yeah, I know." He gave me a reassuring smile. "It's just not going to be the same around here. It's all changing."

He wasn't wrong. Some of the gang was still around, but others had gone off to college or just drifted out of our orbit. Avalon was behind us, and while there were new possibilities ahead and new memories to be made, it would never be the same.

CHAPTER 11

Higher Learning

I still had a year of high school left when I came to the conclusion that I'd outgrown it. Nothing that seemed to fit everyone else, that guided their feet and kept them grounded, applied to me anymore, and my budding awareness of how out of control my life was becoming made me feel even worse. Even my teachers turned a blind eye to my obvious self-destruction, so I said fuck it all. There was no sense lingering where I no longer belonged. Luckily, I had options.

Rockland Community College, often referred to as RCC or "the Rock," offered a kind of combo year for local high school seniors. I could complete my high school diploma with college credits, which I could later parlay into an associate's degree or even use to transfer to a four-year university. With that opportunity lying at my feet, nothing in the world could have kept me in high school for another year, so in the fall of 1990, I started my college career.

And I fucking loved it.

Most of my fellow seniors were still clocking seven hours a day, five days a week, but me? I had class for about three hours a day, and my early days didn't even start until 11 a.m., so I could party all weekend, sleep in on Monday, and still make it to class on time. Plus, Paul and most of our friends were already taking classes there, so there was no downside I or anyone else could see.

Mom and Gene, both educators, were thrilled I was getting a jump on my college education, and even still living at home, I was enjoying more freedom than I ever had. Cruising around town in the middle of the day had gone from truant to perfectly legit, and an afternoon high became an entirely feasible indulgence. Coke was still an elusive treat, only manageable two or three times a week…but nonetheless manageable.

By winter break, the taste of freedom I'd experienced had me hungry for more, and rather than complete the school year living at home, I started looking for my own place. My cousin Matt, at that point studying to become a drug counselor in the wake of his own recovery, was in the market for a roommate to share an apartment in Mahwah. The timing was perfect.

The vibe at our place was chill, and the location was reasonably close to campus. Sure, Matt's new chosen profession ran completely counter to my psychotropic lifestyle, but we all allow for some contradictions in our lives, and if Matt struggled at all to reconcile those things, he never made it my problem.

With some strategically placed partitions, Matt and I managed to transform a one-bedroom apartment into a two-bedroom that afforded us each our own personal space. The place wasn't huge, but like any first apartment, the most important thing was that it was my own space, and that gave it its own gravity, drawing my friends to hang out and party. Even Paul, who was still living at home while he got his associate's, turned up on a regular basis, as did Mark, Omar, and even Brandon. They'd swing by between classes and on the weekends, and we'd get high just like the good old days.

I even scored points with Michael, who I'd pick up from school some days and bring over to watch movies and grab the kind of junk food forbidden to him at home. Even a ten-year-old could find a little freedom to indulge his vices in my domain, and I liked that. I liked it a lot.

After Joey, I'd been in no rush to pick up another boyfriend, and it had never occurred to me to consider Brandon an option. He'd always been a friend, some guy I worked with and got high with. I didn't know he used to do coke before we'd met and quit. When he learned I had gotten into it, he picked the habit back up. We'd go off and do lines all weekend, and being at the Rock together made it easier to hang out, so we hung out all the time.

One night we got coked up and ended up in bed together, and after that we were an item. It just seemed to make sense at the time. It was nice to be part of an "us" again, and this time with a guy who wasn't going to get on my back for partying too hard, because he was right there alongside me.

Pretty soon, I was doing coke every day, and between that, school, and Brandon, I was completely fried, but not enough to slow down. *Never* enough to slow down. At the rate my habit was blowing up, a few odd jobs here and there weren't going to keep the party going, so I needed to find a steady job.

At eighteen, I was finally old enough to waitress, so I scored a gig at the local Chi-Chi's. It wasn't bad. It never captured the same vibe as Bennigan's—nothing ever could—but it was easy, and the tips were generally good. My new coworkers weren't my people like the old ones had been, but our spirits were kindred enough for me to wonder how I managed to keep that job as long as I did.

We'd drop acid before our shifts in the alley behind the kitchen, laughing uncontrollably in the rank stench of dumpster juice and stray cats, only to steal away behind the prep line in a vain attempt to pull our shit together. Any composure crumbled the second we remembered where we were and why, sparking another round of hysterical laughter we could only pray no one heard. Then we'd shuffle out onto the floor to try and salvage our jobs.

I wouldn't recommend serving sizzling fajitas in this state. Hallucinating dancing skeletons in the flames makes it considerably more difficult to carry the platter through a crowded dining room.

Several times during my shift I'd take an order, run some food, then quickly escape into the bathroom, where I'd lock myself in a stall, grab a dollar bill from my apron, and do a line off the toilet paper dispenser. A quick flush was all I needed to conceal the incriminating sound of snorting cocaine on the job. One would think, between the pot, psychedelics, and now a steady diet of coke, that my habit had reached critical mass. I was certain it had.

Until…there was crack.

I was no angel. I had long since ditched any pretense of innocence, but crack? That was a brand-new frontier, and when I found myself faced with it, I hesitated for a moment…but just a moment.

A fellow waitress, an older woman who was even farther gone than I was, took me into the city with her one time after I'd expressed some interest in whatever it was she was using. We drove down a dark street, and some guy came up seemingly out of nowhere to drop several tiny, five-dollar vials of crack through the rolled-down window.

Soon after my first experience with the white rock, I was buying my own stash to smoke in my very own pipe. I shouldn't have been surprised. It wasn't that far a leap from where I'd already been for some time. I had dealers I could page at all hours for whatever fix I was looking for. What was a late-night drive across the George Washington Bridge to pick something up?

"Hey, Brandon? Whatcha doin'?" I had just finished my shift at Chi-Chi's and was lingering near the kitchen, anxiously twirling the phone cord around my finger.

"Uh…nothing. Why?"

"I'm heading into the city to get a hookup."

"Shotgun," Brandon said, needing no further explanation.

"I'll pick you up in ten." I hung up without even saying goodbye.

The drive to Manhattan from Rockland is usually thirty to forty minutes in regular traffic, but at that time of night we were halfway over the bridge in twenty. Every corner we turned led onto a street that seemed darker and grimier than the last until it straight up looked like we were driving through the third act of a Charles Bronson movie. Lo and behold, there my guy was with the stuff I was looking for, and I picked up as many vials from him as I could afford. We were three blocks from the bridge when I realized I'd left my pipe at home.

"Shit! Shit, shit… Motherfucker!" Brandon growled. "Slow down."

"What?"

"Slow the fuck down!" So, I did, and as we rolled by a parked car, Brandon leaned out the window and snapped its antenna right off. When I eyed the broken antenna in his hand, he shrugged and said, "The shit's not going to smoke itself." And he had a point. Within seconds, Brandon MacGyvered that antenna into a makeshift crack pipe and took a hit. At the next red light, he held the "pipe" to my mouth and lit the end of it. I took a huge hit, blowing the smoke and hitting the gas as the light turned green.

We'd barely hit the Palisades Parkway when we felt compelled to pull over. We rolled into a parking spot at the first rest stop, right off Exit 1, and ran into the restroom. We crammed ourselves into a stall, tweaking and blowing crack smoke down the toilet to flush away any trace of what we were actually doing. We could see the legs of a random stranger in the next stall over, but we didn't give a shit. The rush was immediate, hardcore, and it pushed my high to the limit. Crack was the most violent high I'd ever experienced, slamming into me with the force of a freight train, and yet it yielded such a peaceful bliss. Each rush only lasted minutes, but it was right where I wanted to be, where I *needed* to be. And I had Brandon to come along for the ride, one that even Mark, one of the hardest partiers I'd ever had the pleasure of partying with, wouldn't take.

I loved Mark. He was the best friend I'd ever had, and the further I drifted into my multiple addictions, the further I drifted away from him. We didn't talk about why, but we both felt it and knew if something didn't change, our friendship would just decay until there was nothing left. We agreed to meet on campus one day before class, just to catch up and hang out like we always used to. He even offered to spring for bagels and coffee. I would have met him anyway, but he definitely sold the plan with the promise of free breakfast.

I never made it. He waited for me, long enough to eat both his bagel and mine once he admitted to himself that I wasn't coming. And even then he lingered, chain-smoking for God knows how long, wondering where the hell I could be and why I would stand him up like that. Even now, thirty-plus years and a fully accepted apology later, the thought of him waiting there in front of two lukewarm coffees while I was at home, sleeping off a weekend of crack and God knows what else—it fucks me up a little.

At the end of the spring semester, I'd fulfilled all the requirements for my high school diploma and could return to RCC in the fall as a full-fledged college student. It was enough to make me consider turning over a new leaf. Even in the midst of my spiral, I was aware of what was happening to me and figured the start of my sophomore year would be the perfect time to get it together and find my focus.

Two days before the start of the term, I was chilling out in my apartment. Matt was out for the evening, so I had the place to myself to just take it easy, do a few lines of coke (no crack; I'd resolved to be responsible), and call it my last hurrah. I would be sober again in twenty-four hours, just in time to get a good night's sleep and start my first day of classes fresh and prepared.

That's not what happened.

What was meant to be some mild partying before "Take Two" of my college experience turned into a full-blown coke binge. I locked my door, and before I knew what had hit me, I'd been up for two solid days, high as a fucking kite, having left my room only to pee. In that time, I'd played solitaire with feverish intensity for hours on end, journaled vigorously, cleaned my room down to the reorganization of every last drawer and shelf, and had intense conversations with just about everyone in my address book who would answer the phone. What I had decided to ignore, to deny even to myself, was what any cokehead knows perfectly well: The party doesn't stop until you run out of coke.

If you've never seen someone tweak on a two-day cocaine high, allow me to paint you a picture.

As I left my apartment for my first class of the year, I in no way resembled the go-getting student I'd aimed to be when my binge began. I was skinny and pale, eyes bloodshot, and my teased-out '91 hair was veering from trendy to trashy. I couldn't stop snorting and swallowing from the days' worth of cocaine clogging my nose, and I was so on edge that every movement was a sharp jerk in one direction or another. I can't imagine I was fooling anyone, except possibly myself, and I have no doubt that as I twitched my way across campus, I looked like a complete lunatic.

My first class, as irony would have it, was Criminal Justice. My goal of remaining discreet wasn't entirely unrealistic, despite being so wired

I could have shorted out the lights, but when the professor introduced himself as an actual local judge, the background hum of paranoia in my head got a lot louder. My jones for another line went from zero to *right fucking now!* in about three seconds. I excused myself, not waiting for the professor's reply before walking right out the door. I did a line or two (or maybe five, who knows?) in the bathroom and returned to class, flickering and crackling inside like an old neon sign.

I spent the rest of that class and many others like it unable to sit still, talking a mile a minute. When I wasn't ranting incoherently, I was grinding my teeth, eyes bugging out of my head. I would do lines between, sometimes even *during* classes. I was frankly a mess, but somehow I got away with it. I always got away with it, because no matter how far down the rabbit hole I went, I learned the rules of the game before my feet even hit the ground. There had never been a system I couldn't work, at least for a little while. College was no different.

I managed to do well on my tests despite barely showing up to class, and my coke-fueled papers were well received. But after a while, class attendance became an issue, and it was clear I was headed toward flunking out. I now had two goals, to pass my classes and to keep feeding my habit, so I did what came naturally and always seemed to work: I found a loophole and thoroughly exploited it.

One forged doctor's note later, the dean informed my professors that my absences were due to a legitimate medical issue, and I couldn't be penalized for them. Held accountable only for my actual work, I not only managed to pass all my classes, I made the dean's list. As for keeping the party going, Chi-Chi's paid for some of it, but not nearly enough, so I resorted to other means of making cash.

"So, let's just go over it one more time," Brandon said as we lingered about fifty feet from the campus bookstore.

I nodded, tore the first page out of my memo pad, and handed it to him. "This is a list of all the books I bought at the start of the semester. You go in, grab all the books on the list, and *discreetly* leave them at that spot by the door I showed you." I pulled a forged receipt from my pocket. "Then you leave, I go in and grab the stack, and use this copy I made of the original receipt to 'return' the new ones."

Brandon glanced down at the list, then up at me. "You think this will actually work?"

"If you can play it cool and not look suspicious, you fuckin' spaz," I said with a sly grin.

Smiling, Brandon shook his head, kissed me, and headed into the bookstore.

The scam worked exactly as planned, and between the two of us and the few classmates we later enlisted, we pulled it off several more times before the semester was out. Not much was computerized in 1991, so forging those receipts was pretty easy, and we were long gone by the time any inventory discrepancies popped up. I don't think our activities went completely unnoticed. I'm fairly certain we were the reason the bookstore installed a security system the following semester, but we duped them while we could.

At eighteen, my life had become a buffet of weed, psychedelics, coke, and now crack. The refrain was always the same: get high, barely make it to school, get high, roll into work, get high, get high, crash if I had the time, and repeat. With that routine, it becomes surprisingly easy to simply forget to eat, because compared to a howling jones, hunger is just a petty little nagging in your gut that barely registers, if it all. But then I would come down after days without food and realize I was absolutely ravenous, practically tearing my car apart for enough loose change to buy a twenty-five-cent burger from McDonald's. When Brandon was with me, we would share that one burger because twenty-five cents was often all we could scrape together after days of binging. We would stare at the sad little burger even as we tore it in half and inhaled it.

It didn't matter how many tips I pulled in from waitressing or how much cash Brandon's parents would slip him for the month. A few hundred dollars could be gone in an hour. It was never enough money. It never is, so you resort to doing whatever you can to get more.

It was the middle of winter, early into my final semester at the Rock. I hadn't been to class in days, but by the grace of my forged doctor's note, it wasn't an issue. Brandon and I had been binging for at least two days, and the only thing I could remember was a quick trip to Dunkin' Donuts, during which I'd smuggled toilet paper out of the restroom. I'd run out at home, and a girl's gotta do what a girl's gotta do.

I scrambled into the kitchen and started ransacking the cabinets, grabbing random cans, boxes of pasta, and bags of rice that had been in there for God knows how long, so I could return them to the grocery store for cash. I completely cleaned the kitchen out, even stuff Matt had bought for himself. I was jonesing way too hard to give a fuck. I didn't make much money off of it, but there was enough to keep the party going just a little longer. When there were no non-perishables left to return, we scoured laundromat floors, parking lots, and sidewalks for loose change, praying to catch the promise-filled glint of a few coins.

I smoked everything down to my last vial, and when that was gone, I started tearing my bedroom apart, my mattress up against the wall, furniture strewn about the room, and me on my hands and knees, combing the carpet for some tiny crumb of crack I might have missed. When that didn't work, I'd play a game of "bad carpet," smacking the floor to see what crumbs might fly up. It worked fine if what I found actually turned out to be crack, but if some lint or kitty litter made its way into the pipe, it would explode and turn the stem black. That kind of stuff wasn't flammable, and the sour, nasty smoke it produced tasted absolutely revolting. And even knowing that, I'd roll the dice.

That craving, that comedown…there's nothing that can quite describe it, but it's torment to the point of panic and severe depression, and it doesn't go away until you pass out. I would have done anything for one tiny final blast, just *seconds* of euphoria. And when even that was gone, all I could do was lie there on my rug in the fetal position.

I was getting by in school, but even with my doctor's note, I was losing traction pretty quickly. My spotty attendance at Chi-Chi's had gotten me fired, I barely left the apartment anymore, and I'd started dealing coke just to feed my habit. Matt would be working the graveyard shift at a rehab and would call in to see how I was doing. I'd be cutting an ounce of coke on our glass coffee table and weighing out little baggies as I snorted a line or two, all while trying to convince him I was just fine.

Eventually, Matt rightly figured that if my junkie behavior was so blatant he could no longer ignore it, the line had been crossed. Just like when we were kids, he had my back, though I wouldn't appreciate it for quite some time afterward. He made a phone call, and a few days later, on my mom's invitation, I swung by the house only to walk straight into a half-assed intervention that consisted mainly of my parents telling me that I was going to rehab.

Maybe I could have fought them on it. I was a legal adult, and they couldn't *make* me do anything. But I was just too run down. Every addict has these lows, these brief periods of exhaustion where you know you need to change and more importantly *want* to change, but they never last. This one lasted just long enough.

Less than twenty-four hours after my intervention, I was on a plane to Arizona.

CHAPTER 12

Treatment

I'd been so exhausted with my addiction, so eager to be done with it, I didn't put up a fight about going to rehab. I actually *wanted* to go when I boarded the plane, but by the time I was cruising at thirty-five thousand feet, I was already over it and planning how to score my next high.

I needed to escape, but I couldn't exactly get off the plane mid-flight, so I'd just have to find someone at the airport I could ride all the way to my next fix. Fuck Rockland. Maybe it was just time for a new start, and why not Arizona? I tanned well. I could simply go missing…just like that. If I could find a hookup on the plane, all the better, and you *know* I tried.

But of course, none of those half-baked plans panned out. I was picked up at the gate, herded into a van with a handful of other lost souls who didn't want to be there any more than I did, and shuttled off to rehab.

Whoever thought of building a rehab in the middle of the desert, right in the foothills of the Santa Catalina Mountains, knew what they were doing. It wasn't until I had detoxed that I was fully able to appreciate just how Zen the environment was, with its adobe-style buildings, clear, open skies, and total isolation from the city beyond.

After a few days in detox, I was moved to one of the four *haciendas*, each with its own fire pit, hot tub, and a little outdoor nook set aside for the smokers. I would often take my morning coffee out to the smoking nook and let my mind wander as I stared out into the tranquility of the Arizona desert, surrounded by sand and cacti. I'd even hear the occasional rattlesnake, which was an oddly soothing sound from far enough away.

I'd return several times a day to keep myself centered, and the sight of the desert sky at twilight, painted in hues of amber and violet, did as much to calm my nerves as the nicotine fix. I felt bad sometimes for the non-smokers, who had no such crutch to lean on in their recovery, but not bad enough to forfeit mine. I needed it too much.

In the beginning, I would have done anything to escape. "Don't take away my drugs and leave me in my pain" was my constant prayer. I was wishing for the impossible, for a way to make my problems go away without ever having to actually deal with them, never realizing that's not how it works.

Without anything in my system to take the edge off or any friends around to distract me, I was sober and alone with my thoughts for the first time in years, and I had nothing but time to reflect on the road that had taken me from sweet little girl to hardened junkie. I was feeling things, really *feeling* them, for the first time since childhood, and I didn't like it. Acknowledging that even as a small child, I had still been a person, still had feelings, and none of the adults in my life could get out of their own way to see it—it stoked a raw, unyielding pain that I could do nothing but sit and stew in. I was a fucking *person*, yet no one had seen me. I'd been so casually discarded in order to comfort others, to maintain their status quo. How was that love?

It occurred to me that being shut down and silenced in the wake of my abuse hadn't just affected that one situation. I had lost my voice and never found it again. The only way I could communicate my pain after that had been to take care of myself by any means necessary. If that meant scamming and working the system and breaking all the rules, so be it.

But look where it's gotten me, I thought. *They still can't see any of it, because I'm not hurting* them. *I'm just hurting myself. Maybe it's time to knock it off. Maybe I should actually give this place a shot. You know, since I'm already here.*

Rehab actually ended up being a pretty good time. For the twenty-eight days I was there, I felt like I'd actually found a community of people who got it, who knew what it was like to need whatever each of us needed. Whether it was drugs or booze didn't matter; it was the *need* we had in common, the hunger that never seemed to go away, the hunger for whatever numbed the sadness, the guilt, the shame, or whatever else it was that hurt so badly.

Each hacienda had about a dozen rooms, each shared by two patients, that opened right out onto a courtyard, motel-style. There were common rooms where we could come together and hang out between meals and therapy, and the patients in each hacienda more or less kept to each other. The greater community came together for big lectures, in the dining hall for meals, or at the pool and gym, but for the most part we stuck to our haciendas. The people in mine were the ones I really went through the program with for the four weeks I was there.

Though mutual confidentiality prohibits me from naming names, the drummer from a certain band that was enormously popular from the mid-80s through the early 90s happened to be lodging only a few rooms down from mine. Although he was twenty years older than me, we actually became really good friends—like, *charging out of our rooms to have a huge pillow fight in the courtyard* friends. He showed me how to drum with pencils in the big community room where we'd hang out to pass the time when there was nothing to do. We would walk around the property and shoot the shit, and the fact that we were twenty years apart and one of us was a freaking rock star didn't even factor in. Then one day he completed his program and checked out, and off he went back into the real world, never to be heard from (at least by me) again.

That's just rehab. You're stuck in this crucible, and everything is so intense. You bond over your traumas and your current condition, and it feels so real at the time, and then when you're done, you're done. It's not common to keep in touch with your fellow inpatients afterwards, and I didn't take it personally. I don't think any of us do.

There was group therapy, of course—hours a day, every day—but I never got much out of it. Others did. I saw these amazing transformations, cathartic releases that came from raging on inanimate objects with foam bats, screaming and releasing all their hurt and fury. They would break down sobbing eventually, some because they were victims, some because they were perpetrators. Seeing a 6'5" rageaholic fall to his knees weeping is a sight. I know that none of us knew they were abusers until they "came out" in a sobbing fit, admitting the wrongs they'd done, but come on, clinical staff. What even is your screening process?

Putting a survivor like me in a therapy group with a guy like that? Expecting an abuse victim to empathize with and support an abuser? It felt like my trauma was the fuel being burned to power someone else's recovery. I couldn't object or make a scene because the moment wasn't about me. I had to support all my fellow patients, even this one. There was no way I was going to feel safe enough to open up after that. It was game over right there. I shut down completely.

The people around me were tapping into their deep-seated pain, salving their wounds and coming through it all with a fragile, growing hope, but while they healed right in front of me, I just hit autopilot. I went through the motions, mumbled the Serenity Prayer, told my counselors what they wanted to hear, and by the end I was praised for what hard work I'd done and how much I'd accomplished. I would just sit there, thinking, *Lady, I didn't do anything. I'm still a hot mess, but okay. Whatever makes you happy.* I was still running, always running.

There were other things to occupy my time when I got a break from therapy: volleyball, swimming, and walks in the semi-contained wilderness. But what really reached me, the thing that truly calmed my spirit, was the horses. Horseback riding was available for recreation, but there was also equine therapy, a therapeutic exercise based in grooming the horses and earning their trust. Horses are incredibly intuitive creatures. They can sense your vibe behind the chillest poker face. There's this exercise where you need to lift the horse's hoof to clean its shoe. If you're nervous or hesitate, the horse will know, and that foot ain't moving, but if you're confident and serene, up it goes. Well, I'd never been uncomfortable around horses before.

Being in a stable again brought back such a sense of joy and peace, evoking that summer at sleepaway camp with Stacey and JD. I hadn't been around horses since then, and the freedom I had felt being close to them came flooding right back. I would ride out under the open sky to clear my head and soak up the tranquility of the desert as often as my treatment schedule would allow. When I couldn't do that, I'd talk to the horses and feed them apple slices I'd swiped from the dining hall. It's amazing how such a little thing could bring me so much peace.

Even at my darkest, when it seemed I had no one else in my corner, Paul had always been there, able to vibe with me without a word, because we'd survived the same horrors. To the world, Paul and I were this pair of fun, wild siblings everyone knew and admired, and we let them believe we had it made, but when we looked at each other we saw the truth no one else could. We could see in each other's eyes how fucked up and broken we were. Maybe neither of us could help the other find their way, but we could at least be lost together.

About two weeks into my program, I was walking through the detox area on my way to my room when I saw Paul slouched on a huge, puffy couch, looking absolutely miserable.

"You've gotta be shittin' me," I said, walking up to him.

"Surprise." There was no mirth behind his smile. "Whatever the staff here is reporting back to Mom must be real impressive, because… hey." He waved.

I crashed down beside him. "Jesus," I murmured.

Paul laughed despite himself, and I sat with him for a while before I had to leave. It was one of the only times we had a conversation of any length or depth in rehab. As siblings, we were strongly discouraged from socializing. The staff felt it might create some kind of emotional crutch that could hinder both our recoveries, so we didn't talk much. We'd pass each other all the time, exchange a nod or a wave, and keep on moving without a word. We knew each other's pain. We'd shared so much of it that little needed to be said. We couldn't hang out, we could barely acknowledge each other's existence, but in what small way we could, we were still there for each other.

My rebelliousness was never completely repressible, even at my most compliant, even when all it drove me to do was find a place to relax. Early on in my stay, I figured out the skill and timing required to sneak out of my room after lights out and walk very slowly past the night counselors, to the perimeter of my hacienda. On the side of the neighboring building was a ladder right up to the roof. I spent several nights on that roof, staring up at the stars. The sky is pretty big out in the desert, enchanting in its own way and just a little intimidating. It certainly helps to remind you of your place in the universe.

On a patient's last night, there's a little ceremony—a clap out—where everyone claps, sings, stomps their feet, and cheers the graduates on to send them back out into the world with love and encouragement. It's exhilarating and hopeful, and it even made me kind of believe it was going to work.

I didn't keep in touch with many people from rehab, and the ones I did didn't stay on my radar for very long, but I know the statistics. More than a few of them saw that place or one like it again, possibly even a few times. Some of them made it out only to fall back down. And some didn't make it out at all. No matter what it compels you to do, what drug it tells you to abuse, it's the same disease, and sometimes the disease wins. I wouldn't let it beat me, though. Not yet.

Not long before my own clap out, I learned I wouldn't be going directly home. Aftercare had been arranged for me at Pathways, a halfway house in Miami. The apartments there were fully furnished two-bedrooms, two girls to a room: a little cramped but a step up from rehab.

I arrived very late at night, so I moved my luggage inside but didn't bother unpacking. I was pretty beat and didn't want to make any noise, so I went outside to the small balcony off the living room for the only surefire means of clearing my head: a cigarette. I sat there silently, looking around and taking it all in: the palm trees swaying in the breeze, the distant sound of traffic below.

A halfway house is neither a hospital nor a prison. It's exactly what it sounds like, halfway between treatment and your new life, which meant a limited degree of freedom. We were allowed on weekends to go out on the town to see movies, shop, grab a meal at an actual restaurant. These outings had to be chaperoned by fellow residents further along in their program than we were, but it was a loose leash and it never got in the way. In fact, it opened a few doors.

I was notorious in my resistance and skepticism toward certain parts of the program. My inability to take meditation group seriously was not a secret. A decent number of my chaperones, on the other hand, took it quite seriously and saw our weekend outings as an opportunity to come at me from a different angle.

On one excursion, I was led by friends to a small shop, one of dozens in Miami back in the early 90s. The chimes above the door sighed music as it opened, and I was hit by a wave of sage and sandalwood the moment we stepped inside. The airy song of Indigenous flutes on the stereo system welcomed us, and the soft trickle of water came from a small, portable fountain sitting on the counter. The shelves were stacked with books, crystals, candles of every shape and color, and several types of incense and their accessories. I felt like I'd stepped through the looking glass.

I walked around that store for hours, examining tiger's-eye stones and sniffing small vials of essential oils, and while I wasn't eager to admit it to anyone, least of all myself, I felt something inside, a calm I couldn't explain, because I had no frame of reference for it.

Spirituality of any kind had never factored into my life. My dad, a lapsed Catholic, hadn't set foot inside a church aside from weddings or funerals since his own confirmation, and my mom came from twice-a-year cultural Jews, a second-generation atheist. I don't know the Catechism and can't speak a lick of Hebrew. The closest thing to religion I was raised with were the complete discographies of Peter, Paul and Mary and The Beatles. As card-carrying liberals, my parents impressed upon us that while other people's religions were to be respected, the idea of anything beyond your five senses was something for other people, not us. They had never considered spirituality of any kind for themselves, much less passed it on to their children. So, I arrived in Miami, having never believed in God or *gods*, spirits, or energy. The only things I believed in were pain and the need to escape it. I was finally ready for so much more.

That first day in the New Age shop, I bought myself a box of incense, some crystals and stones (carefully selected after learning what each represented), a candle, a tiny bottle of patchouli, and a cassette of some of that airy flute music—and I was feeling myself. I left there feeling connected to something. I had no idea *what* just yet, but I felt like I'd walked through some kind of doorway and couldn't go back. There was this whole other layer that had been laid over the same world I'd always known, one I couldn't see but could feel.

When I returned home, I went straight to my room and set up shop. I put the candle by my bed, arranged my crystals and stones, lit the incense, and put my music on. And for the first time I could remember, without the aid of drugs, booze, or even a cigarette, I just chilled.

I returned to that shop and others like it many times. One weekend, my friends took me for a psychic reading. I didn't even understand what a psychic was. I was just going along with it for kicks. The woman who read my fortune was kind and crunchy, and maybe she truly had the gift and maybe she didn't. Honestly, considering the catch-all platitudes common to such readings, the jury's still out on her authenticity, but that's not really the point. Because of what she told me, I suddenly believed there were other possibilities for me, a number of futures I could choose from once I knew what I wanted. And what I wanted counted for something. I finally felt some sense of my own potential and something more to my soul than a background hum of torment and self-loathing.

For most of my life up to that point, suffering had just been the status quo. Even when I'd been free of abuse for years, the malignancy it left behind lingered. But now suddenly…what if that wasn't all there was? What of the spirit and its workings? The simple concept that there were reasons, paths, and guides was nothing but comforting to someone who had felt so alone, so adrift in her darkness. How could I not be intrigued? How could I not wonder?

I started reading up on different faiths and spiritual practices, considering that maybe there was a universe full of mystery and wonder, perhaps even design and harmony. Maybe there was more to this crazy life than self-destruction. I wasn't sure what exactly, but this spiritual journey I'd embarked upon was already opening me up to all kinds of ideas.

Reincarnation struck a particularly strong chord with me. I read *Many Lives, Many Masters* several times, compelled by the idea that I could have lived other lives and might yet live more; that maybe we never truly die, we just get another chance to do better on the next go-around. Suddenly, the world that had always seemed so inherently dangerous and terrifying was so much more—or at least could be. It was almost too big a responsibility, but I couldn't turn back now. I couldn't pretend I had no say in my fate. All I had to do was choose my path, my future, and do my best to make it happen. I was, at the very least, willing to try.

CHAPTER 13

The Best Laid Plans

When you graduated to Phase Two at Pathways, you moved into an actual apartment away from where the Phase One residents lived. You got a job and could have your own car if you owned one. As soon as I could manage it, I arranged for my trusty Volkswagen to be transported down to Miami, and oh how I'd missed her and the freedom she provided.

Over six months after I'd arrived in Miami, I was still sober, several *New York Times* bestsellers into my spiritual education, and the best salesperson by a long shot that the Bayside Marketplace Foot Locker had ever seen. No one could figure why. I had never been the sales type, but I've always been a people person, and while I'd never counted on it taking me very far in a sales job, the size of my paycheck from all those commissions told a different story. I had sobriety, autonomy, and success at a steady, *honest* job. As fledgling adults go, I was doing okay. As recovering addicts go, I was a rock star. But it wasn't enough.

I had no intention of putting down roots in Miami. It had been a nice time, but I never for a second considered it might become my forever home. I didn't know what was next, but I had the feeling it was time to reconsider the world of higher education, so I started researching colleges. I looked at schools all over the country, mostly on the coasts, but none of the settings or programs really seemed to fit. I applied to a few places that looked good, but none really inspired me. Then, late one night not too long before I was set to leave Miami, my phone rang.

"Hello?"

"Hey, Mammano. What's up, girl?" The raspy voice on the other end of the line chuckled, and memories of the great nitrous oxide caper came flooding back.

"Deb? How the fuck are you?! What are you doing? How did you get this number?"

Deb laughed and took a slurp of something. "I had to call your mom. I'm doing good. I'm—oh, shit. Totally forgot the time difference."

"Time difference? Where are you?"

She was five time zones away, in Oahu. She had apparently cleaned herself up enough to transfer to the University of Hawaii, where she was studying nutrition. This led to a lengthy conversation about my newfound devotion to health food and my spiritual awakening.

"You want spiritual? Shit, girl, I roll out of bed, see a sunrise on the ocean. Bitch, it is beyond. The people are chill, there's ukulele music *everywhere*, and the dress code? It's all shorts and flip-flops. You'd love it. Trust me. I know. Like, *I know.*"

She was silent for a moment, then took another slurp of whatever she was drinking and cleared her throat.

"Okay, this is going to sound weird, but hear me out. I had this dream the other night, right? You were here with me in Hawaii, and we were chilling like old times except way better. You should come here. You're *supposed* to come here."

I had absolutely no reason to believe her, to take stock in some random dream, but I did. I'd spent enough time around palm trees in the past year to know a tropical breeze worked for me, but Miami wasn't it. Hawaii sounded like just the right vibe.

Deb and I talked into the night. She told me all about Kalakaua Avenue and its crazy nightlife, bonfires on the beach, and a campus where I could get my degree in whatever I wanted. With her nutrition degree and the same natural business savvy that had gotten me in trouble at Bennigan's, we could open a health food store, all fresh and organic. I couldn't argue that it sounded kind of great. Perfect, actually.

I tied up my loose ends, put in my two weeks' notice at Foot Locker, and made some plans. A road trip seemed the simplest and most fun means of moving back home while I waited for a response from the University of

Hawaii. I knew it would be infinitely better with someone riding shotgun, so I made a phone call, and a few days later, I stood in the terminal at Miami International Airport to greet an old friend as he stepped off the jetway. His curly hair had been tamed with a little time and experience, his mischievous smile just a touch more suave than it had been that first night I'd passed out on his shoulder, but he was still Mark, and this road trip was going to rule.

It was already early evening when Mark arrived, so I drove us straight to the Bayside Marketplace, a shopping center on the water that was scenic and pleasant during the day but a surprisingly hip center of local nightlife after dark. We grabbed a quick meal, then headed for Fat Tuesday, where a wall of slushie mixers churned frozen alcohol in every color of the rainbow. Yes, I had just graduated from a halfway house, but alcohol had never been my poison, and I wasn't concerned. Hard drugs were out. I was done with them, but drinks with my best friend from back in the day at a place that offered infinite combinations of flavors and quality booze? Hell yes. Besides, this was a road trip with Mark. A few drinks and a little weed were simply going to happen, and I was sure I could handle it.

Mark and I sat with our brightly colored frozen drinks, looking out over the bay with a soft, clean breeze rolling in, so close to the boats docked in the marina that I could literally almost touch them. We caught up and reminisced, laughing like we were sixteen again and so happy to see one another it hurt a little bit. But that bittersweet twinge passed, and we each lit a cigarette and proceeded to get mildly drunk.

I woke up, blissfully free of a hangover and proud of myself for it, walked out to the couch to smack Mark's foot, and started getting ready. I'd already packed my car the day before, so a shower and a quick breakfast later, we were on the road. It wasn't long before Mark produced a huge bag of pot he'd flown down with. In a pre-9/11 world, it was mind-bogglingly easy to smuggle drugs past airport security. Just hide it in your shoe and act cool, and you've got yourself all the pot you're going to need for a road trip from Miami to New York.

Mark was gracious enough to take the first shift driving while I rolled my first joint in over a year. Then, much to my surprise, I paused to consider whether it was really a good idea.

It's just a joint, I told myself. *This is totally normal college kid stuff. I had some drinks last night. Didn't black out, didn't even wake up sick. I'm fine. I'm good.* And I was, or at least seemed to be, so I lifted that joint to my lips, lit it, and hit it.

By the time we were crossing through Georgia, the screws were starting to come a little loose. I was behind the wheel, flooring it and giving not a single fuck, with rolled joints on the dash. And Mark, my best friend and brother in mischief, was not loving it.

"Nik, slow down!" Mark chuckled, but I could hear the nerves behind it. "It's like *The Dukes of Hazzard* down here and we *will* go to jail if we get pulled over." He said it with love, smiling the whole time, but his meaning was perfectly clear. *Nikki, I'm happy to smoke up and have fun and shit, but you are always pushing it.*

He was right. He wasn't judging me, but he had my number. It was so easy for me to careen right off the deep end, and I never even knew it until I was in freefall. Only a few days out of Miami and I was already back on that slippery slope. I knew then and there I had to check myself, and I was grateful Mark was there to remind me.

The next stop on our epic road trip was South of the Border, a popular tourist attraction at the border of the Carolinas. We rolled up just in time for a much-needed bathroom break before killing the munchies with some gloriously greasy burritos. We hung around for a while afterward while our lunch digested, then made one last loop through the souvenirs, bought some fireworks, and took a few pictures to capture the moment before heading back out.

We were just a little over nine hours from home, and though Mark offered to trade off, he ended up falling asleep in the passenger seat on the way. He'd done most of the driving while I'd been busy getting stoned, so I figured he deserved the nap. I let him sleep until we hit the Garden State Parkway.

"Hey. Wake the fuck up," I said, jostling him. He sat up straight and looked around groggily as dawn broke to our right.

"Holy shit, Nik. You drove the rest of the way?"

"Just about. Another forty-five minutes, give or take, and we'll be back in New City. God help us." We laughed and pulled over at the next gas station for some caffeine.

Summer was on the way out when I arrived home in New City. It didn't take much to get the old Bennigan's crew together again, and I spent the remainder of the summer of '93 hanging out with my people while I planned the next chapter of my life.

Seeing my old friends wasn't just like old times—it was better, because the last time I'd seen them I was such a hot fucking mess they hadn't known what to do with me. But this Nikki…post-rehab Nikki? I was drinking moderately and smoking just enough weed to achieve a mellow high. I was careful not to let myself get too baked. I wanted to be present enough to actually enjoy the moment and the people I was with, and I managed to do just that.

I love the fall—the colors, the crispness, the perfume of rain and dead leaves. It's my absolute favorite time of year, and I didn't even have to bother with school until January, so I could enjoy it at as leisurely a pace as I wanted. I had plenty of time to contemplate how far I'd come and where I was headed. Long drives alone up and down the Palisades Parkway, hypnotized by the autumn foliage, became a staple of my routine. I'd leave the windows down, the wind sliding over my skin as I blasted the classics like "American Pie" and "Bohemian Rhapsody" and newer favorite "Closer to Fine."

The leaves were already turning when my packet from the University of Hawaii finally arrived. With my checkered academic history, I wasn't sure I'd get in, but there it was, a thick envelope with several forms and a course catalog inside. I sat down on the front stoop, flipping through the catalog and enjoying a cigarette under a nice, overcast sky when the phone rang. I took one last drag, stamped out my butt, and headed inside.

"Is this the parent or guardian of Michael Mammano?"

"I'm his sister. Is he okay?"

"He's not feeling well and needs to go home, but he would have to be signed out by an adult, so…"

"It's cool. I'm twenty. I'll come get him."

I'd only seen the local junior high once or twice, having moved to New City just before high school, and I didn't know my way around. The woman at the front desk was kind enough to point me in the direction of the nurse's office. Halfway there, a balding man approached me with a paper cup of something hot.

"Excuse me," he said in a stern voice that wasn't making a request. "Where's your hall pass?"It took a second to sink in. I'd always been short and looked a little young for my age, so his mistake wasn't at all odd, but I laughed out loud all the same and kept on going. "Where do you think you're going, young lady?"

"Dude, I am *in college,*" I said proudly, then I jangled my car keys at him and went the rest of the way to the nurse's office.

I'd spent the entire fall just partying with my favorite people. Being home was better than I could have guessed. I was actually happy to be there, and everyone was happy to have me.

My flight was set for a few days before Christmas, so I could settle into Deb's beachside apartment and spend a few weeks getting the lay of the land before classes started. It was an early-morning flight, so the whole crew agreed to stay up with me and see me off.

We partied all night long, stretching a few hours into a last hurrah that made us feel immortal. We drank and danced, then hit the diner for some pie and disco fries to sober up. I felt loved and alive and ready to take on whatever came next. After some food and a little time to sober up, we headed to Newark International Airport, where we passed the time until my 5 a.m. flight hanging out in the parking lot, giggling as we hotboxed the car with pot smoke. When the time came, everyone came inside with me to see me off.

We sat on the floor by the gate for at least an hour, some of us even lying down, just talking and laughing, taking up space without apology, wondering just what was next for all of us. I leaned against Mark, my head on his shoulder in a bizarre recreation of that first hangout immortalized in a tacked-up Polaroid four years and a lifetime ago. Some small part of me wanted to just linger in that still, peaceful moment forever, and that moment seemed to dilate until we were just floating in it. Suddenly, we looked up to find that a handful of other people had settled by the gate, and soon after, the announcement to board came.

We all hugged and said our goodbyes. Paul was the last. We hugged, and he patted my back. In lieu of a long, sentimental goodbye, he simply offered a quiet "See ya." Then I grabbed my bag and boarded the plane.

I reached my seat and spaced out as I gazed out the window into the predawn darkness, grateful for one last hangout sesh with my friends as I flew off to Hawaii. And, well…we all know how that turned out.

Part Three

Paradise Lost

CHAPTER 14

Lockdown

I was arrested on a Thursday—January 26, 1995. Within a week, I'd been shuttled to OCCC. My cell was small and dark, barely enough room for a bunk bed, a toilet, and a sink. My only window was blacked out, so after lights out, I couldn't see a thing.

On my second night, I jerked awake at the sound of the door and flinched at the blinding light from outside. Two pairs of hands grabbed me, pulling me from my top bunk and dragging me out of my cell—guards. I asked them what was happening, but they didn't answer. They just marched me along so fast my feet barely touched the stairs down to the first level, where they shoved me into a room and locked the door behind me.

Once the shock subsided, I sat at the metal table and waited for… fuck, I had no idea. I had more than a passing suspicion I was about to be raped or worse. Given my surroundings, assuming the worst seemed to make sense. Time, or at least your perception of it, expands considerably in prison. I was probably only in there a few minutes, but it felt like hours, and just as I was about to start climbing the walls, the door opened and a guard came in, holding two huge paper bags. It wasn't one of the guards who had dragged me in there. I knew him.

"Oscar!" I whispered, afraid it was all a dream, like saying his name too loudly might make him evaporate. Despite all the business I did with OCCC, it had never occurred to me I might run into a client, but there he was. Oscar gave me an uneasy smile and took a seat, setting the bags down on the table.

"I was processing some new-arrival paperwork, and your mugshot came up."

"Yeah? Good picture?" My poorly timed attempt at humor completely failed to lighten the mood. Oscar just shook his head, confused. He knew me as this savvy, cutthroat dealer who could take care of herself. Getting caught didn't exactly fit that image.

"Holy shit, Nikki. What the fuck happened?"

I brought him up to speed, telling him all about how I'd been profiled by the feds, set up by a friend who'd sold me out. He asked if I was all right, if anyone had hurt me yet. The "yet" was not comforting, but I kept the conversation moving. I realized very quickly that in prison, protection was key. I was a little slower on the uptake with what Oscar was offering. Fortunately, as he was leaving he spelled it out for me.

"That's all yours," he said, nodding to the bags on the table. I peeked inside quickly to find smokes, toiletries, food, candy, and more. He must have cleaned out half the commissary. "There can be more of that, and an eye or two on your back…if you don't talk."

It's hard to believe that up until that moment I hadn't considered the power I possessed. There were probably a dozen guards walking the premises at that very moment with meth in their pockets that they'd bought from Oscar, who had bought it from me. A few words in the right ears, a few answers to questions no one had even thought to ask, and I could take the whole prison down, earning myself some leniency, likely even walking free. Someone as far along in the process as I was, already booked, transferred, and awaiting trial, rarely had that kind of get-out-of-jail-free card in their pocket, and I can't believe I didn't use it. I mean, Oscar was a nice guy and all, but I felt no loyalty toward him, not enough to rot in jail to cover his ass.

But he was a known quantity, and even if exposing him and the other guards would get me a deal, there was no telling how long that process might take or what might befall me in the interim. An assurance of some limited security and a few creature comforts carried a lot more weight at that moment than a chance at freedom. There are times you ante up and bet everything, and maybe this was one of them, but I wasn't about to chance it. The house almost always wins.

A normal person would call their parents at that point, but normal was something I'd given up on a long time ago. I didn't look to my parents for the promise of comfort or salvation, just another reminder that I'd screwed up yet again and had made things harder on everyone else. It was always about everyone else. I always seemed to come last in the discussion, and what I didn't need at my lowest point was an itemized rehash of what had gotten me there and what a selfish, crazy disappointment it made me. So, no, I didn't call home. I didn't call anyone.

I didn't get to see the other modules at OCCC, but it's safe to assume they looked and functioned more or less the same as mine: two floors of cells arranged in a square around the guards' station, tables on the first floor where our meals were brought to us by male inmates.

Unlike us, the men were allowed to have jobs outside their modules, which required them to move around the complex a bit. Sure, it was for work, but it was still more fresh air than I got.

The women were allowed out a few times a day for a smoke break, when we could chat and feel at least a little normal. Once or twice a week we got an hour out in the yard, where I could look past the cinder block tower and barbed wire fence to a lush, green mountain that was so close yet so far. If one of us was really lucky, we'd get called to medical, giving us a change of scenery for ten, maybe twenty minutes, but otherwise one day was the same as the next.

Up at 5 a.m. for a head count, standing outside our cells as the guards checked us off their list, one by one. Then we had to clean our cells. Toilets, floor, and beds had to be perfect, and without much else to do, it was easy to be meticulous. After that, breakfast.

I ate so much bread in that place—not toast…bread. At every meal. A hardboiled egg…four slices of bread. A lunch meat surprise…four slices of bread. Meatloaf for dinner…four slices of bread. You wouldn't think someone would gain weight in prison, but seriously—just count those carbs.

The rest of the day was mostly spent walking around the module. TV, when we could watch it, was a great distraction. I was wandering through that area on one of my first nights when one of the women called me over.

"Hey! Hey, was that you?" I just looked up at the TV to see some boring news story that had nothing to do with me. The inmate turned to one of the others. "Was that her?"

"Yeah, that was her. You missed it, hon."

The arrest of one of Oahu's premier meth dealers—yours truly—had made the evening news, giving the girls in my module something to buzz about. They waved me over to have a seat, asking me all kinds of questions. It was a bizarre, twisted, and fleeting moment of celebrity, but we all seemed to enjoy it, and after that icebreaker I kind of had…friends?

We didn't braid each other's hair or anything, but we sat together at meals and played cards and would join any and all meetings we could. It didn't matter if we didn't fit the bill for attendance; many a non-addict showed up for Narcotics Anonymous, and people without a drop of faith would show up for Bible study. *Any* group would be packed just so we could have a break from all the nothing we had to do. Many of us never knew how long our daily nothing would last…how long *any* of it would last. Someone could linger there for weeks, months, years, for all we knew. But then some guard's voice could call one of us for "bag and baggage" over the loudspeaker, and after picking up what few possessions you arrived with, you carried it out in a plastic bag, and that was the last anyone heard of you.

You really come to appreciate certain things in prison—everyday things you otherwise take for granted like, say, showering. There were only a handful of shower stalls, wedged in amidst a row of cell doors, and you needed to book time in one.

On my second or third day, I went down to the guards' station, signed up for a turn in one of the shower stalls, and signed out a razor, a privilege violent offenders weren't afforded. I was mildly concerned about having only a thin plastic curtain between me and the guards (and everyone else, for that matter), but I was a floor up, and they barely seemed to be paying attention, far more interested in their magazines and conversation.

I was lathering my hair with some of the shampoo Oscar had included in my goodie bag, when I heard a scrape of metal on metal and felt a rush of cold air. When I turned around I was standing face to face with a naked woman I'd never met before in my life. Before I could think, she grabbed the razor I'd signed out and held it up.

"Make a sound, and I'll cut you," she breathed. This woman stared at me with an intense, almost angry frown, then ran her hand over my head to scoop up some lather. She raised her arm, smeared the lather onto her armpit, and started shaving. She sighed, and this weird look of serenity passed over her face as she groomed herself right there in front of me. All I could do was stand there, careful to keep my head out of the shower stream. Standing naked in a slippery shower stall was not the time or place I wanted to anger someone holding a razor.

When she was done clearing her armpit, she looked up at me with those intense eyes, and I leaned my head forward. She accepted my offering without a word, as though it were just matter of fact, and lathered up her other armpit. I stood there awkwardly until she scoffed at me.

"You can rinse your fucking hair," she said.

"You're not going to…do your legs?"

"Don't be stupid," she sneered with her arm over her head, never taking her eyes from mine as she shaved her armpit smooth. "Ain't no room in here for that."

I just nodded and leaned my head back into the water, rinsing my hair, and when I stood erect again, she held the razor out to me. Not knowing what to expect, I plucked it from her fingers, and her sour grimace twisted up into a smile. "Thanks," she said before peering outside the shower stall, waiting for her moment, then hopping out.

I stood there, the shower stream drumming against my back and the floor of the stall, staring at the spot where she had been just a moment before. A single-occupant shower stall had never seemed so spacious. "What the fuuuuuuuck?" I whispered…and then rinsed the razor to use it myself.

"Right in there *with you?*" Roxy asked me over the phone the next day. It was the first time I'd talked to anyone on the outside since I'd gotten to OCCC. Luckily, Roxy was never far from her phone. I leaned against the desk at the guards' station, the only phone we had access to, and conditional access at that. I knew I had to be careful not to say anything incriminating, even if the guards were only half-assing it and barely listening anyway.

"She just hopped right in like it was nothing. And apparently, this is totally a thing. Old-timers do it to fresh blood all the time, and they're not always looking for a razor."

"Ooh…baby…that is not the kind of female bonding I think you're looking for."

"Not from them. I'll be taking the shortest fucking showers in history from now on. I can tell you that." It was nice to actually laugh. It was the first time I had in weeks. "How's Bella? Is she okay?"

Roxy paused for a long time, then sighed and said, "She's…not great. She lost her job. And she lost you. And…it's rough. But I'll keep an eye on her as much as I can."

"Thanks, Ma."

Talking to Roxy had made my day. I hadn't expected any contact with the outside world once I was at OCCC, not any phone calls and definitely not any visitors, so you can imagine how jarring it was to me when later that week I heard my name called out from the guards' station.

"Mammano, you got a visitor!"

I bolted up out of a very comfortable slouch, slightly suspicious that I was being jerked around. I never got visitors. Anyone on the island who might think to come see me would know better than to come within a hundred feet of OCCC. But the excitement of getting out of the module for even a few minutes got the better of me.

I walked into the visiting room to find a short-haired woman in a tailored pantsuit, an Islander from the look of her, sitting at the table. She jumped up, revealing she was rather short, though she made the most of her stature. It could have been the soft butch power suit, but I think it was just how she carried herself.

"Nikki? Reinette Cooper, your lawyer."

I shook her hand, deeply confused. "I have a lawyer?"

Apparently, I did. Keilani, well aware that I was going down for her and still hadn't given her up, had reasoned the least she could do was help get me out of prison. But her growing agoraphobia was stronger and more justified than ever, and out of self-preservation, she wasn't going to touch anything near me with a ten-foot pole. Instead, she gave the money to Bella, who took it straight to Reinette, who now stood before me, gesturing to the chair with a cordial smile.

"I think our best strategy right now is to see if we can get the charges dropped on a technicality."

"We can do that?"

"We can try." She looked me dead in the eye. "I'm going to get you out of here, Nikki, but we've got our work cut out for us. I'm not going to sugarcoat it. You are in some seriously deep shit, and the case against you is strong. You're looking at thirty years, easy, so if you don't want to piss away the prime of your life, you need to pull it together and help me help you."

"Yeah. Yeah, no fucking problem." I was in. Whatever it took, I was in.

My brief moment on the local news had turned into a reliable conversation starter among the inmates, but I already knew my story. I was way more interested in learning about everyone else, and poker games were usually the best time to do it.

Liberty House Lucy was named for the chain of bougie department stores that, at the height of its prosperity, had about fifty locations throughout Hawaii and Guam. Lucy was a shoplifting genius, truly gifted in the sleight of hand of stealing shit. She was always talking about getting "back to business" as soon as she got out and promised to score me some of the highest-quality merchandise once we were free women (in exchange for some quality meth, of course).

The skittish, giggling girl to my left rolled her eyes and called bullshit on Lucy. I don't remember her actual name. We all just called her Cooch. Why, you might wonder?

"So, we're trying to get away, right? And the cops, they're already on us, so I'm just trying to fly out of there, but I've got all the goods, right?" And then she explained in graphic detail how in her haste, she had stuffed a whole load of diamonds and other jewelry up inside her vagina. Not quickly enough, apparently, because the cops had caught her anyway. "So, they bring me down to the station. I'm booked, strip-searched, everything!" Her voice kept getting louder and louder as she stood up, gesticulating wildly. She got up on her chair to provide us all with a visual aid. "They look here, they look there, it's getting real personal, know what I mean? But they couldn't find it. And I'm almost free and clear and out of there, when they tell me to cough. And then…pop!" She thrust her hand away from her crotch, miming the explosion of rings and loose jewels. "It all fell right out my cooch!"

We were all dying, heaving with laughter. I'd barely remembered to turn my fan of cards face down. Didn't want to lose that round on account of a giggle fit.

"You nasty, girl," squawked a rawboned old lady as she cruised by on her scooter, shaking her head. Edie was an old-timer. Most people get transferred somewhere else long before they clock the time there she had, but she'd been around so long no one knew when she'd gotten there or what she'd done to earn it, only that she could no longer walk and needed that scooter to get around. But we all figured if she was still around and getting by at her age, it might be wise to leave her alone. You find a lot of people in the pen you're better off leaving alone. My cellmate was one of them.

Rhonda was cranky and paranoid, but fairly quiet about it. And listen, if I were stuck limping around prison on a prosthetic leg, I'd probably not be in the best mood most days either. She wasn't aggressive, at least not until backed into a corner, which was exactly what happened when I started to notice my shit was going missing. I'm not really the type to go around pointing fingers, but the list of suspects was pretty short, so one day I finally asked her.

"Fuck you!" she snarled, hobbling toward the door. It wasn't hard for me to jump ahead of her and block the way. "Move, bitch! I don't have your shit!"

"Where's it going, then?"

"How the fuck should I know? Ask the guards, maybe?" She had a point. They would have access to our cells and could easily raid them any time with impunity, but my gut said no. I had Oscar's protection, and while it was only good for so much, my commissary had never gone missing before I'd started bunking with Rhonda. "You want to check my stuff? It's right over there. Go ahead." But I didn't. I could see from where I stood what was there, so I just let her by.

My stuff kept going missing. Smokes, chocolate, noodles, toiletries… they were all slowly but steadily disappearing, and I didn't know where to until one day when a guard busted Rhonda in the act. And wouldn't you know it, he unfastened her prosthetic leg, tilted it over, and out spilled about as much as someone could fit inside, all of it mine.

They couldn't arrest her. What she'd done hadn't, strictly speaking, been a crime or even a violent infraction, so she got a slap on the wrist, and that was that. It didn't foster goodwill between us, though. Not long after that, we got into a fight, and it was the last I saw of that cell.

From time to time, if a situation got out of hand and needed to be controlled, there'd be a lockdown. It could be hours you were confined to your tiny little cell with your cellmate, or it could be weeks; there was no way to know.

The guards, with the aid of the medical unit, were not shy about medicating the inmates for any reason they could come up with, and make no mistake: There were times when they just made shit up. My fight with Rhonda had just been the excuse they had been waiting for. The moment one of us was even the slightest inconvenience, we were put on something. In my case, some meds that my body really didn't like.

So, there I was, on lockdown with someone who was clearly not on the right medication, because she would just talk to herself all the time—seriously, *all* the time—and then she'd turn toward me and start jabbering on about some shit I couldn't even understand, much less remember now. And all of this was going on while my body was taking a bad turn.

Holy fuck, I remember thinking. *I have to get the fuck out of here.* But I was stuck in there without any relief from my cellmate's insane babbling or the medication I should never have been on in the first place. I continued to feel sicker and sicker until I started to shake. I pushed past my new cellmate, who was ranting as she paced the narrow strip of floor, and banged on the door with what little strength I had. The spasms in my muscles would cease for a long moment, then return, rapid-fire. Then finally, they started constricting to the point where I couldn't extend my arms or legs, and I crumpled to the floor. Lucky for me, a guard heard my banging and decided to respond. They rushed me to medical immediately.

Once I was stable, I begged them to take me off the meds, and to my surprise, they did. Being free of that crap didn't make things easy. I still had work to do around the module. One day, I was cleaning the guards' bathroom, a fairly routine chore I was often assigned, when I reached the sink and froze where I stood. Right there on the porcelain, forgotten by one of the guards, was a meth pipe. The bulb had been burned black, and the puddle of meth along its bottom had already hardened, so there was no telling how long it had been there or who might come looking for it. All I knew was that the nearly used-up product had almost certainly been mine, supplied by Oscar from the last stash I'd sold him.

That remaining residue wasn't much, but it would have been enough to send me far, far away, if only for a little while. It was a vacation I could have used, one my body was begging for—my mind too. I was surviving at OCCC, but surviving isn't enough, and with the results of Reinette's efforts still up in the air, I was just as on edge as when I'd first gone into detox. And now, here in front of me, lay an opportunity to escape it all for a little while—on my own product, no less. How poetic was that? If only I'd had a lighter.

I had half a mind to throw the meth pipe out. That tiny bit of spite might have felt good for a few hours, but it would have only pissed the owner off, which meant he'd take it out on us. It wasn't worth it, so I left it there and finished cleaning up.

Reinette had really sold me on this "technicality" strategy, and busted her ass trying to make it work, so when it didn't I started to get really scared. The plan had seemed so airtight, so very doable, that if it was a bust, what hope did I have left? Reinette didn't give up, though. She just circled back around to square one and commenced with Plan B.

Having come so close to getting out, prison started to feel even smaller, even more suffocating, until after a month of practically climbing the walls, I broke down and played a card I'd been avoiding at all costs. After more than a year of radio silence, I called my parents.

Asking my mom and Gene for help was the last thing I wanted to do for a lot of reasons, not the least of which would be the inevitable catch. It was not an easy conversation. I sidestepped more questions than I answered, and I still gave away too much, enough that could and probably *would* be used against me down the road.

"Again, Nikki?" My mom's voice sounded so weary.

"Look, if you're not going to help…"

"Of course I'm going to help you, Nikki, but…" She paused, and I held my breath. "How many times can we go through this?" But what she meant was, *How many times are you going to disappoint me? How many times are you going to ruin the Hallmark card?* Tempted though I was to call her out or simply hang up, I was in prison, so I swallowed my pride, weathered the guilt trip and the scolding, and once she'd gotten it out of her system, she called my grandparents to ask them to post my bail.

"But you're getting out?" Roxy said to me over the guard station phone.

I played with the cord, leaning against the desk. "Sometime in the next few days. I just don't know when."

"Honey, you made it this long. You're going to be all right, just remember you're getting out, don't forget to breathe, and when that time comes, you call me. I'll come get you."

I discreetly wiped my eyes, thanked Roxy, and hung up. She was right. I'd lasted this long. I just had to hold out a little longer.

I was in my cell, sitting on my bunk and brooding over how the minutes seemed to keep stretching into days, when I was called for bag and baggage. I jumped down and breezed through the door, almost breaking into a jog, not giving a thought to the commissary I was leaving behind. Fuck it. Who cared? Within a couple of hours, my discharge was processed, and on my way out the door, I was handed the personal effects I'd arrived with.

My clothes barely fit. All that bread and little yard time had packed on a few pounds, but it was fine. I could find something new to fit me.

I walked out the front door of OCCC and into the sun, throwing my head back, and taking a deep breath of free air. Jeremiah's car sat on the curb. I'd never been happier to see such a dinged-up, rusty piece of crap. Jeremiah was at the wheel, Roxy riding shotgun. Bella stepped out of the backseat, and I strode right up and fell into her arms.

CHAPTER 15

No Rest for the Wicked

My stay at Roxy's would only be for a few days, after which she'd pull up stakes as she always did and move on to her next hotel suite, and since she couldn't host me forever, it seemed like a fair enough time for me to go back out on my own. For a few days, though, it would be nice to be back with "Ma" and Bella and even Jeremiah.

Bella wasn't looking great. I could see the toll her worsening meth habit had taken on her. She had that look, weary and hyper-aware at the same time, and while I'd been the one living on prison food for the past two months, she looked even more excited than I was that first night when Jeremiah brought in a pizza for dinner.

After we ate, I took a shower, the first one I'd actually been able to relax in for months. When I came out, Bella was snoozing on the couch, so I sat beside Roxy.

"So, what's your plan from here?" she asked.

"My lawyer told me about this new plea deal that's on the table. Overpopulation in the prisons is kind of a thing now, so they want to keep people out if they can. So, as a first-time offender—on the books, anyway—I could get a reduced sentence if I plead guilty. I'd be a registered felon for life, but it would mean less time."

"How much less?"

"Next to thirty years, does it matter?"

Roxy couldn't say it did.

The truth was that under this new protocol, some people in my position could get away with probation and no time at all, but given the gravity of my case, that didn't seem likely for me. As for my next move, I didn't know. I didn't have much choice but to take things one step at a time. But as for what I'd be doing for money…

I figured that Roxy must have found another supplier while I'd been in prison. She had done right by me as well as she could have, hanging onto my Beretta and the few personal items I'd left with her, but she still had to make a living. She'd moved on to another dealer, as had most of my clients, and with good reason. Rumors always circulated when someone in our world got nabbed and locked up. *Did she talk? Is she going to turn someone in? Is she a narc now?* There's no shaking that reputation once it's stuck to you, and no one of consequence was going to come anywhere near me for a long while, if ever again. I didn't blame Roxy for taking care of business. Life moves fast in the fast lane, and it had moved on without me, probably for good.

A few days later, my mom and dad, divorced for over a decade, flew out together to see me. Reinette said it would be a good idea and helpful for my case. I was sober when they arrived. Sure, I was basically homeless and my days at Roxy's were numbered, but I figured I'd make the most of the amenities while they were available to me, especially if my parents were going to get their first look at me in years. A fresh outfit and combed hair wasn't going to fool them into forgetting why they were there, but it might help convince them I was still me.

They kept the conversation nice and light for the first hour or so, and then came the talk of rehab. I wasn't interested in repeating that experience. For one, it hadn't really worked the first time. And two, I'd just been released from captivity, and while a rehab facility and a prison are very different settings, to someone who doesn't want to be there, one surrender of control over yourself looks pretty much like another. So, I resisted and changed the subject every time it came around.

My mom was relentless. Maybe it was due to my experience with this side of her, maybe I was still raw from my time in prison, but I dug my heels in and refused. She kept on pushing.

After two days of this back-and-forth, my dad decided to fold, which I saw coming. He'd never been one for follow-through, and he wasn't interested in watching me and my mom continue this argument ad nauseam, so he grabbed a flight back to the mainland, leaving us alone to hash my options out. We didn't get anywhere. I got lecture after lecture about taking responsibility for my lapses in judgment from someone who could barely acknowledge her own and the ripple effect they'd had on me.

No headway was made, but I still wanted to see her before she left to give it one last try. I somehow convinced myself this was also the right time to come out to her, so I brought Bella along, the two of us looking as put together as we could manage. When my mom showed up, she eyed Bella warily, trying to figure her out.

"Mom…this is Bella…my girlfriend."

She stared at us both for a moment, then just Bella, then back to me.

"Are you going back to rehab?" she asked.

"I…no," I said. There was nothing another stay in rehab could teach me that I didn't already know. I had the tools. It was just a matter of choosing to use them, and I'd made that choice. I would have been happy to explain that to her, but I don't know how much of a difference it would have made even if she'd given me the chance instead of turning around, getting into her rental car, and driving off.

After that, I stayed clean just long enough to show up to my hearing sober. The judge assigned to my case, Marie Milks, was stone-faced and looked like she hadn't smiled in several years. Yet somehow she had agreed, after looking over my case, that I had a fighting chance, and Reinette's play for a reduced sentence worked out. I pled guilty, and Judge Milks signed off on the deal. My sentence itself was to be determined at a later date, and whether it would consist of probation alone or some jail time was up in the air. It was now mid-April; I had to report back for sentencing in June—and keep my nose clean until then.

I would remain free, at least for a little while, but what could I even do with that freedom? My business had dried up completely. My customers had moved on to other dealers, and even if they hadn't, Keilani wouldn't have supplied me. The Crystal Queen of Waikiki had been deposed and didn't even have a crown left to sell. I had no home, no money, no prospects, just a court date to dread for the next few weeks.

By this point, I had been out on the street for a while. I'd occasionally crash at Roxy's, but she wasn't in the market for a roommate, so I had to make do as best I could. I was basically homeless. I tried to stay clean during that time, but my resolve disintegrated, and the vicious cycle played out over and over.

My wounds, never fully healed, continued to bleed and sting, so I salved them however I could, which led me down roads that only ended in more pain—pain I couldn't ignore, because it wasn't going anywhere. It would always be nipping at my heels. I couldn't hide from it, but I could run.

Trying to stay clean and getting over a raging meth addiction while you're homeless is all but impossible, and I figured what did it matter if I used a little before I went back to prison? I wasn't being monitored, no one was going to know, and I needed to survive until then.

I showed up to Reinette's office when she told me and I was sober on my day in court. I'd like to say Bella was my rock at that time, but meth and street living bring out the worst in people. It brought out the worst in us, and we had a pretty intense fight that led to us breaking up, so I was alone when I stood before Judge Milks for my sentencing.

I got five years, more in principle than practice, because Milks reduced it to one year right there on the spot. And that single year was deferred due to prison overcrowding, so I was to report back in January to serve my year, followed by ten years of probation. I thanked the judge, keeping as cool about it as I could. It was a year in jail, but next to thirty, that was nothing. My recent brush with incarceration hadn't been fun, but I could weather a year of that.

As we left the courthouse, Reinette saw the grin on my face and checked me. "This is good news, Nikki, but you are not of the woods yet. You've got six months before you report back. You cannot be caught anywhere near drugs. You cannot leave the island. You will report to the probation office today and at every appointment for a check-in and drug screening. Fail just one, and the deal's off. Straight to prison, no excuses, no questions asked. You got it?"

I got it. So, I went to the probation office and met with Bill Waxman, the officer assigned to my case. He gave me the time and date of my next appointment, and I walked out of there a temporarily free woman. I called Keilani immediately.

"It's done," I told her. There was silence on the line for a long moment, then she told me to come on over and hung up.

Our reunion was sweet, though the first ten minutes, we just sat in her living room, not knowing what to say to each other. Finally, she broke the ice.

"I shouldn't have sent Tāne to threaten you. I should have known you'd never…" She paused, then nodded, eyes distant. "You came through, Nik. Thank you."

I shrugged. Sure, I never rolled over on Keilani in order to save my own ass, but it wasn't like I was her willing patsy, taking the fall for something I didn't do. It was my mess as much as hers. I'd just been the one who'd gotten caught. Still, it's always nice to be appreciated, and given my circumstances, I couldn't afford to turn away any goodwill I'd banked.

"I could kill for some sushi," I said.

Keilani smiled. "I can make sushi happen."

An hour later, we'd picked up right where we'd left off: A long talk over dinner bled into a night full of junk food, video games, and darts, just like old times. I was invited to stay the night and never asked to leave the next day.

Keilani had taken up a new hobby since I'd last seen her. She was now cooking meth in her own apartment, not enough to supply herself with all the product she needed, but enough that it cut her business costs by a noticeable margin. She would cook, then dry it out in the spare bedroom. I would wake up to find large chunks of glassy meth drying out in trays on the floor, the dresser, and pretty much anywhere there was space to lay it out. Was I supposed to do anything but roll out of bed, fill up a pipe, and smoke it? I couldn't think of an alternative. And I knew I was on borrowed time, that I was fucking up my probation and could very well land myself in jail for a lot longer than a year, but all those very real concerns just faded to white noise with several baking sheets of fresh meth just sitting there in front of me.

I figured a week at Keilani's would be fine. I'd enjoy my little vacation in her second bedroom, and then head back out onto the street, show up for my check-ins with probation, and kill time until January.

I didn't leave in a week. I'd been at Keilani's for twice that time before I realized I'd missed my first check-in, and I convinced myself that it wasn't that big a deal. Even if I'd missed the first appointment, I'd be fine as long as I showed up for the next one. It was better, even. It would give me an opportunity to clean myself up and get myself together.

About a month after I'd shown up on Keilani's doorstep, a month of meth and good food and a soft bed in a luxury apartment, Keilani came into her guest room and sat at the edge of the bed. She was smiling softly, but I could tell that whatever she was about to say wasn't going to make me very happy.

"I'll never forget what you did for me. That's why I let you stay here as long as you have, but you're still too hot. You're still going to have to deal with the fallout. I can't have any connection to that. I'm sorry, Nikki."

I nodded. "Can I stay the night?"

"Yeah," she assured me. "Hang around another day or two. See if you can find somewhere else to stay, but after that…"

No more needed to be said. I got it. Underneath my cool, however, I was shocked. Keilani had always been a survivor, and I knew how she felt about liabilities, but she hadn't given a single hint over the past month of laughing and chilling out that I might count as one. It was so out of left field, but what could I do? I couldn't fight it, couldn't convince her otherwise. This was just how it was.

Two days later, having still not found anywhere to go, Keilani followed through as she always did, and it was time for me to leave. She handed me a thick wad of money and a large bag of meth, and I was on my way. She didn't need to tell me that this was it, that all ties, personal and professional, were being severed here. I could feel it in the way she hugged me and closed the door. She had no intention of ever opening it for me again.

I was still the infamous haọle everyone talked about, but the rumors were far less flattering than they used to be. Had I really made a deal with the cops? Gotten back out on the street to narc on my friends and former customers? Of course not, but that kind of thing had happened often enough that no one had trouble believing it, so everyone kept their distance. The market was closed to me.

I considered going to Roxy, just to have someone to turn to, but there was only so much she could have done, and associating with me had clearly become the kiss of death. I couldn't bring any trouble down on her.

The funny thing about living on the street…it can be a really small world in its own way. People rarely stay put. You're always looking for fresh turf, new people to hit up for money, so the faces are always changing, and since you're one of those faces, you bump into the same people over and over. You're the only ones who notice. The people passing you by do everything they can *not* to notice you.

Finding Bella didn't take long, and when I did, whatever our big fight had been about didn't matter anymore. We were just happy to be together again. The fact that I had a bunch of drugs on me didn't hurt our reconciliation. Don't get me wrong. Bella truly cared about me. She was a comfort and safe place for me to go in many ways, but I was always the one who took care of things. I got us high, I got us fed, I found us places to crash. I was the provider, and we smoked through the supply I provided pretty fucking fast.

We soon fell in with a small cluster of panhandling street kids. I was twenty-one, and an adult in the eyes of the law, but still a kid at my core. Fucked up and jaded, but a kid. We were like a guild of orphans in our way, some bizarre, meth-addled version of *Oliver Twist*.

The general strategy was to cover as much ground as possible, so we'd go our separate ways and meet up again later. Always one to make the most of a good hustle, I took to panhandling rather well, always coming back to the group with a five-dollar bill or ten dollars' worth of singles and loose change. We'd then pool our earnings for a carton of lo mein or some Spam and rice that we could all share. We'd linger in a parking lot or sometimes an alleyway, starving as we passed around our communal carton of food, each taking a single bite and savoring it until the carton made its way back around the circle. It was never enough, but we made it work.

It wasn't a bad crew. Not all of us were addicts. Some were runaways or throwaways, kids who had fallen through the cracks, but we all had enough in common that it was worth our while to stick together. When it all got too much, we found brief little moments where we could rediscover just being kids, chilling on the beach or going to Zippy's for donuts. That was always an event.

There was a whole ritual to Zippy's. We'd walk in, see all the hot, fresh donuts behind the glass, and each pick our favorite. I was partial to the powdered Long John. At times, we barely made it to the parking lot before tearing the bag open and letting the sweet scent of fried dough and sugar burst out as we stuffed our faces.

That was how we survived; we stuck together…most of the time. If one us had "the load"—extra drugs, food, or whatever—we'd usually share, but not always. It was a game of survival, and we were all desperate to win.

CHAPTER 16

Streets and Alleys

I traveled pretty light, nothing in my bag but a flannel for when the sun went down, a toothbrush, my Beretta, and a little lock-pick set. I also carried around a little journal to doodle in or write down things I didn't want to forget, but I rarely had the downtime. Believe it or not, being homeless is a full-time job.

Contrary to everything *Aladdin* might have you believe, living on the street is not an adventure. It gets really old, really fast, and some nights you just want a bed. Waikiki had no shortage of those; there were hotels on practically every corner, but none of them wanted a bunch of dirty street kids loitering in their lobbies, so the main challenge was getting inside.

The simplest scam could accommodate four, maybe five of us at a time, and since the young guy working the front desk set off our gaydar, our boy Keoni would have to be the face for this operation. It was actually a great choice. Keoni positively radiated charm. While he chatted up the concierge, asking which rooms might be available, he eyed the wooden rack of tiny cubbies over his shoulder, the keys to each available room just hanging there. If they weren't claimed by midnight, they wouldn't be. While Keoni distracted the concierge, we snuck past them to the stairs.

After a few minutes, Keoni made some lame excuse for not booking a room after all and slipped away to give us the number of an available room. Once we found it, two of us would go up to the door and pick the lock, which, in the era before electronic keycards, was a simple matter of skill and dexterity. Speed was also a factor, because a surveillance camera wouldn't pick up *how* someone was unlocking a door, but standing in front of it for several minutes would definitely look suspicious.

While Keoni and I picked the lock, the others hung back in the stairwell. Once given the signal, they would filter in one at a time, each minutes apart. It was a tedious process, especially when you were dead tired, but once it was all done, we had ourselves a place to crash for the night.

We all showered and hopped into bed, sleeping in shifts so that we didn't stay long enough for the maids to find us in the morning. That night, I pulled my shift, crawled into bed beside Bella, and slept more soundly than I had in weeks.

"Wake-up call," a scratchy voice boomed. I blinked awake to find hotel security standing over me, the manager over his shoulder. I shook Bella awake, on fire with adrenaline. *Shit! What if they looked in my bag? What if they found the gun?*

Fortunately, they hadn't. Bella and I had their full attention; the others had already left. Maybe to go for a stroll, get high—who fucking knew? All that mattered was that they left us high and dry and in the spotlight. I should consider us lucky that security and the management were satisfied with escorting us out and not calling the police. I don't know what would have happened to me if I'd been turned over to them.

When we ran into Keoni on the street later, I shot many a "what the fuck, man?" in his direction, and after he apologized and agreed he owed us, I let it go. He offered to treat us to a midday high, which was a laugh, considering not one of us had a pot to piss in, but he reminded us of a tried-and-true way to get some cash. The second Keoni saw it, his eyes lit up. Jackpot.

At a table several yards from the sidewalk, a man gazed absently at the ocean as he took a bite of his sandwich. He ate carefully, the way you do when you've got an office job and want to keep your dry-cleaning bill low. He seemed like a nice enough guy. Nice enough guys were the easiest marks.

"His name's Austin." Keoni said, pointing to Mr. White Collar. "He was a few years ahead of me at Moanalua. Liked to surf but wasn't very good. He dated this girl, Lena, for most of high school. She was crazy popular, so if you say you knew her, he'd buy it. I already scammed him a couple months ago, so I'm out."

I nodded. "Austin. Moanalua High. Lousy surfer. Lena. Got it." I strolled up to my mark as he was washing down the last of his sandwich with a beer and put on my game face.

"Austin?" He looked up, already trying to figure out if he knew me. "Nikki. From Moanalua. I'm a friend of Lena's. I saw you wipe out that one time." I smiled as if I hadn't seen my old friend Austin in years. He broke into a nervous smile.

"Oh…hey. How've you been?" The poor bastard was trying so hard to fake it. I improvised about ten minutes of small talk, then went in for the kill with some bullshit about needing a cab but forgetting my wallet at home. By the time I was done, Austin thought spotting me a twenty had been his idea, a nice knight-in-shining-armor moment to help a cute girl from the good old days.

That twenty bought just enough meth for me, Bella, and Keoni to share. We didn't have anywhere to go and lounge around while we got high, so the three of us found an alley deep enough to give us some cover from the street (and any cops that might happen by) and huddled in a circle, passing a pipe around until we were good and tweaked out.

You'd think we'd have at least considered buying some food with that money, but hunger was easy enough to ignore as long as we were tweaking. It got harder once we came down, and harder still if we'd forgotten to eat for several days.

I stood outside the McDonald's, begging the passers-by for just enough to get a burger or one of those molten-core apple pies. I didn't care if I burned my tongue. Bella and I were ravenous. Sadly, no one was feeling generous that day. I couldn't even get enough loose change for a snack, much less a meal, so I swallowed the last of my pride, marched my ass inside, and begged the cashiers for food. They called the manager, of course.

"Look, kid," he said, eyes darting around apologetically. "I can't give you anything, okay? It's against policy."

"You give people free shit all the time if you fuck up their order. How is this different?"

"You're not a paying customer." That made absolutely no sense to me, but he just kept on going. "If you get food poisoning or something, we're liable, and you could sue us."

"Oh, yeah. I'll call my lawyer," I said, gesturing to my street-soiled clothes. The manager sighed, taking my point.

"Okay, listen. I can't *give* you anything, but every night at closing, we have to throw out any unsold food. There's nothing wrong with it. It's just policy. If you happen to be out back by the dumpster…we didn't give it to you."

I didn't put a lot of stock in what he said. I figured he was just trying to get rid of me, and he was. But on the off-chance his offer was legit, I went into the alley around back later that night, my stomach howling, and right on cue, the manager emerged with bags of perfectly good food and tossed them in the dumpster.

I jumped right in, grabbed as many lukewarm Big Macs, fries, and apple pies as I could carry, and brought them back to Bella. That night, we ate like queens on our thrones of cardboard and moldering newspaper. As I lay awake with her head on my shoulder, I looked up. Even in the grime of an alley, I could see the stars.

We went back several times, even hooked our friends up with the info, and the manager let it go as often as he could. If he saw one of us hanging around, he didn't ask any questions, but I suppose he had to maintain some plausible deniability, so we tried not to press our luck and just appreciated the relief whenever we could manage it. It never lasted.

Bella's feet were bothering her. With all the walking we did, our shoes had seen better days. Her black boots were rough and busted, the soles worn clean through in places. They had another few days in them, maybe a week. After that…

The Payless on Kalakaua was the easiest solution, but scamming some shoes out of that place was a two-person job. While Bella tried on different shoes to find the right fit, I circled her perimeter to make sure no one was watching. I was losing patience with how picky she was being. This wasn't a scam we could pull every day, and the longer she took, the more likely we'd get caught. By the fifth box, my nerves were shot. I was ready to grab a random box in Bella's size and shove it in her hands.

"Can I help you?" one of the salesgirls asked as she approached. Fuck!

Bella politely declined while I slipped out of view. We'd walked in separately and needed to maintain that illusion in case I needed to cover her exit. As soon as the salesgirl left, I poked my head back around into the aisle and mouthed to Bella, "Choose. Now!"

She shook a box at me to indicate she'd made her choice, then stuffed her worn-out boots into the box and put it back on the shelf while I went up to the sales counter to cover her exit with a little misdirection.

"Oh! I'm so sorry!" I said, deliberately bumping into the shopgirl, drawing her attention away from the door. After a few more apologies for my clumsiness, she forgave me just to shut me up, and I slipped out.

"I hope you like those shoes," I said, joining Bella at the end of the block. "And they better last, because Payless is going to be off-limits for a good, long while."

Bella's nails dug into my arm, she was holding onto me so hard. Her face was hidden by her lank hair, but when I could see it, it was all twisted up. I held her as she hung her head, tears leaking from the corners of her eyes. It had been a while since we'd gotten high and longer still since we'd eaten, and Bella was teetering on the edge. I didn't know what to do for her. We were exhausted and hungry, and by that point I'd scammed just about everyone in that neighborhood for one thing or another. We were completely out of options. And then, I looked up, looked around, and realized where we were.

I'd known Keoni to frequent this corner when the day's panhandling hadn't pulled in enough. After sundown, cars would start pulling up to the curb, and whatever the drivers were looking for, they could find for a price. I'd never known how Keoni found it within himself to do it, but now I understood.

Since I was little, my body had been up for grabs in one way or another, and yes, my promiscuity as I'd gotten older had been with my consent. And maybe, according to the math, sex work may not have been the hugest leap, but it was still a line in the sand, and there are some lines that, once crossed, there's no going back. There's no unknowing what you're capable of. You'll always know what you did and that, push comes to shove, you can do it again. I didn't know if I could live with that, and I didn't want to know.

Johns were pulling up left and right, drawing the attention of professionals from all along the gender spectrum. The reality of what I was signing up for began to sink in. Was I really going to do this? *Could* I do this? I glanced down at Bella, leaning against a streetlight, and made my choice.

To say I strutted my stuff would be wildly inaccurate. I did not strut my stuff. I merely made my stuff available, but it turns out guys driving around looking for hookers tend not to place too high a premium on enthusiasm, because a car pulled up within seconds. It was a cab like any other, the driver off-duty. He told me to get in, but I couldn't just leave Bella there on the corner. She was practically delirious, tears leaving tracks in the grime on her face, so once I assured the driver it wouldn't cost him extra, I eased her into the backseat, and off we drove.

I left Bella asleep in the cab before heading inside the driver's house. I didn't know what to do or how the guy expected me to act. I just kind of froze as he laid me down on the bed and took my clothes off.

I don't remember much of that first time. I wasn't really present for most of it. I just kind of left my body and went somewhere else. It had been a long time since I'd had to pull out that old parlor trick, but it turned out to work as well as ever.

Afterward, I rented a cheap motel room for the night, where Bella and I could sleep on an actual bed for the first time in a while. While Bella slept, I went out and used the last of the night's pay to buy a rock or two of meth, returning with every intention of smoking some more, but I crashed before I could.

As soon as Bella and I woke up, we got high. After what I'd done for the money, I needed it. As I looked around the motel room, I realized that at that moment, every one of our needs had been met. We were fed, high, and at least somewhat rested, having slept in an actual bed with clean sheets. Much as the thought of ever hitting that street corner again made my flesh crawl, I couldn't argue with results. Prostitution was inarguably a more effective and reliable way for us to survive, and while not pleasant, it was surprisingly easy. Johns weren't looking for romance or an act; all I had to do was tune out and let it happen. Once I realized that, I never looked back.

It got easier after the first time. It's a horrible thing to think, but it's true. It was never something I wanted to do, and I'd have stopped the second I had an easier and more lucrative means of providing for myself and Bella, but there wasn't one. We had bellies to fill, habits to feed, and a powerful desire to sleep under a proper roof. The large cardboard box we found discarded behind some store was better than a bed of newspaper, but not enough. I didn't have drugs to sell, and I didn't have anything approaching the stability to get a legitimate job, but I always had my body, and a commodity like that was always in demand.

Sometimes I worked alone, sometimes with some of the other homeless junkies who'd taken to hooking long before I had. I'd known about Keoni, of course. He'd made no secret of it. In fact, he'd tried to get me in on it several times, insisting we'd make a great team and could pull in some serious money. I'd always resisted before, but now that I'd taken the leap… hey, what was a little monetized group sex between friends, right?

We always made more money in groups. Most of our customers were pretty vanilla, though some stood out. This one guy would hire a bunch of us at a time, always an even number of guys and girls, and insisted upon a very particular dress code. The girls would have some sort of costume like a French maid getup, and the boys' uniform? Tighty-whities. I shit you not.

Our patron never joined in. He never spoke a word to us, dirty or otherwise. He just sat in the corner, touching himself and getting off to the sight of college-age kids going at it, taking one of the best, wildest things about being young and turning it into something ugly and humiliating. The best we could do was pretend it didn't happen and use the money to fucking *party.*

“How much have we got?” one of the others asked me as I fanned out the bills, counting them. Our voyeur extraordinaire had already left, and it was just the six of us, some sitting there barely dressed.

“Enough for some meth,” I said. “And some pizzas.” The food had been an afterthought, but a welcome one. And it worked out. Within the hour, we were chowing down and cracking jokes like we hadn’t just engaged in a paid orgy. It was the only way to deal. We couldn’t dwell too long on what we were doing. It would only have torn us up inside.

When you’re a sex worker, at least at the street level, you develop a sixth sense pretty quickly. It’s just basic self-defense. You vibe on someone, then weigh the risk against the money. And it usually works if you’re paying attention, but every once in a while some sicko slips past the radar, and you end up in over your head, just hoping like hell you’ll make it out unhurt or, at the very least, alive.

This one tweaker…he was intense, on edge. He smelled like amphetamines and sour sweat, the smell of someone who had been too high to remember to shower for at least a few days. And whatever. I wasn’t in this for a good time. But then he got rough. Usually when that happens, you can guide the guy with an “easy” or “careful,” and they kind of listen to you. This guy didn’t respond until I spoke up a second time, then he slapped me, threw me on the floor, and kicked me in the side.

“Shut the fuck up!” he bellowed as I cried out. Then he kicked me again, and I screamed again, because it fucking hurt. “*Shut the fuck up!*” he howled, and I would have, but every time his foot smashed into my ribs or guts or back—I’m damn lucky he didn’t rupture a kidney—I struggled like hell not to make a sound, gritting my teeth until all that came out was a grunt, but that was enough to continue the cycle. I eventually realized he wouldn’t stop kicking me until I stopped screaming or crying. Even once I did, he kept on going until he ran out of steam. I had to stifle any reaction or else risk incurring a fresh beating. When he’d finished, he left me there on the floor, sore and bruising as I caught my breath.

I remember thinking, *How am I going to work? Who's going to want to have sex with some girl covered in bruises?* But it never got in the way. Johns don't often ask questions, and their standards aren't terribly high. Richard Gere was not swooping in to save me. So, I kept on working, my bruises faded, and soon all that was left was the memory of that beating and a loss of confidence in my weirdness barometer, which opened the door to other experiences.

"It's good money," Keoni said, flicking his cigarette butt into the gutter. I'd tricked with Keoni before. That wasn't an issue, but I had my doubts about anything anyone tried too hard to sell me. He was riding the line.

"How good?"

"This bitch is white collar. We're talking at least twenty-four hours under her roof, getting high and eating real good for as long as we're there, plus a little cash for the road."

I took a little more convincing, but that night I accompanied him to this woman's high-rise apartment, which was very upscale. That was promising. While Keoni greeted her, I eyed the place. There was enough around to steal, but none of it would have been worth burning a possible repeat engagement, so I curbed the impulse.

"Nikki, this is Joanne." Keoni stepped aside so she could get a good look at me.

"Hi, Nikki." She bit her lip as she sized me up. "Jesus, you are tiny."

"Uh…thanks."

What else was I supposed to say to that? I still needed to eat, so I stuffed my panic down and just tried to stay in the moment, however horrible. Keoni and I undressed and climbed into bed with Joanne. The fact that neither of us were into it didn't matter as long as she got off. After all, she wasn't paying us in pleasure. She was paying us in drugs and food, which we got once she reached her first orgasm and rolled over, flicking her hand in the direction of the kitchen.

We raided the fridge and stuffed our faces, and once Joanne had cleared her head, she rambled out of the bedroom and gave us some meth. As I wiped my mouth with the back of my hand, I wondered who she'd gotten it from. Could she have possibly been a former customer? A year prior, would she have been just three or four middlemen down the chain from me? I didn't bother to ask. It didn't matter.

Keoni and I went back to Joanne a few times. On one occasion, she looked me over, then handed me a razor, looked down, and told me to shave. So, I did. When I was done, she walked over slowly with this sickening smile.

"You look just like a little girl," she said in an unctuous voice. I fought the urge to squirm as she caressed my cheek and ran her hand all the way down between my legs. Then she kissed me, and I froze, suddenly feeling just like a little girl again—seeing, hearing, smelling, and feeling all the things that little girl had known: a funky kitchen, dark hallways, cigarette stink...naked strangers and hands touching me everywhere, hands that were too large, hands that devoured me.

Despite all that, I came back to Joanne's a few more times, because as sick as it felt, as triggering as it was, that damage had already been done, and my addiction wasn't going to feed itself.

A month or two later, weeks after I'd last seen Joanne, I was strolling down Kalakaua Avenue when I stopped short in front of a store's display window, in which I could see her face on one of the TVs. I ducked inside to listen to the news report and learned that Joanne had been found face down with multiple stab wounds in the Ala Wai, a river that ran right next to her high-rise. She'd only ever slept with young guys, the younger the better, and had likely gone too far with some kid, triggering them until they snapped and shanked her. It was horrific to think about, but I wasn't about to shed any tears over it.

"How much?" the broad-shouldered man asked as I leaned in through his passenger-side window.

"Depends on how you're paying."

He nodded and leaned over, opening the passenger door, and I got in.

The houses grew more and more spaced out as we reached the north shore. Hawaii has this image of being a quiet, peaceful place, and it is, but there's a line separating the silence of peace from the silence of desolation, and we'd crossed it. The farther we drove, the more nervous I got, and I was thankful for the Beretta in my bag. I never wanted to use it, but knowing it was there as an option was somewhat reassuring.

We talked for a bit in his living room, then he led me down the dark hallway to the bedroom. I just stood there waiting while he strolled around the room in no particular rush to do anything. I, on the other hand, was eager to just get it over with. He stopped in front of the closet and stared into it, then he pulled out a coat and walked over to me. He brought it to his face, and inhaled deeply. He looked up at me with wide eyes—a little too wide—and an oily grin.

"Ahhh...fresh blood," he said. He took another deep whiff of the coat, and that's when I saw the stain on it, a stain I knew was actually blood.

I was standing not two feet from a complete psychopath.

"Smell it," he said, holding the coat up to my face. Just the thought of it made me sick, but I was in full-on survival mode, so I leaned forward and pretended to sniff at the coat. It must have been convincing enough, because he didn't ask again. He just looked at me with those wide eyes and that awful grin, then steered me over to the bed. I spent the next several minutes staring at the ceiling, frozen. Terrified.

He didn't want to kill me. He just wanted me to know that he could in any number of ways and get away with it, and there was nothing I could do. My Beretta was in my bag, and the bag was in the living room.

When he was finished, he drove me back to Waikiki and dropped me off on the corner where he'd found me, with the agreed-upon cash in full. I never spoke of that encounter with anyone on the island. I just prayed I'd never see him again, and fortunately I never did, but I never stopped wondering when that winning streak might end, when he might show up again and proposition me for another job I'd be too scared to refuse.

I couldn't find a better gig, so I used whatever steam I had left to keep on hooking anywhere I could: alleyways, park benches, pay-by-the-hour motels, cars, dirty peep-show booths, and on one occasion a broken table beside a dumpster. And every time, a little more of me bled away until I was one step above a blank slate. Tabula rasa.

From the start, Bella hadn't loved the fact that I was hooking, but she found a way to handle it. What she couldn't handle was her addiction. I can't blame her. I wasn't doing a great job of handling mine. We'd grown so tight, relying on each other, caring for each other, but eventually the exhaustion, desperation, and straight-up paranoia set in. I can't even recall what we broke up over *that time*, but it left me without the only constant I'd come to rely on.

Everything had fallen away. My girlfriend, my family, my dignity, myself…it was all gone, and now there were just dirty alleys, creepy men, and food I fished out of dumpsters. Throughout my entire spiral, I'd been reluctant to reach out to my family. I'm not sure why I found myself at that graffitied pay phone, calling home. I wasn't expecting anyone to save me. I knew that ship had pretty much sailed. I wasn't asking or even looking for forgiveness. I didn't owe anyone any apologies. But if I was circling the drain, I wanted something that at least resembled closure.

"This is a collect call from…" The brief recording of my name interrupted the automated message. "Would you like to accept the charges?" My mom did, and the call connected.

"Where are you?"

"A pay phone on Kalakaua."

A long silence followed. I'd have thought she'd hung up if I couldn't hear her breathing.

"How are you?"

I mostly kept my voice from shaking. "Not great. I'm hungry—most of the time, actually. And I'm tired. I'm just so tired. And I don't know what to do, but I just wanted…I don't know."

She sighed and sounded like she was going to say something, so I shut up. She paused a long time before she spoke again.

"You reap what you sow, Nikki."

If she said anything after that, I didn't hear it. Did it really matter? *You reap what you sow.* Only I wasn't. I was reaping what she'd sown, what they all had, and I knew it. It didn't make what she said hurt any less.

I didn't slam the phone down on the hook. My hand wasn't steady enough for that. I just hung it up and cried, feeling hollowed out, gutted, and completely alone in the world. I'd gone too far and burned my bridges, and I was too fucked up now for even my family to bother saving.

It was easier, apparently, to just let me go and grieve me. I was as good as dead. I was a ghost.

Shortly after that, at some point in November, I took shelter for the night in a motel room after some John had gotten his money's worth and left. And that's where you first found me, staring at my reflection in a cracked mirror, alone, completely tapped out, and running on empty. I looked down at my Beretta and considered going out on my terms. I even got as far as pressing the barrel to my temple, but I never pulled the trigger. I just collapsed, slept it off, and went back out onto the street the next day.

I was up and about the next morning, looking for a fix, when I felt a wave of nausea and ducked into an alley. After vomiting up everything in my stomach, I started thinking about how I'd been getting queasy more frequently than usual. And while some of my discomfort could be mistaken for withdrawal, there was something about it that just felt different somehow.

Oh. *Ohhh…*

It wasn't certain. At my stage of addiction and malnutrition, a girl's period can get a little cagey, but I had to know for sure.

It was somewhere around noon when I stumbled into a drug store and headed straight for the pregnancy tests. I couldn't afford one. I couldn't even afford a cup of coffee, so I'd have to improvise. I'd never been a very good shoplifter, but I worked with the skills I had. I cased the store four or five times, mentally rehearsing my exit strategy. The doors were in my line of sight. If I made a beeline and played it cool, I could make it.

I stuffed the test down my shirt and started moving. My paranoia begged me to glance back at the counter to make sure the cashier wasn't watching, but I forced myself not to. It would be a dead giveaway. I sailed right through the sliding doors and onto the sidewalk, heart pounding in my ears, and headed for the family eatery a few doors down to make use of its restroom.

Home pregnancy test technology has come a long way in the past thirty years. Nowadays, you pee on the stick, and in a minute you've got your verdict, but in 1995? I must have lingered in that stall, staring at that plastic stick, for a solid five minutes that felt like twenty before I saw blue. Pregnant.

What am I going to do? I'm so far gone, how would I even find my way back? Is it even possible?

I stared blankly ahead at the metal door in front of me until a pair of voices snapped me back to reality. I swung the stall door open and stumbled out to find a woman at the sink, helping her daughter, maybe three or four years old, wash her hands. It was so ordinary, so simple, and it hit me like a sucker punch, triggering thoughts and feelings I'd thought dead a long time ago.

As I stepped out onto the sidewalk, the sun shone down on me, bright and unrelenting, as though to say, *Wake up, bitch. No more stalling, no more fucking around, no more dwelling on whose choices got you here. This just got bigger than that and bigger than you. What you do next is your choice.*

Make it.

CHAPTER 17

Aloha

To say I was overwhelmed would be beyond understatement. I couldn't even take care of myself. How the fuck was I going to keep a kid alive? At the rate I was going, would I even live long enough for it to be an issue? I couldn't say, but I had to do something.

I knew of a shelter where I could get a hot meal and some medical attention, but it was miles away, so there wasn't much time to waste. I didn't make it there that night. Early detox and a pair of very sore feet got the better of me, and I fell asleep at a bus stop along the way.

I woke just after dawn, squinting to keep the sun out of my eyes, to find a crowd of people staring at me for taking up the whole bench. There were several businessmen wearing suit pants and Hawaiian shirts (local white-collar attire), and a trio of high school girls in private school uniforms, burdened only by their backpacks and perhaps the looming terror of a pop quiz.

As I sat up, raking my ratty hair back from my face, I fought a wave of nausea. That really would have been the icing on the humiliation cake, not only being a pregnant homeless junkie, but one who'd puked all over herself in public.

I didn't blow. I forced it all back down and took deep breaths until the nausea passed. And still, even though I'd made room on the bench, no one would take advantage of the freed-up seats. They just eyed the bench with disgust like I'd tainted it. Well, fuck 'em. I'd never been as respectable as those businessmen or as innocent as those girls. All that potential, a future of infinite possibilities, seemed so far behind me. But maybe, just maybe, if I got my shit together *just enough* and gave my kid a shot, I could say I'd done something right with my life.

Once the nausea subsided, I became aware of the gnawing feeling in my belly and started looking for whatever might pass for breakfast. My first instinct was to think small, the way street kids do, but my hunger quickly overrode my good sense. I walked myself right into one of those breakfast places that always smells like eggs and powdered sugar. The seating host looked horrified.

"Can I help you?" It was as diplomatic as he could be. I looked like shit, dirty and unkempt, and not at all matching the charming vibe of the customers having omelets and pancakes with their families.

I apologized up front, well aware he had every reason to turn me away. I wasn't exactly good for business. But I pleaded for him to spare something, anything. It didn't even have to be fresh. I was willing to accept food they were ready to throw away or maybe some leftovers the busboy hadn't gotten to yet. Anything.

Just then, the owner walked up to us. The young greeter looked so relieved to pass the buck it put about five years on his life. The owner looked me over, drumming his fingers on the little podium, and his eyes softened. "I'm going to have to ask you to step outside."

"Please..."

"Please just wait outside, miss," he said in a firm but gentle voice. "Don't go anywhere. Just wait."

He emerged about ten minutes later and handed me a to-go container heavy with food: French toast, bacon and eggs, and home fries. He nodded when I thanked him, his tight smile making it clear that he very much wanted me to enjoy the contents of my Styrofoam box, but somewhere else. He handed me some plastic cutlery and went back inside. I found a place to sit, got comfortable, and dug in. I was tiny and underfed, and looking at me, it was probably hard to imagine how I had room for all that food, but I didn't leave a crumb.

When I got to the shelter a few hours later, I learned that the doctor who volunteered at the in-house clinic wouldn't be there until Monday. It was Saturday. I was willing to wait it out, but every bed was already taken. All they could offer me was a blanket and a spot on the floor with a dozen other people. I laughed. Of course that was all I could score. I'd probably used up all my luck on breakfast.

I continued to detox over the next few days, which were utter hell. Withdrawal is bad enough without heaping morning sickness on top of it. I remember dragging myself to the bathroom one morning, hardly able to see as I shambled into a giant room with toilets, sinks, and showers all together, past a bunch of girls who were standing around chatting. After I emptied my stomach, I pulled myself to my feet, stumbled into the shower fully dressed, and turned on the rough jet of water. It spewed from the crude showerhead, drenching me and my clothes, but I could barely bring myself to notice.

The shelter was not what anyone would consider ideal living, but it was a lot better than the street. I was able to wash and rest while the last of the drugs worked their way out of my system, and there was on-site medical care if I needed it. The dormitory looked like a huge gymnasium with bunk beds and cots. There were some mats on the floor to accommodate any overflow, and there was always overflow. Homelessness in Hawaii was, and still is, a very real problem, and shelters never had space to spare. That was my main incentive for following every one of their rules. You get kicked out, someone else gets your bed right away, and you're not getting it back.

During my detox, and especially on account of my pregnancy, they were kind enough to waive one of their major rules: no hanging around during the day. You're only inside for meals and to sleep at night. While I was working the drugs out of my system, they let me sleep, but once I was well enough to stand, I had to fill my days the same as anyone else, whether that meant wandering around town or loitering outside the building. But the first thing I did was see the doctor. He confirmed what I already knew. I was pregnant, about three months along. So, what now?

I had no idea who the father was, so whatever choices I made for myself and for this kid were all mine. I didn't have anything in the way of a plan. I just knew I wanted this baby, to love it, to raise it, but I couldn't do that on the streets and in the shadows. If I was going to give it any semblance of a normal life, that meant facing my legal demons, and there was only one person I knew of who could give me a fighting chance.

I flagged down a cab and asked the driver to take me down to the courthouse. Reinette's office was right across the street. The driver was happy to take me there until I told him I couldn't pay. Honesty is generally the best policy, but in hindsight, given the circumstances, I probably should've just kept that detail to myself. He refused to let me in the cab, but I told him I was pregnant and desperate, that I needed to do right by my baby. I actually begged. He sighed, grumbled for me to get in, and drove me down to the courthouse.

There was no one in Reinette's office when I got there. The front door was unlocked, so I knew she'd be coming back, but if she was in court, I could be waiting there for hours. Well, it wasn't like I had anywhere else to be, so I took a seat in the waiting area and picked up a magazine to pass the time.

Around 4:30 p.m., I lifted my head at the sound of the front door. Reinette stood there, staring down at me. I can only imagine how awful I must have looked. It must have defied words, because Reinette was one of the most eloquent people I've ever known, and all she could manage to say was, "Where the fuck have you been?"

"I'm pregnant." It was all I had to work with, and I could barely choke the words out.

Time just stood still for a long moment. Neither of us knew what to say, much less do. She looked so pissed off, I half expected her to take me right over to the courthouse to get cuffed and thrown back in jail, but she just walked over and sat beside me.

"Okay," she said, rolling it around her brain. "I can't promise anything, but given you're pregnant, I *might* be able to convince your PO to give you one more chance."

"I understand."

"I mean it. You've fucked up really bad. I like you and I want to help you, but you need to want it. For real."

"I want it." I nodded, realizing just how much. "I want it."

"Good," she said, glancing down at her watch. "Office is still open. Let's go."

I followed Reinette across the street to the probation office, which was about to close. The receptionist told Reinette that Bill, my probation officer, had finished all his appointments and was about to leave for the day, but Reinette insisted. She knew he'd see her. She was right.

A very long fifteen minutes later, Reinette emerged from Bill's office and called me inside. Every nerve I had was shot, but I forced myself to stand and head in. Reinette joined Bill at his desk, where he sat and gestured to the chair in front of me. I sat.

"Reinette told me about your situation, and to be perfectly honest, I'm not so sure another chance is something you deserve or what's best for your baby." He gave me a thorough once-over, as though he were still debating which way to go. Finally, he said, "But Reinette has assured me you can do this, so last chance. Last one, as in no mistakes, no appeals, no more do-overs. This is it."

And there were strings. A lot of them. I needed to show up every week for a drug test, every one of which had to be clean, and I had to attend an outpatient rehab program. I was due (as per my original probation agreement) to show up in about a month's time for my year in prison, but Reinette intended to petition the court to postpone my start date for a year and drew up the paperwork immediately.

"What does it even matter, though?" I asked her. "If I go back to jail, I still lose my kid."

"This time next year, that kid will be six months old, and if you're still clean and can show the court you've turned your life around, that you're taking care of that baby…" She pointed to my belly. "There's a decent chance I can get your sentence changed to probation."

"Seriously? That's it? Probation?"

"A shit ton of it, but yes. But you need to be out here to make that happen."

It sounded like a plan that anyone with a little faith in humanity could support. Unfortunately, the judge assigned to my case wasn't known for pulling punches. Marie Milks was appointed a circuit court judge in 1984, the first woman to achieve that honor in the state of Hawaii. She hadn't gotten to where she was by going easy on drug offenders in a state with a massive meth problem. This was going to be a hard sell.

Judge Milks's face was inscrutable the whole time Reinette argued to delay my sentence, a stern expression that gave away nothing. When Reinette finished, Milks looked directly at me.

"I'm not lifting your sentence," she said. "You've already gotten a better deal than most would in your position. But I will postpone your incarceration for one year. If, in that time, you're caught within ten miles of any illegal drugs, even if they're not yours, I will take your baby away from you, and you will serve the full thirty years. Do you understand?"

She knew she was asking the impossible, and that there was no way I—or anyone, for that matter—could guarantee a drug-free radius of ten miles around them at all times. There's nowhere you can possibly go, no way to know what your neighbor has in their apartment. Even in the poshest gated communities, there's always a Keilani running something illegal out of her luxury condo. But Milks didn't literally expect that of me. She was making a point, and what she was really saying, once I read between the lines, was that I was fresh out of wiggle room. One step out of line, even the slightest fuck-up, and I was done.

Going cold turkey and staying clean, especially while homeless and pregnant, would certainly be a challenge, but I could do it. I had to do it. I had an obligation to myself and to that baby growing inside me.

I was in line for dinner at the shelter. One tray, one meal: That's what everyone gets told up front. Among the volunteers working the line were a couple and their son, who was about twelve. Was I part of a lesson in kindness and civics for this kid? A cautionary tale? Both? I don't know. But when I went back up with my tray for a second portion, the kid didn't hesitate to grab the ladle. His mother gently stopped him, looking at me with genuine compassion before ruefully reciting the shelter's one-serving policy.

"I'm pregnant," I said, and their faces relaxed. How relieved they must have been that I presented the one exception to the rule. The father patted his son's shoulder, and the kid loaded me up. This kid, only ten years younger than me, looked me in the eyes, and I could see what he was thinking. *That's not going to be me, dirty and homeless and neck-deep in my own personal hell.* And I couldn't blame him. *I* certainly didn't want to be where I was. It doesn't make it any easier to take, especially not from some kid who didn't even know what a real mistake was yet, but I took his kindness at face value and ate up.

At times, the shelter wasn't enough. If we didn't make it back in time for scheduled meals, we didn't eat, and we'd be out on our own all day, so I'd panhandle outside restaurants with zero shame about working the pregnancy angle to feed myself. It was amazing just how much food I could buy when I wasn't spending the bulk of my earnings on getting high. Appealing to people's sympathies got even easier once I started to show.

Every once in a while, a family would take pity on me and invite me to come and sit and eat with them inside whatever restaurant I'd parked myself outside. And they almost always encouraged me to order whatever I wanted. I mean, come on. Once you're at the inviting-a-homeless-pregnant-chick-to-your-family-dinner stage, you're probably not going to begrudge her the entrée of her choice. And if they offered dessert, you bet your ass I got dessert.

I kept myself fed, but it wasn't enough. I missed having someone at my side, someone whose hand I could hold. And specifically, yeah, I missed Bella. We'd seen each other through a lot of shit. Granted, most of it was of our own making, but that wasn't the point. She had always been a comfort, someone to walk with, hurt with, and sleep on the streets with. And if I was really going to do this, I couldn't do it alone.

Keeping Judge Milks's warning in mind, I was risking a lot looking for Bella. I had to check around all our old hangouts, places we could have been found at any time, and all of them were hotbeds for the kind of criminal activity that would land me in the pen for three decades. I had to be careful and ready to walk away if things didn't pan out. Whatever happened, I couldn't linger at the scene.

When I found Bella, I half expected her to tell me to fuck off, but she was just as happy to see me. I told her everything that had happened, that I was exhausted and just done, and she didn't try to tell me different. She was tired too. Convincing her to get clean didn't take much. She'd wanted a new beginning of her own for a while, but it's easier said than done, especially when there's no margin left for error.

Bella took a moment to weigh the pain of withdrawal and the difficulty of maintaining sobriety against dealing with the world and her own shit without anything to anesthetize it, but in the end her better instincts won. She nodded and helped me to my feet, and we headed back to the shelter so she could detox in a clean, safe place and stay with me.

The shelter ultimately didn't agree with us, and after a while, we left, thinking we could find some other way to put a roof over our heads. We were less than successful, but our spots at the shelter were gone the second we'd forfeited them. It was not the smartest move on my part.

Bella and I weren't on the street long. The unsustainability of that situation was driven home the night we'd fallen asleep behind a restaurant, Bella sitting up against the wall, and me on my side.

"Oh my God! Oh God!" Bella shook me awake, screaming. "Roaches! Get up! Get up!" I could feel them a split second before she said anything, and as soon as those thoughts connected, I screamed. I stumbled to my feet—at four months along it wasn't too hard yet—and swatted away the fat, brown creatures scuttling along my clothes. A few had gotten inside my shirt, and I had to shake them out. I tousled my own hair like a fucking maniac, making sure there weren't any stowaways getting comfortable. We never got back to sleep that night, not after waking up covered in bugs.

The roaches really were the point of no return, and they lit a fire under my ass to move to the next stage of this. If I was serious about making this all work, I had to get off the street, period. But there was always the question of money, and I was not only fresh out of cash, I'd run out of ways to acquire it. All but one, and much as I hated even considering it and probably wouldn't have if it were just my life on the line, it *wasn't* just my life on the line anymore. It never would be again.

God fucking help me, it was time.

"Mom?" I kept my voice low, humble. She'd like that. "I'm…I need help."

"I don't doubt it."

"Mom, please don't make this harder than it already is. It's not what you think. This is for real. I'm on the street and I need—"

"You need money. No."

"I'm pregnant." I could always count on dropping that bomb to stop the conversation cold. "I'm having it, Mom. Whatever I have to do, I'm going to do. But I have to get off the street."

I told her my plan: There were public assistance programs, all things I could arrange, but not if I was living on the street. I needed someplace to rest and clean up while I set everything in motion. It took some convincing, but eventually she bent.

The money went about as far as I needed. I got a motel room for a few days while I signed up for welfare and found a small one-bedroom apartment. It was barely more than a studio, but after the life Bella and I had been living, it was a palace. My welfare checks covered the rent, and food stamps kept us fed. It wasn't glamorous, but it was enough.

Over the next five months, I showed up for all my appointments with Bill and passed every drug screening. Otherwise, the remainder of my pregnancy was more or less what you'd expect: heartburn, swollen ankles, back pain, all worth it when I thought about the life growing inside me.

My maternity outfit consisted of a belly shirt, an old flannel, and one pair of green army pants with a button fly that did not survive the experience. As my belly continued to swell, buttons kept popping off until at last I had to rely on a safety pin to hold them closed. And that was only through my sixth month. After that, it was sweatpants all the way to the finish line.

I managed to stay clean through all of this, and I'd say I don't know what possessed me, but I do. Motherhood is a hell of a drug.

I went into labor two short weeks after my twenty-third birthday. I was in labor for days—I'm talking *days*—and I pushed and screamed and felt like I'd rip myself in two, but I didn't. And when it was all done, I had this beautiful baby girl in my arms. I had Evie.

I looked down at this baby and knew at that moment that whatever I had to do to take care of her, whatever I had to work at, whoever I had to be, I would do it and be it. I'd had no idea I could love anyone that much. I'd always considered love something I wasn't fully capable of, but now I knew different.

Bella had managed to call my mom at some point while I was in labor, and she arrived at the hospital the day after I'd given birth. It was an awkward reunion at best—neither of us could think of much to say—but I was struck by the way she held Evie and sang to her.

This wasn't the mother who had sacrificed me on the altar of her social life, who had always been so concerned with appearances and people's perceptions. This wasn't the woman who had damaged me in so many ways over the course of my life, then blamed me for living in the wreckage. Who was I even looking at?

My mom stayed for about a week to help out and bond with her granddaughter. And while I had renewed my commitment to moving on, it didn't erase the pain. I didn't know then that healing is a lot more complicated than crying "do over!" and calling it a day. But for a short while there was peace between us, as much as there had ever been. She cooked meals, fed and changed Evie so I could sleep, and even took me to buy some new clothes now that my maternity sweats would no longer fit. She bought some clothes for the baby as well, and the whole time there was this warmth coming from her. And it made me wonder…

All the dismissiveness, the unwillingness to admit fault or hear anything that might contradict her own point of view—where had all that come from? What wounds had *she* suffered to make her that way? I didn't know if I would ever learn the answers to those questions, but I could accept that and her. I could at least try.

I did my best to keep looking forward. I had severed ties with my past and everyone in it except for Bella, but sooner or later, I wound up in the orbit of some old friends who just assumed I was the same person. When Keoni asked if he could crash at my place for the night, I should have said no, but less than a year ago, I'd been sleeping in alleys and helping him scam our way into hotels just to get a little shelter. What, was I too good for him now?

"One night," I said, through the cracked door. "And only if you're clean. No meth or anything else. Not even cigarettes. I have a baby." He assured me this was all cool, but when I found some gear on the small table in the living room the next morning, Keoni passed out next to it, I immediately lost my shit. "Are you fucking kidding me?!" I screamed, shoving him awake. He told me to chill out, but I had no chill to spare.

Bella walked out into the living room to see what all the noise was about. I just ducked back into the bedroom, scooped the baby up into my arms, and threw her diaper bag over my shoulder. "I'm taking Evie for some fresh air. Which *she needs*," I growled pointedly at Keoni. "When I come back, you're going to be gone, and take all your meth shit with you."

I stormed out of there, holding my little girl, my mind racing at how close I'd come to blowing everything. If word of this got back to Bill or Reinette, or especially Judge Milks…

Somewhere inside, though, I knew my fears were bigger than this. It wasn't just about my close call, but its implications, how easy it had been to fall into a scenario that violated my probation. My next move was completely counterintuitive and even hypocritical, considering what had sent me out my own door in a fearful rage, but I needed to talk to someone I knew and trusted, someone older and wiser than me.

A quick call to a cell number I could never forget, and Roxy told me which hotel she'd set up shop in for the week. Within an hour, she was holding Evie, smiling at her and making baby talk while I killed a bottle of water, still calming my nerves.

"She's so beautiful," Roxy said.

"I know. And it would be so easy to fuck it all up and lose her." I knew myself. I could turn them all away for a while, but sooner or later I'd slip and it would all be over. I'd lose my baby and probably never see her again, and that would be my story. "I don't know what to do, Ma." Roxy handed Evie back to me. When she spoke, her voice was firm and a little sad.

"Baby, what you see? This is me. This is who I'm always going to be. Me and my 'kids'? This is our life. It's not for you anymore." She took my free hand, trying not to cry. "You've got to get off this island. There's too much here gonna drag you back down. Save yourself and that baby while you can. Go."

"I can't," I told her. "I legally can't."

"You can find a way. You always do."

I fought her a little, going a few rounds, trying to think of a way I could solve this problem without cutting Roxy out of my life forever, but she didn't back down. She just kept telling me no, and I knew in my bones she was right. I reached for her, and she waved me away, as though she couldn't afford to mess up her makeup or outfit, but her glistening eyes told the truth. Always a lady. Well screw it. Before she could stop me, I hugged her tight and thanked her for everything. Then, just as I was about to pull away, I felt her hand on my back, and we said goodbye, both knowing that even if I never got off the island, I could never see her again.

Thirty years later, I still don't know what Roxy's doing, if she's safe or even on this plane of existence. But wherever she is, be it some hotspot on Kalakaua Avenue or some eternal realm beyond the physical, I hope and pray it is the most fabulous scene, brighter and more colorful than any club we ever partied in. I see her sometimes in my mind, tall and resplendent, dancing to a thumping beat in a swirl of color. I'll always be grateful to Roxy for sending me away and for saying goodbye, and I'll never forget the mother of misfits, the true queen of my underworld, in all her glory.

When I told Reinette about my decision to leave Hawaii, or at the very least Oahu, she didn't seem the least bit surprised. In fact, she looked relieved. She'd already been gearing up to request that my sentence be commuted and insisted this was only going to make her argument easier. I didn't see how.

"Nikki, you've been clean for six months. And in that time, you've stayed away from any past associations, had a baby, provided a clean, safe home for her by legal means, and renewed your ties to your family. What would be the point of throwing you in prison and separating mother and child now?"

"You really think that's how Milks will see it?"

"I'd say there's a pretty strong chance, especially if you're looking to remove yourself from all your triggers and seek out a strong support system." I wasn't sure what she was getting at. "Your family in New York. That's your trump card."

New York? I just wanted to get the hell off Oahu and start fresh on Maui or the Big Island. Moving back to New York and cohabitating with my parents had not entered my mind as a possibility. And what about Bella and *her* chance to start over? I couldn't just leave her behind now.

Reinette wasn't unsympathetic to any of that but firmly insisted that this was my strongest chance to avoid prison for myself and the foster system for Evie. I had to choose what was best for me and my daughter.

A newborn, Evie wouldn't be safe to fly for a couple of months anyway, and it would take that time to draw up and file extradition papers to be approved by Judge Milks. But Reinette, being Reinette, presented my case and convinced Milks that sending me to jail and taking Evie from me would undo all the progress I'd made. Letting me go back to New York to rebuild my life was a better chance for both of us.

Milks commuted my one year of jail time to ten years' probation and agreed to extradition, under the proviso that Hawaii could call me back at any time to review my case and put me back in jail if I fucked up. I found those terms more than fair. I signed the papers, and it was done.

The day of my flight, Bella came along to the airport to say goodbye. For how long, neither of us knew, but I think I was probably a bit more optimistic than she was.

"We're going to think of something," I assured her. "I am not going to just leave you here. I promise."

She smiled and nodded. I could tell she didn't really believe me but knew I believed it, and this wasn't the time or place to argue. She had my parents' phone number. I'd written it down in several places just in case she lost it.

Bella said goodbye to me and to Evie, and I boarded the plane. As we took off, I looked out the window onto the fresh, beautiful landscape I'd taken for a paradise when I'd arrived only a few years ago. I knew now that it was partially true but also an illusion masking the ugliness I'd spent the last several months clawing my way out of. Would I ever be back? I had several reasons both for and against, but for now, Hawaii was behind me, one eastbound flight away from being my past. It was goodbye to all that and hello to the new life awaiting me. I looked down at Evie in my arms, then again out the window and whispered…

"Aloha."

Part Four

The After-Party

CHAPTER 18

History Repeating

I'd been a runner, a drifter, a mover, and a shaker, but that was done, twenty years behind me by the time I got the therapy I'd desperately needed for most of my life. I'd given it a shot a few times. Either I hadn't been ready or the therapist in question simply hadn't been a good fit.

Finding the right therapist is not so much about finding a good one, because "good" is subjective. It's all about their style, their personality, how equipped they are on a personal level to give you the right kind of care. Plenty of therapists are incisive or effective or down-to-earth. A therapist who checks two of those boxes is a rare find. By some miracle, Barbara checked all three. She had a warmth about her that didn't press against my defenses so much as lean on them, wearing them down so softly and steadily that I barely noticed.

Few people tell their therapist the story of their life in a perfectly straight line. There are always digressions and backward leaps to things you skipped or forgot, things you assumed were trivial, only to learn they were tremendously significant. I did my best to make as much sense as possible, starting with my childhood, through my wild and wayward youth, and all the way up to the birth of my daughter and escape from Hawaii.

"So, when you left Hawaii, you moved back in with your parents?" Barbara asked.

"My mom and stepdad, yeah."

"That must have been a pretty huge adjustment."

A laugh crested in my chest but broke into a sigh on the way out. A huge adjustment? That was putting it mildly. I collected myself and looked back to the summer of 1996, when, after three years in Hawaii, I reunited with my family.

The flight home to New York was the first time I'd ever flown with a baby. The entire twenty-four hours leading up to the trip had been exhausting on every level. Saying goodbye to Bella had only made it worse, and I was totally drained. Fortunately for me, Evie didn't make a peep the entire trip. She just slept on my chest, giving me plenty of time to think and even get a little sleep myself. Both legs of the flight were like some kind of spell unraveling, some dream clearing away like mist.

I stepped out into the terminal, holding Evie against my hip like a skateboard, her eyes soaking up everything. Waiting there at the gate to greet me were my mom and Gene, my grandparents, and Michael, who had already been taller than me when I'd left but only by an inch or two. Now fifteen, he had nearly a foot on me.

My mom lifted Evie out of my arms with a broad, sunny smile, while I took a hug from Michael, who had held out for about as long as he could. The kid held on to me like I was going to disappear at any second and didn't let go until I agreed to ride in the back with him on the drive home. I was happy to see him but so wiped out all I could do was smile and pat his knee.

I'd made it clear that while I was coming home to live under my parents' roof, I was now an adult and a parent in my own right, and I was going to need a little more space and privacy than my old bedroom could provide. Since Paul was out of the nest and living in Arizona, I staked a claim to his old room, the second largest in the house, complete with its own bathroom. In anticipation of this, my old room had been converted into a nursery, furnished with a crib, a changing table, and some toys. Not bad for a fresh start. Not bad at all.

After all the stress and trauma of pregnancy, childbirth, and rebooting my life, I felt like I'd been holding my breath for years and could finally exhale. I spent most of the first week in my room, sleeping. I'd have Evie throughout the night, then, once my family woke up, I'd hand her over to someone and crash. I kept to that pattern for just over a week, and then a switch went off in my head. I knew I had to get up and start living, so I pulled myself out of bed, showered, and made the choice to swim rather than sink.

The first friend I called was Mark, and he came right over. He was exactly the same and completely different, still funny and charming, though a lot more grounded. He still smoked like a chimney and even indulged in the occasional joint, but he'd left the hard drugs behind, and it was a good look for him. He'd also been living his life authentically as a gay man for a couple of years, which had done wonders for his peace of mind. But despite a calmer, more casual demeanor, his mind was as sharp and quick as it had ever been, and within minutes he had me laughing again. I was so damn happy to see him.

Mark became a regular fixture around my parents' house for the first time in years, coming around to hang with me and play with Evie, who would eventually call him "Unca Mark." We'd take Evie with us to go get food and do typical twentysomething stuff…just now with a kid in tow.

Gradually, I started meeting up with other friends, and it was pretty great, but a little weird. Only a decade earlier, in the mid-80s, having a baby at twenty-three would have still been fairly common, but this was right around when holding off on kids until you were pushing thirty was becoming the standard. I was the only one of my friends with a child. The rest were years away from even thinking about it. So, in that regard, I stood out—still loved, still welcomed, but staring across this line that set me apart. I wasn't young and free to do whatever, whenever. I was a parent, and that always came first, so the first time I left Evie with my mom in order to meet up with some friends was a big deal.

I'd been home for months at that point, never parted from my daughter for more than a few hours, and even then, never more than fifty feet away. But there I was, wandering the Nanuet Mall with my friends, window shopping and consuming an ungodly amount of empty calories in the food court, and it was just perfect. But after a few hours of that, maybe one more than I'd planned, I was ready to get back to my kid. Retracing the hamster-liberating footsteps of my crazy youth was all well and good, but how much could it really compare to that beautiful, chubby little face?

I walked in the door around 5:30 p.m. and heard a familiar creak coming from the kitchen: Evie's baby bouncer. I found my mom at the stove, hair pulled back with a clip, looking almost deliberately disheveled as she pushed something around in a pan. She was tapping the bouncer with one foot, keeping the baby bobbing up and down as she looked around quietly. She glared at me with pursed lips.

"Where were you?" I didn't understand. She knew exactly where I'd been. Shaking her head, she let out a tight, exasperated sigh. "I will not be raising your child."

It took a second to register, then I laughed. I hadn't even been gone the whole afternoon. I'd spent a few hours at a suburban shopping mall fifteen minutes from the house, and my mother was staring me down like I'd been out all night, clubbing. Like she hadn't encouraged me to take a little time for myself and agreed to babysit. I could suddenly see it all, this melodrama she'd concocted and staged: the poor, put-upon grandmother left to raise the child of her selfish, irresponsible daughter.

I shook my head, laughing at the absurdity of it all, picked Evie up, and said, "I was gone for three hours. This whole scene you made up is ridiculous. It is not real." I took Evie down the hall to my room and shut the door. The honeymoon was over.

Regina Beckmann was still my mom's best friend, but she'd been so far out of my orbit for so long that I'd almost forgotten. After all, she'd lived so far away for years, first in Southern California, then up in New England, it wasn't like they hung out daily, but they visited each other on a fairly regular basis. It wasn't something I'd given much thought to until my mom told me Regina and her husband were coming to stay with us for a few days.

I didn't really know how to respond. It wasn't my house, so it wasn't really my place to object, not that I would have thought to. Even after everything that had happened when I was little, I still thought of Regina as my aunt and felt obligated to show her and her husband the respect and affection they were supposedly due. Some part of me knew how insane it all was, but I just sort of compartmentalized it. I walked into the kitchen one morning with Evie, stowed all the weirdness of that moment in the overhead, and sat down to breakfast.

We're cool. This is cool. This is not at all insane.

So, I ate, and we talked. I even forced a laugh or two. Then, after what I judged to be an acceptable time, I retreated back to my room with Evie. We were on the floor, playing, when Regina knocked on the door. Not having a reason to send her away, I invited her in. She told me once again how adorable my baby was (which is never a bad thing to hear), and then asked if we could talk.

Sure. Why not?

Regina sat down on the floor, smiled blandly, then after a short, awkward lead-in, said, "Jacob wants to talk to you. Would that be okay?"

Would that be okay? Was she fucking serious? How was that even a question, and whose idea had it been—hers? Jacob's? My mom's? I didn't know, and to be honest it didn't really matter. It was an insane proposition any way you sliced it. I had nothing to say to Jacob and no interest in anything he might have to say to me. But I had a feeling this wasn't entirely about him, the same feeling that told me Regina had already cleared this request with my mother.

I'd been out of sight and out of mind for a long time. Between Hawaii, Florida, rehab, and my apartment in Mahwah, I hadn't been a mainstay of the household for close to six years. I'd been easy to ignore for the sake of their friendship. But now that I was back—older, sober, and a lot savvier—I could throw a wrench in everyone's plans if I decided to call bullshit on their lies and delusions and all the pain that they'd put me through. It would be easier for them to get me to fall back in line. If they could get me to accept Jacob's apology and absolve him, well, there'd be no take-backsies after that. I'd be agreeing to let it all go and never mention it again. And if I did mention it, well, that would be *my* problem.

I should have said no right then and there, but I agreed to Jacob's request, knowing that if I didn't let him off the hook (and, by extension, our mothers), something awkward or unsettling would always linger in the air between all of us, and the blame would fall on me. It was on me to get over my pain for everyone else's sake. It always had been. I could say "all forgiven" and everyone could enjoy the good times again while I quietly swallowed my pain…or I could refuse, take care of myself, and always be resented as the selfish girl who couldn't just let everyone be happy. When those are your only choices, it's not much of a choice at all.

Not long after that, Jacob was ringing my doorbell, and my mom welcomed him in with the warm hug she always had for him. The love and affection she showed him was so sincere. I couldn't understand it. Every time she laughed with him or his parents, it just made me hate myself a little bit more, because I was the outlier. My pain was the crack in the glass ruining their perfect picture, so I'd learned long ago not to bother fighting it.

Jacob and I went to a duck pond in a nearby park. He drove. I asked him to stop at a store on the way so I could pick up some bread. Feeding the ducks was the perfect distraction to dilute the weirdness of the moment. It sure as hell beat looking him in the eye as he unburdened himself. We sat on a bench and tossed chunks of bread into the water, and Jacob said—whatever it was he said. I honestly can't remember much of it. He apologized, and I said it was okay even though it wasn't, because that's what everyone wanted.

At least the Beckmanns were off in Rhode Island, which was hardly around the corner. They weren't part of our everyday lives anymore, but my mom made no secret about who her best friend was, always dropping news about what they were doing and what was going on in their lives, and she and Aunt Sally would go visit them whenever they could. And now that I'd signed away my right to object ever again, there was nothing I could say about it.

My sporadic phone calls with Bella were beginning to cause me concern. She'd sounded fine at first, but with every call she sounded increasingly distracted and uneven, and whenever I asked her about it, her explanations never added up. I knew that she was backsliding. Without me and Evie there to ground her, Bella would keep drifting further and further until the undertow pulled her down. I couldn't let that happen. She needed me as much as I needed her. I'd told her I wouldn't leave her there to rot, and I meant it. Making it happen was another story. It would be difficult… but not impossible.

The money wasn't an issue. There was always money floating around in my family. My grandmother had squirreled away plenty over the years in savings, investments, and stashes of cash she kept around the house. Her children had adopted that practice, though not as frequently, so from time to time some bond would mature or some policy was cashed out, and one of us would get a grand or two to save for a rainy day. Shortly after my return, one such windfall came my way, so I had a small fund to work with. Bella could get a job, and we would only be staying with my parents for a little while before we could get our own apartment. Even with that plan in place, my mom was a little resistant to the idea of Bella coming to live with us, but after nearly losing me, she was willing to bend a little.

A couple of weeks later, I picked Bella up from the airport. When she stepped into the terminal and I saw her, I knew she was going to be okay. We were going to be okay. She hugged me and kissed Evie, and we went home.

I was still getting the hang of being a mom, only six months or so into the experience when I applied to Ramapo College. School had never been my scene, but I wanted to have every possible advantage in providing for my kid, and I knew the longer I waited to go back to school, the harder it would be. A better time to finally complete my education wasn't going to come along, so I buckled down and made it work.

Bella got a job on the production line at a pharmaceutical company. It wasn't glamorous, but it was steady and enabled her to contribute financially. Fortunately, her sobriety, once rooted in routine and responsibility, became unshakeable. Within a year of being home, we were able to get our own apartment. The truth is our relationship had fizzled out a long time ago on the streets of Hawaii, but we were still a team, still a family, and as far as we were concerned, raising Evie was just as much her responsibility and privilege as mine.

It was mid-afternoon when Bella woke up, having worked overnight on the production line. "What time is it?" she mumbled, walking out into the living room, where I was playing with the baby.

"Just a little after four," I said without looking up. "You were out pretty cold. You gonna be all right to—"

"I'll be fine," she said, insisting that she just needed a shower and some coffee. I had, of course, been up with the baby in the early morning and was gearing up to head out to class. Bella and I worked out a pretty good system when it came to Evie. She would watch her while I was at school until I came home to relieve her so she could work the graveyard shift, and if she pulled some overtime or fell prey to a week or two's worth of sleep debt, I'd take Evie to school with me, push her stroller up the steep hill to the campus from the parking lot, and park her next to my desk. I was lucky she was never a very fussy baby. A snack and a toy, and she was good to go while I jotted down notes about the history of broadcast news or whatever other topics fed into my communications degree.

Ramapo was my third attempt at college in six years and the first time I really stuck with it. It shouldn't have come as much of a surprise, but it turned out when I actually did the work without bullshitting, trying to scam the system, and doing tons of drugs, I was a fantastic student. Who knew?

I'd been home about a year. I was living independently of my parents, going to school, and waitressing part-time to contribute what I could to rent and expenses. I don't think I ever valued a few consecutive hours of sleep more in my entire life than I did then, but we were doing okay, stable enough that I actually had the time and wherewithal to wonder about certain things and certain people I'd lost track of.

In 1997, the internet was less than a decade old and still hammering out its identity, but one thing it was good for even then was connecting with people. In some cases, reconnecting. One day, on a whim, I did some intense online detective work that these days could be accomplished with a five-minute Google search and found the current whereabouts of Kim, an old friend of mine from elementary school. Why her, of all the people who had drifted in and out of my life? A lack of closure, maybe?

Kim had moved away from Teaneck in fourth grade. There's not much you can do at that age, so we'd lost touch. At the time it felt like she'd moved across the country, but in reality, she hadn't even crossed state lines. She'd been right there in Jersey the whole time.

I debated what to do with her phone number for a few days but eventually got up the nerve and called her. She assured me in a very excited voice that she remembered me and insisted we meet up as soon as possible to catch up on the last fifteen years. I didn't even think twice about how I'd have to curate that information. Telling only half the truth about my life had become second nature at this point. But a nice lunch with an old friend? Sure, I could act like I'd had a semi-normal life for an hour or two.

Rather than going out, Kim invited me over to her place for lunch. She looked great, and we laughed and helped each other remember things we'd forgotten. The whole visit was oddly disarming, enough that I revealed "Hawaii not working out" ran a lot deeper than I'd implied over the phone. I didn't go into detail, but I shared that I'd dropped out, gotten involved with drugs, and that coming home had been my Hail Mary. Kim wasn't put off by any of it, sympathetic but not all that surprised I'd wandered down such a dark and twisted path since last I'd seen her.

"I had a lot going on," I said. "I guess I've always had a lot a going on." I shrugged it off and took another bite, but Kim just looked at me as if she were wrestling with something. "Hey, I'm okay now," I assured her. "It's fine."

She grabbed my hand and said, "Come with me. I want to show you something," before leading me to her room. She pulled an old jewelry box out of a drawer. There wasn't much jewelry inside, just a random assortment of mementos gathered throughout her life, few of them of any monetary value but all precious to her for one reason or another. Among them was a sheet of paper that had been folded over several times. She solemnly handed it to me, and I unfolded it to find a note, written in a child's handwriting.

Please help me

Nikki

"I wrote this?"

Kim nodded. "I found it a couple of years ago when I was going through some stuff I'd saved. I didn't know what it meant back then—I'm not sure I do now—but I knew it was something important. I should have told someone. I'm sorry."

I waved it away, and she stopped. "It's okay," I said, looking straight ahead. I couldn't look her in the eye yet, but not because I blamed her. Hell, I'd never have thought to blame anyone but myself. I didn't even remember writing that note, but clearly I had, folding it over so many times, as if each fold would keep it more of a secret. To think I was dropping breadcrumbs even back then. If only someone who could have actually made a difference had spotted the trail and followed it to me. But then again, would it really have mattered? After all, I'd come forward with how I'd been hurt and how I was hurting in no uncertain terms, and how much help had I ever gotten for my trouble?

And what was I supposed to do about it now? How much could I explain…how much did I really *want* to explain to make this question mark go away? I knew Kim knew something and I had to let her know how desperate I'd been when I wrote that note, but I also hadn't seen her in fifteen years. I wasn't about to spill my guts to someone who was essentially a stranger to me now.

"There were some years there where my life pretty much sucked all the time, and I was a kid, so I didn't really know how to fix it and couldn't see a way out. But that was a long time ago, and I'm fine now." I gave Kim a soft smile I doubt was very convincing but put her at enough ease to take my word for it, and I was grateful the matter was closed.

"You say you never reached out, but you did," Barbara said. "Your cousin had to force the issue, but you did end up confronting the adults in your life with what was happening to you. Were you ever able to talk to anyone about this?"

I shrugged. "My mom took me to see a friend of hers a few times." To clarify, I added, "A therapist."

"Who belonged to her social circle. And how did that feel to you? Were you comfortable opening up?"

I snickered. "Not really. It was weird. I saw this woman at social events. She knew me. She knew my family. It's probably why my mom picked her. The whole thing with Jacob and Harvey and all the others, you think my mom wanted anyone to know about it at all, much less that it happened right under her nose? No fucking way. Of course she picked someone from her circle."

I stopped and looked over to Barbara, who was eyeing me, waiting for me to hear myself. And then I did. I think that might have been the moment I finally started to get it.

"It was never about me, all that damage control. My mom, Aunt Sally, Regina…it was never about me."

CHAPTER 19

The Motherhood

As the millennium approached, I was a single mother and college student cohabitating with my best friend, sober and barely out on my own but managing to keep my head above water. My part-time waitressing wasn't pulling in quite as much as I'd have liked, so I made some extra cash on the weekends bartending at a local gay club.

I'd spent a lot of time in gay clubs, but never one so evenly split between men and women. There were two bars kitty-corner across the dance floor, the men's bar up front and the women's at the back. Alcohol had never been my poison, so my sobriety wasn't at risk. I'd mix drinks and flirt for tips, and most nights it was a pretty good time. Others…

"If I have to make one more fucking piña colada…" I grumbled. Frozen drinks were a major pain in the ass. Keeping up with everyone's orders is enough of a dance without stopping to grind ice and clean the blender every five minutes. That night, I was knee-deep in piña coladas, daiquiris, and margaritas, ready to throw one at the next person who asked.

"It's a birthday party," the other bartender said. "Just power through. The tips will be worth it."

I took her word for it as the music changed from ear-splitting techno to chill techno and conversation became possible once again.

"Could I get a Coors Light?"

I nodded to no one in particular, grabbed a bottle from the trough, and looked up to find a woman with olive skin and sleek black hair leaning on the bar. She took the bottle and thanked me.

"Thank *you*," I said. "All these fancy frozen drinks…"

"Yeah, I get it. Sorry about that."

Ah, she was with the party. So, I'd just been complaining to this woman about her friends. Wonderful. Fortunately, she didn't seem to take any offense, gave me her name—Val—and chatted me up for a few delightfully uneventful minutes. She kept smiling, and I kept smiling, and once my coworker gave me the all-clear, I headed toward the ladies' room, signaling Val to follow. We spent the next ten minutes making out in one of the stalls, barely managing to pull ourselves together and head back out before anyone noted our absences.

When I got back to the bar, it was too busy for my coworker to even notice me, and surprise, surprise, we were running low on margarita mix. I dashed across the dance floor to the men's bar for some.

"Hey, Felix, I need to borrow some mixer," I said to one of the bartenders. He wiped his forehead with his arm while making two different drinks in the chaos, barely acknowledging me before doing a double-take and smiling playfully.

"Ooh, girl! Who you been kissin'?"

I froze, suddenly self-conscious, then checked the mirror behind him to find lipstick smeared all around my mouth like a kid with too much ice cream. Felix dabbed a napkin in some water and handed it to me, and I cleaned my face off before retreating to the women's bar, hoping anyone who saw my flushed face would assume it was from working hard and nothing else.

I played the rest of the evening pretty cool, glancing at Val from across the room, which she seemed to like. We kept smiling at each other like we'd gotten away with skipping school. It was obviously a step up from the *guys* I'd dated, fond as I'd been of them, and coupling with Bella had been mixed up in so many other things—self-discovery, addiction, codependency—but with Val, it was just flirting, easy and uncomplicated.

She came around again the following weekend and the weekend after that: sly, sensible, and just a little mysterious. Things proceeded rather smoothly, and after a few months of dating, she showed up for my college graduation. After nearly a decade of false starts, I'd finally earned my bachelor's degree, still clean and sober, ready to step into whatever my life—my *real* life—was going to be. Bella and my family were also there for my big day. Evie wore a little blue, flowered dress, and we twirled around together on the vast lawn.

About a week later, I asked Bella if she could watch Evie for the evening so Val and I could go out to dinner. There was only a slight delay in her response, but it was enough for me to assure her there was no pressure. It was short notice, and I could find someone else.

"Nah, it's fine. I'll get some time alone with my girl," Bella said, lifting Evie up off the floor. She smiled at her, then turned that smile toward me, and it faded a bit. "It's getting serious, yeah? With Val."

"I guess so. We're not rushing it." Progress for me, really. Taking some time to feel things out and think them through went against all my instincts, but in this new stage of my life, I'd resolved to try some new approaches and see if they worked out better than what I'd always done before. I couldn't imagine they'd be any worse.

So far, taking things slow with Val was working out pretty well. We were getting serious. Bella was right about that. We'd already talked about moving in, but there were a lot of factors to consider, most importantly my daughter.

"Val and I agreed if we're still going strong in a year, we'll move in together. That was a couple months ago."

Bella nodded somberly, and I was about to apologize when she said, "Hey, we knew that sooner or later, you'd meet someone or I'd meet someone, and this…" she gestured to the apartment, "…would start, you know, winding down. It's okay, Nik. We're okay."

We'd both been well aware that playing house came with an expiration date, and while it was bittersweet that the end was finally in sight, our little experiment had been a success. It had done more for both of us than we ever could have hoped. It had gotten us clean, gotten us to a safe place, and set the stage for both of us to move on to whatever came next. And now it was time to start letting go.

As for Val, she understood that Bella and I weren't romantically involved and hadn't been for years, so there was no reason for us to stop being roommates right away, especially with several months left on our lease. Besides, Val and I had already agreed to wait a year before moving in together, practically an eternity in lesbian dating time.

We waited a year and one day.

Val was the vice president of a thriving family business, stable in a way I had only ever aspired to. She'd been living in Nutley when we'd met but was checking out real estate in the neighboring town of Montclair, and our year-long delay had given her plenty of time to find the perfect house.

Giving your kid a nice home in a clean, safe neighborhood is a dream come true for any parent, and our house was smack in the middle of one of the most picturesque streets I'd ever seen in my life: one gorgeous house after another, each with its own unique style and layout while still managing to blend in seamlessly with the rest of the neighborhood. There were seasonal decorations, well-tended lawns, and SUVs of every model and color.

I often felt like a tourist on vacation, seeing how long I could blend in with the locals before anyone caught on. I'd sometimes pause and let it sink in all over again that this big, sunny house was *my* house, a home Val and I had made together. I loved that it was a synthesis of our aesthetic tastes, which were, for the most part, very compatible, but I still wanted some space set aside to call my own, one little corner where I could just vibe, chill, and find a moment of peace whenever reconciling my old life with my new one grew too overwhelming.

I claimed the sunroom off the master bedroom for this purpose, and Val was content to let me have it. I perfumed the space with incense and decorated it with candles, small statuary, and books—*Be Here Now*, *The Seat of the Soul*, and of course Kahlil Gibran's *The Prophet*. My meditation room was a dash of bohemian groove in my otherwise conventional home, where I was always able to find my center. I could sit and breathe, finding guidance in the writings of Thích Nhất Hạnh, Caroline Myss, Eckhart Tolle, and of course, Deepak Chopra. And like any lesbian worth her salt, those Indigo Girls lyrics were always humming at the back of my mind.

And I wondered how long would it be till *my* soul got it right? At the rate I was going, I just might be able to heal it enough to find some peace and maybe even a little wisdom within this lifetime. For once, I felt like I was on my way.

The real challenge of blending into my new world began when Evie started preschool and I plunged into the suburban shark tank that is "the Motherhood." In some ways, I actually preferred dealing with gangsters and drug dealers. Say what you will about chronics and criminals; with them, you always know where you stand. Suburban parents are a lot trickier and certainly less direct.

Learning to navigate the bourgeois politics of upper-middle-class parents was quite a learning curve, but at the end of the day, it wasn't so bad. Overall, most of the moms were lovely women who welcomed me into the fold. Would they have been so eager if they'd known who I'd been only a few years earlier? Probably not, but why bother telling them? How would that conversation even go down? *Sure, Janet. I can totally help you bake some cupcakes for the nursery-school picnic. Just let me pee in this cup for my probation officer, and I'll be right over.*

Yeah, best to keep certain details to myself.

My new friends got to know the new me, and to my surprise, the very foibles I'd expected to keep me on the fringes of this little world ended up drawing me in deeper. My sly jokes, my meditation room, my commentary on the everyday quirks of suburban parenthood, and the stories of my wild past (just the PG ones, of course) made me a hit with everyone. After a lifetime of being the hopeless, fucked-up junkie, I was suddenly the hip, young mom of the group, and I kind of loved it.

I somehow became the mom other moms came to for advice or just to talk about life, as though I wasn't figuring it all out as I went along. Something about me just vibed "wisdom" to these women, and I went with it. It was hilarious when I stopped to think about how I'd become this everyday oracle, someone *with it* enough to have the answers they sought. I guess all those years of surviving had given me an insight into people that resonated. Against all hopes and expectations, I'd somehow arrived.

As I pushed my cart down the aisles of Whole Foods, I was amazed and grateful how I could give my kid fresh produce, starkly aware of what a far cry it was from pinching some restaurant-goer's table scraps. Despite my knack for adapting to new circumstances, I was taken aback by just how well and how quickly I'd assimilated into this affluent suburban community. I knew the lingo, the common topics of conversation, and all the faux pas to avoid, offenses which, with a little perspective, were nothing compared to my wild past.

I'd been an addict, a thief, a whore, an inmate, and a federally wanted drug lord. Meanwhile, the scandalous youths my new friends traded stories about over day wine usually amounted to a joint between classes or a tequila-fueled spring break.

Amateurs.

Despite how far I'd come, my mother still didn't approve of how I managed my life. I didn't really take it personally. She didn't approve of how *most* people managed their lives, and from her perspective, I was barely managing mine at all.

I don't really love the term "control freak." It's thrown around far too easily, most often at women for the crime of knowing what they want, so I don't like to give it too much oxygen. Sometimes, however, the term applies.

For as long as I could remember, my mother had a very strong opinion about everything. She was very particular and very neurotic, and if everything wasn't in its proper place, you may as well have been living at ground zero. Control freaks perceive their surroundings in one of two states, perfection or abject chaos; there is no in-between, so the fact that I might leave some mail on the dining room table for a day or two or a plate out on my counter for a few hours marked me as a walking disaster.

One day, Michelle, an acquaintance I'd met in a kickboxing class (because why not?), had come over for some help with an editing project. Video editing had been an essential component of my degree, and I did occasional freelance work on the side when I had the time to spare, so I was more than happy to give her a hand. We were sitting at my kitchen table when my mom stopped by to drop something off. I can't remember what it was, but she asked me to bring it in from the car, so I introduced her to Michelle and went out to get it.

I was gone for maybe two minutes, then came back inside for a bit of small talk before my mom took off. With a sweet smile, Michelle told her how nice it had been to meet her, but her cheerful mask dropped the instant we were alone.

"That was so weird," she said.

"What? What did she say? Whatever it was, I'm sorry."

Michelle shook her head. "No, she didn't offend me or anything, but while you were out there, she started looking around and saying, 'Oh, I would never keep my house like this. It's a mess. I'd never do this.' And then she talked shit about you until you came back in. Like, literally until she heard the doorknob turn. It was bizarre. For the first thirty seconds, I assumed she was joking, because who would do that? I don't even know her."

I sighed, disappointed but hardly surprised. "Again…I'm sorry."

Michelle shook her head, not needing an apology as much as an explanation.

"I just don't get it. Even if the things she said were true, which they're not, she's your mom. Why would she throw you under the bus like that to a stranger?"

I shrugged it off, and we got back to work, but I spent the rest of the afternoon stewing. Not only had my mother made my friend uncomfortable, she'd shit-talked me in my own home, *about* my own home, for absolutely no reason. My house was beautiful and always clean. Maybe there'd be a jacket thrown over a chair or a healthy bit of clutter that comes with raising kids, but it was hardly chaotic and *never* unsanitary.

I didn't have an answer for Michelle. I had no idea why my mom had felt the need to humiliate me like that, to paint me as a failure to my friend. What had her goal been? What could she have possibly gotten out of it? It wasn't an innocent bit of conversation, as she'd no doubt have claimed if I'd called her out. I could hear the entire script play out the way it had so many times before.

What? Who, me?! I would never say something like that! Only…you did. *Ugh, you're being too sensitive.* No. No, I'm not. *It was just a joke!* It's only a joke once you can't get away with it. *All right, well, then I guess you'll just have to return me to the mom store and get another one!* The thing was…I'd had another mom, a drug-dealing drag queen in Oahu who had loved me enough to send me away and never see me again, to lose me in order to save me. My own mother had never made any such sacrifices. I'd *been* the sacrifice for more important things.

I'd spent my entire youth drowning, scorned for it by the very people who'd thrown me in the water, and now that I had swum back to shore, coughed up half the sea, and picked myself up to walk in the sun, my mother had the *audacity* to criticize my stride?!

This hadn't been the first time she'd pulled some shit like this, and I knew it wouldn't be the last. There were always little asides and passive-aggressive comments insinuating I was failing as a mother. She came at me several years later with this pained look on her face, giving me some bullshit about how I wasn't feeding my kids (Val and I eventually had another child, but I'll get to that), how they would tell her all the time that they were hungry. Then she acted out their plea in this maudlin whimper. "Nonny, I'm hungry…I'm so hungry…."

As if I didn't make their lunches every day. As if they didn't have a fridge and pantry, as well as a deep freezer in the basement, full of quality food. My kids got three square meals a day plus snacks, and we're talking nutritious, filling food. They were always hungry because they were growing kids with bottomless stomachs. And no matter how many times I explained this to my mother, showed her the fridge and the pantry, had her over to the house for a dinner I'd cooked myself, every conversation was always a complete reset, right back to square one.

The critique went beyond tidiness and even nutrition. She pulled me aside on one occasion to lecture me about how my children were dirty and I wasn't bathing them properly, which was complete horseshit.

My girls took a bath or shower almost every night. That bathroom was full of shampoos, body wash, and fresh towels. They went to bed clean, they went to school clean, so what the hell was my mother even talking about? It made no sense.

Then, eventually, something clicked. I realized it didn't have to make sense. It was never meant to. I had come so far from where I'd been only a few years ago and built a beautiful life with my beautiful family in our beautiful home, and none of it fucking mattered, because to my mother, it would never be beautiful enough.

CHAPTER 20

Living Proof

The August air was sweet with citronella and jasmine as Evie and her friends giggled and chased each other across the backyard. The kids were still sweaty and flushed from a day of jungle gyms and ice pops. I watched them from the patio along with the other moms as we exchanged the details of our perfectly imperfect suburban lives.

After everyone said their goodbyes and I put Evie to bed, I retreated to the third floor of my charming eighty-year-old house, where we'd fashioned one of the rooms into a makeshift home office. I sat myself in front of the clunky PC, where I did little more than check my email every other day and write papers for my grad school night classes, and considered what I might do with all the hours I'd gain once Evie started pre-K in a few weeks. A master's in counseling would look great on my résumé once I started hunting for a job, but how much of that cred would be undercut by a criminal past that wasn't entirely past? The cold, hard truth was that most prospective employers would see five years of probation still ahead of me and make their judgments without looking much deeper.

I always knew getting my life back on track would be difficult. I'd had no idea it would be quite so complicated.

My thoughts drifted to that day in court five years earlier, when I'd gotten the unlikely opportunity to start over, and to Reinette, who had fought to secure me that chance. We'd lost touch after a few phone calls and Christmas cards, but every so often I wondered how she was doing and what she might be up to. Her number was still in my address book, faded but legible, so I called and left a message on her answering machine.

She called me back the very next day, asking countless questions about me and Evie before I could even ask her for an update.

"Your timing is uncanny," Reinette said "I was just thinking about your case. I'm actually in the process of becoming a judge, and before I do, I've got a few loose ends to tie up."

"And I'm one of them." Rather than deny it, she just chuckled.

"Tell me, Nikki…how would you like to close your case a little early, shave off the last five years of your probation?"

She was right. The timing *was* uncanny. Talk about an offer I couldn't refuse.

Reinette and I talked for a few weeks while she petitioned the court for an early review of my probation. If the court agreed to hear her argument, she would have to do a little research and file a few documents, but all signs pointed to the closing of my case being a simple matter of paperwork.

The signs lied.

I was making a snack in my newly remodeled kitchen when Reinette called, her voice lacking the optimism I'd gotten so used to.

"There's good news and bad news," she said, her disappointment audible even over the semi-crappy phone connection. "The good news is that Judge Milks agreed to hear your case."

I slouched against the kitchen counter, bracing myself for the worst. "And the bad news?"

"She's still a stone-cold hardass. I could sing your praises till I'm blue in the face, but she's not going to take my word for it. You're going to have to come back to Hawaii for a hearing in October."

A pang of nausea came and went, and I took a deep breath. "I have to?"

"You could decline, but if Milks can't see you for herself, in the flesh, there's no way she's going to rule in your favor."

As bad news went, it could have been a lot worse. Still, this meant a decision in my favor was going to be a lot iffier than we'd been hoping. Winning Judge Milks over was going to be a lot more involved, and I was going to have to *get* involved, in person. If I could convince her of my progress, I might be free. If not, I'd have spent a lot of time, money, and energy to still be looking at five more years of the legal system breathing down my neck, always paranoid that some teenager getting caught with a dime bag on my block was going to void the terms of my release and send the life I'd worked so hard to build crashing down around me.

I stood in my shiny new kitchen, all stainless steel and granite countertops, clutching the receiver. Sure, the worst that could happen was the denial of my request, and I'd be back where I was before Reinette's call in August. But as long as my probation hung over my head, so did everything that came with it, including the constantly looming threat of reincarceration. Living with that much paranoia wasn't good for the soul, much less my blood pressure.

Val and I sat up in bed that night, talking, Evie asleep between us. She took the news about as well as could be expected. After two years of hearing stories about my shady past, she understood what was at stake and why I needed to pursue any possibility of having my case dismissed. She needed it too; my baggage wasn't doing her any favors.

"Okay, so we'll go," Val said matter-of-factly. "Might as well make it a family trip."

She was right, of course. Looking down at Evie, I knew immediately that the judge needed to see her. She was living proof of everything I'd accomplished, and if Judge Milks could see us together, I just might have a chance.

In an act of optimism or perhaps just plain old wishful thinking, I booked a ten-day trip for the three of us. We set our arrival on the day before my court date, so that we had the time afterward to either relax and celebrate or to rest up to face another five years of uncertainty.

It's a ten-hour flight from Newark to Oahu, and it feels like longer at the back of a packed plane with a five-year-old in tow. Not that Evie was much trouble. She was almost as quiet on the plane to Hawaii as she'd been on the trip out five years prior. She barely made a peep the whole way there.

I spent the entire cab ride to the hotel staring out the window, reminders of my past rolling by. Every hundred feet, I was faced with a corner where I used to deal, an alley where I turned tricks, even a lamppost Jeremiah had danced on. It was like watching a movie cut together from memories of another life. Some made me smile, others cut me to the bone. The entire island was littered with ghosts of my past, so far from what my life was about now, but as clear as if it had all happened yesterday, and I wondered—was part of me still that girl? And if so, did it show? Would it show in court? Unwilling to be haunted a moment longer, I turned away. Thankfully, we'd reached the hotel.

The Moana Surfrider was a five-star resort, the staff waiting outside in their crisp white uniforms to greet us with leis. The concierge checked us in with a broad smile, the kind I would never have received back when they used to catch me lurking around, up to some kind of illicit business or other. I wondered what they'd think if they knew this mild-looking, casually dressed mother they graciously welcomed was once the same tweaking, homeless hooker they'd have called security on for sleeping on the beach outside.

Wild.

I tried that night for a solid eight hours, so I'd show up to court looking fresh and alert, with all my shit squarely together, but sleep didn't come easy. My nerves wouldn't allow it, and a sedative was, for obvious reasons, not an option. Even if I wouldn't be risking my sobriety, which I would, I wasn't about to chance showing up in court groggy and spaced out. All the more reason I probably should have booked the flight a day earlier to sleep off the jet lag, but it was too late now. It was well past midnight when I finally relaxed, the sight of Evie sleeping soundly beside me easing my nerves just enough to allow a few hours of peace.

We arrived at the courthouse right after breakfast, where Reinette greeted me with a huge hug. We'd been talking back and forth for months, discussing strategy and what to tell the judge, but seeing her in the flesh brought it all back: everything she'd done for me back then, how hard she'd gone to bat for me. The life I'd built had been possible in large measure because of her. I returned her hug and introduced her to Val and to Evie, whom she'd last seen at only a few weeks old—a lovely moment that passed far too quickly.

"Okay, so just a heads up: There will be some reporters here, mostly from your original case." I wasn't surprised. One of Oahu's biggest meth dealers going before one of the toughest judges on the island had been pretty big news back in the day and apparently still was. "Just try to ignore them. Now, the prosecution is not going to take it easy on you—"

"Wonderful."

"—but if we play this right, we get your case closed, and you walk out of that courtroom with all of this behind you, so eyes on the prize." I nodded, and she patted my shoulder. "Attagirl," she said with a wink.

As promised, the courtroom was full of onlookers and press. I followed Reinette past them, projecting more confidence than I actually felt, and we took our seats at the defense table, across the aisle from the two prosecutors whose sole purpose was to reduce me to the mess I'd been five years ago.

When the honorable Marie Milks took her seat, she eyed me from the bench with every drop of skepticism she'd had for the pregnant, strung-out prostitute I'd been when she'd last seen me. Evie, sitting behind me and looking like an angel in her white cotton dress, didn't even seem to register for Milks. Off to a great start there.

Milks called the prosecution first, and just as Reinette had warned me, they didn't pull any punches.

"Ms. Mammano's request to have the remainder of her probation voided is preposterous, especially in light of the leniency she's already received. We're talking about a felon convicted on multiple counts. For someone with her degree of involvement in the local drug trade to simply walk away with little more than a slap on the wrist would set a very dangerous precedent, especially in light of the near epidemic crystal meth has become here in Hawaii. The people strongly urge Your Honor to enforce the remainder of her probation."

Judge Milks appeared inscrutable, barely blinking. The floor dropped out from beneath me. If I hadn't been seated, I would have lost my footing. I turned to Reinette, feeling a flush of panic, and she just nodded to me, her eyes calm and reassuring.

As Reinette delivered my defense, she was careful to keep eye contact with Judge Milks but glanced back at me here and there with an encouraging smile. It went a long way toward preventing me from dissolving into a sweaty, tearful mess.

"It's true, Nicole Mammano has received a great deal of leniency from this court. And she's shown her gratitude for it by not only complying fully with the terms of her probation but exceeding them beyond all expectations. In five years, she hasn't missed a single appointment with her probation officer, hasn't failed a single drug screening, and she's currently finishing up her master's degree in counseling so that she can assist other addicts in their own recovery.

"She hasn't just complied with the bare minimum. She's worked hard and proven herself, so, while living with the stress of probation for another five years would certainly be inconvenient, she could do it. The question is, should she have to? Or has she proven that she deserves to finally put the past behind her?"

The silence that followed as Judge Milks considered Reinette's words was deafening and seemed to drag on forever. Finally, Milks pinched the bridge of her nose, then leaned forward, looking straight into my eyes. Her frown, whether from disdain or ambivalence, was like a punch to the gut.

"Ms. Mammano, have you anything to add?"

Oh, fuck. I'd known from the beginning that the judge might call on me to speak for myself, but I'd convinced myself it wasn't likely. I'd made a bullet list with Reinette of the major points I'd need to hit, but suddenly none of that mattered. I felt something swelling in my chest, smothering my nerves and my fear. It was pure, simple gratitude.

I rose slowly, Reinette beside me. Whether that was protocol or just support I still don't know, but I appreciated the gesture, because at that moment I was sure of how Judge Milks saw me. To be honest, it was how I still saw myself in quiet moments when I was alone: the same meth-addled fuckup whose life had imploded on the streets of Waikiki, hiding behind a crisp haircut and a fitted button-down. Standing there in front of the woman who knew my sins—not even all of them, but more than enough to condemn me—there was nothing else to do but speak from the heart.

"Five years ago, you gave me a chance. I took that chance and did everything with it that you asked of me. I'm clean. I went back and finished college. I'm in a master's program now." I turned and nodded to Evie, who sat behind me, wide-eyed and probably very confused, but not scared. "And this is my beautiful daughter." There were probably a hundred more things I could have said, but none of them mattered. There Evie was, living proof. I turned back around and looked up at Judge Milks's stern face. "So, I guess I just want to thank you."

Judge Milks rested her face on her palm, studying my file for the longest thirty seconds of my life. I could only guess what she was thinking. You don't become the first woman appointed to the circuit court by falling for every sob story, and her record was evidence that she hadn't. She saw lies, mistrust, and failed promises every day. She had a nose for bullshit, and the benefit of the doubt was not a tool she kept in her front pocket. She wasn't likely to serve it up a second time, not with those odds.

I was screwed. I just knew it. And then, Judge Milks picked up my file, wiped away a tear, and shook her head.

"No—I want to thank *you*. I was hesitant to give you a second chance. In my experience, they tend not to pan out. I had my doubts, but you proved me wrong." She sniffed, then straightened up and held my file even higher for the whole courtroom to see. "From now on, when I give others second chances, it'll be because of you." She nodded with a soft smile and banged her gavel. "You're free to go."

And just like that, I was.

Reinette hugged me, then gathered up her things as onlookers and members of the press approached me with kind words and congratulations. Even the prosecutors, who had just brought their A-game to keep me in the system, shook my hand and sincerely wished me the best of luck. Val beamed at me, relieved, and Evie—well, she had no idea what was going on, but understood that it was time to cheer and celebrate, and was happy to jump in. I was indescribably proud of myself, not just for winning the day, but for actually deserving it. In my eagerness to convince Judge Milks of my worthiness, I'd ended up convincing myself.

Reinette shook her head as she walked us outside. "I cannot believe you made her cry. Marie fucking Milks. You made *Judge Milks* cry." She chuckled. "*Now* I have seen everything." Val and I laughed, and she squeezed my hand as we stepped out into a warm Oahu breeze.

Glancing at her watch, Reinette said, "I'd say let's grab a bite to celebrate, but I've got to catch my flight home." She'd day-tripped from

Maui for my hearing. "But listen, why don't you all come visit me before you leave, and we can have that celebratory meal?"

We happily agreed, thanked Reinette another four or five times, and parted ways. Rather than head straight back to the hotel, Val and I thought it would be nice to walk for a bit, so we set off down the sidewalk, each of us holding one of Evie's hands as we breathed in the salty air. Evie's tiny hand grounded me, a good thing, because I could have floated away, I felt so light.

It was over. I was walking the streets of Oahu not as an addict or a dealer, not as a convicted felon, not even under probation, but as a free woman with nothing left to drag me down and hold me back from a future that beckoned me forward, gleaming with possibility.

For the next nine days, we made the most of our family vacation. Since Evie had left Hawaii at just a few weeks old, we wanted to make as many memories as we could. I must have taken a hundred photos, but I would challenge anyone looking at that little girl smiling on a sandy beach to say it was too many.

We visited the Polynesian Cultural Center, walked the beach, and gazed at nightly fire shows. Like tourists, we attended a luau and listened to men in delightfully loud shirts sing beautiful Hawaiian songs, strumming their ukuleles as hula dancers rolled and swayed to the music, emulating the waves behind them. Evie blended right in, passing for a native Islander with her silky black hair, light brown skin, and little grass skirt.

Reinette made good on her offer, treating the three of us to lunch in Maui at a fabulous restaurant and following it up with a trip to the beach, showing us where lava had flowed into the sea long ago and hardened into black rocks. We capped it off with some snorkeling in water that was impossibly blue, watching schools of tropical fish swim by.

In all the years I'd lived in Hawaii, there were so many things I'd never done, some of them so simple and amazing. I'd missed so much, thrown away so many opportunities. The realization made me sad—but also reminded me how rich my life could be now. Despite the seesawing emotions and constant reminders of where and who I'd been, I had no desire to use drugs at any point during that entire trip. Not once. I wanted to experience every moment of it as the real Nikki, and I finally could.

And I did.

CHAPTER 21

Family Dysfunctions

My parents are absolutely in love with New England, and most summers, they rented a house in Massachusetts or New Hampshire to enjoy some local color, fresh seafood, and craft fairs for a week or two.

One year, they got a rental in Cape Cod and invited me and my family to spend a few days there. At dinner, Mom turned to me and asked, "How long are you planning to stay? I want to invite the Beckmanns, so I just need to know your schedule."

I'd been very clear in recent years that, while it was beyond my control whether or not my mother chose to maintain ties with Regina and her family, I couldn't be part of it. For my own mental health and continued prosperity, I didn't want to see them, talk to them, or even hear about them. As far as I was concerned, they didn't exist.

I suppose she was trying to accommodate the boundary I'd set by scheduling these visits so that they wouldn't overlap. Partial credit for good intentions, but if you have to trigger my trauma as part of your efforts to avoid triggering my trauma, you've lost the plot.

"Could you please stop talking about the Beckmanns in front of me," I pleaded. "Every time you do, it just brings up memories of what happened."

There was no counterpoint to be made, so none was attempted, and we went on with dinner. I immediately considered my mom's question, though. How long should we really stay? The vibe had kind of been ruined, but then again, I had spoken. I doubted it would be the last reminder my mom would ever need—Rome wasn't built in a day—but surely the coast would be clear for the rest of our visit now that I'd drawn the line.

"Oh, and Regina was telling me about..."

Whatever my mother said, I didn't even hear the rest of it. Three minutes had passed. Three minutes, no more. Val and I froze and looked at each other, silently exchanging the question of the hour: What the fuck? Val was a seasoned businesswoman. She'd made an impressive career out of taking charge and speaking her mind, and in that moment, she was absolutely fucking floored.

"Did that actually happen back there?" Val asked me later in our room. "You literally just asked her to stop. Forget for a second how insane it is that your mom and aunt stayed friends with this woman—"

"I know, I know," I said, pushing it aside, and Val was good enough to take my lead and let it go. I shrugged it all off in the moment, but that night sparked something, a tiny fire that burned away the last of the excuses I'd internalized and any desire I'd felt to make allowances for that kind of bullshit. Val had been right. My mother's behavior at dinner had been thoughtless and hurtful, and I was done letting it slide.

Barbara eyed me patiently from her chair, waiting for me to continue. After a long silence, she said, "So, did you confront your mother again?"

"Not during that trip but soon after. I told her how it all had affected me and how hurtful it had been and why. And I don't know what got through to her that time, but it was like she finally got it. She realized she was losing me and that she had a choice to make." I shrugged, my disappointment still raw years after the fact. "Still, it took her a while to realize she couldn't have it both ways."

"Meaning?"

"I guess she thought it might work, that she could ignore Jacob and somehow stay best friends with his mom, keep the three sisters together and keep all our families together as best they could, but that's not what happened."

Shortly after my mom had arrived in Rhode Island for a visit with Regina, Jacob had walked through the door with his new girlfriend, eager to introduce her. And for all I can and do blame Jacob for, I can't fault him for thinking that scenario would have been perfectly normal. That's what we'd both been taught, a permissiveness our mothers had gone to great lengths to drill into us. There he was, the man who had violated me more times than I could even remember, seeking my mother's affection as sincerely as a child. Much to everyone's surprise, she didn't show him any. She shunned him. It was a ballsy move. How she *expected* Regina to react is anybody's guess, but it did not go over well.

"So, Regina's like, 'What the fuck? If you don't accept my son, then you're out of my life.' Which I can actually understand. Regina stood up for her kid, whether he deserved it or not, because that's what mothers do. I guess my mom really thought she could have her cake and eat it too, be friends with Regina while giving Jacob the silent treatment, but—"

Barbara shook her head. "That was never possible."

"I know. The thing is, I really do feel bad for her. Her biggest fear was losing that connection. She demolished me to hold on to it, and when she finally came around and chose me over Regina, her worst fear came true. She was on the outside."

"So, your aunt remained friends with Regina?"

"Well, yeah. Like *my* aunt was going to cut her off in solidarity? No fucking way."

My brief return to Hawaii had provided the closure I needed to complete my metamorphosis and thrive in my new identity. With that new freedom came a feeling that just about anything was possible. I could start planning for a future, something more than just a stable status quo. That included expanding my family.

Val and I had decided early on that I would carry any children we might have together, so from there it was just a matter of finding the right donor.

In early 2004, I delivered our second daughter, Dani, by C-section. Shortly after I came home from the hospital, Aunt Sally called and asked if I was up for a visit so she could meet the baby. I was still recovering physically and wasn't up for any huge family functions, but a low-key visit in my own home? Sure, why not? So, I made some lunch and readied myself for some fawning over my baby and perhaps some small talk about my C-section, neither of which happened. When Aunt Sally arrived, she said hello and barely acknowledged Dani's presence or my convalescence before she started in on her true objective.

"Nikki, honey…this thing with the Beckmanns…"

I flinched. She could *not* be serious. I hadn't spoken to those people in years. I didn't know them anymore and had no desire to. And while I felt bad that my mother had lost a friend in the process of doing right by me, I wouldn't have changed it. If her estrangement from Regina was even a problem to be solved, it sure as hell wasn't mine.

"Things are so tense right now," Aunt Sally continued. "All the kids are going to be getting married in the next few years, and if the Beckmanns are invited, Matt and Emily won't come to their own brothers' weddings. And you know *that's* not an option, so…" She sighed, shaking her head like she was envisioning some unspeakable tragedy. "I just can't imagine the Beckmanns not being there. You have to make things right with them. We're all *family*."

But we weren't. Aunt Sally's kids were family. *I* was family. Regina was a friend who'd been elevated way too high above her station. Not to dismiss the significance of found family—my dearest friends have come through for me where my relatives have failed time after time—but your loyalties should never lie with people who hurt your kids and your sister's kids, no matter who they are.

But this wasn't even about family. Aunt Sally didn't give a fuck whether or not *I* would be at my cousins' weddings as long as all her kids and her precious friends were there. The thing is, her family was already divided on the issue.

Matt and Emily's brothers were Michael's age and, like him, they'd been too young when everything had gone down with Jacob for any of it to register at the time. In the years since, they'd been raised to view what little they *had* learned through the lens of our parents' delusions: this mutually agreed-upon fiction where whatever had happened to their older siblings hadn't been anything *that* bad. So, they didn't have a gripe. This division between my cousins had nothing to do with me, and yet somehow in Aunt Sally's mind, getting her house in order was my problem to solve.

When I relayed this story to Emily a few days later, her eyes bugged out of her head. She looked like she couldn't decide whether to laugh or scream and assured me her mother had acted completely on her own and hadn't at all represented how she felt. Matt seethed quietly across the table, right on the edge of exploding.

"This is so fucked," he said. "What is she thinking? That if you come around on the issue, I will? As if Jacob didn't beat the shit out of me on a regular basis? He nearly killed me that one time, and Regina just played it all off like it was nothing. Every time. *Every time.* And that's not even going into what he did to you and almost did to Emily! No way. Even if you were okay with it, I would *never* be."

Emily shook her head. "Me neither."

I was grateful to have them on my side, to know I wasn't alone and wasn't being crazy or petty, that the way I felt toward the Beckmanns was not only justified but shared. I considered the matter closed, which was horribly naïve of me, because, though it took a few years, that beast reared its head once again.

My grandmother died just shy of her ninetieth birthday. More than once in those final years, we'd all been sure it was the end, but she always bounced back from the brink until finally, in the spring of 2007, she took another bad turn. After spending some time in a hospice facility, she decided this time to meet the end in her own home.

Living only half an hour away and having a more flexible schedule than most, I ended up stepping in to help with quite a bit of her hospice care, often staying the night. I sat with her, talked to her when she was scared, and set an alarm so I'd be able to administer her meds at the right time throughout the night to keep her comfortable.

It was so bizarre seeing her that way. She'd always been a force of nature, this *grande dame* who suffered no fools and passed her word down as law: the matriarch of my family. And while she could be overbearing at times—all right, most of the time—in those last days, she was so weak and scared, so *human*, that I actually felt bad for her. She wasn't the elegant bully who'd spent her entire life jerking people around in the service of her ego. She was just an old woman at the end of her life, with no belief at all in anything that lay beyond, and she was terrified.

And yes, it did occur to me that this was the woman who had encouraged the cult of personality that had birthed Hippie House, and thus indirectly bore some responsibility for the abuse at the root of all my sad stories. She'd inspired and encouraged that entire community of festering dysfunction, each pathology feeding the others, creating an environment ideally suited to my abuse. She had spurred the competition between her own daughters for her affection and approval, which had led to their own obsessions with control and shaping the narrative, which had in turn led to the piss-poor handling of the aftermath of my abuse and all the suffering that had come out of it. The roots of it all lay in my grandmother's narcissism, and yet, as she lay dying, all I could do was love her.

Death doesn't wipe the slate clean. It doesn't give the dying a free pass for the wrongs they've done, but it does have a way of softening your heart toward them, even if they've hurt you. It's a lot of conflicting emotions to process all at once. Of course, no one is obligated to care for family members who have hurt them, and I'm no better or worse than anyone for the choice I made. Truth be told, had I been more healed at that point, I might have chosen differently, but I didn't then, and I don't regret it now.

Mom and Aunt Sally would come by to spend time with their mother, and for all the annoyance and resentment I felt toward both of them, I could see that watching their mother fade away was probably the worst experience of their lives. Even my grandmother's declining faculties in those final years couldn't knock her from the pedestal my mom had placed her on. To the very end, she remained the gold standard that could never be met.

I knew better. I loved my grandmother but had no illusions about who she was. She was intelligent and frank, cultured and generous, but she was also controlling, often condescending, and at times even cruel. And you can totally see the generational divide between the Baby Boomers and Generation X by comparing how we deal with this kind of behavior.

Our Boomer parents were taught that family ties confer some kind of irrevocable state of grace. Toxic and abusive behavior may not be *okay*, but you are expected to forgive it, or at the very least let it slide, because it's family and that's just what you do. And our parents had bought into that hype like their parents before them and *their* parents before *them*. And then, Gen X came along and said, "No, that's bullshit. No one, even a relative—especially a relative—should get a free pass for hurting you."

It's not that we ourselves are perfect people or, for that matter, perfect parents. I've fucked up like every other parent since the dawn of time. It's inevitable. And forgiveness isn't impossible; it's just not taken for granted. It's not a given. Some degree of accountability and genuine contrition is the bare minimum required. "Oh, that was so long ago" and "I'm sorry I wasn't the perfect parent!" simply do not cut it anymore.

Our parents *hate* it when we take this tack, because it was drilled into them that when it came to family, especially their elders, they were to forgive whatever fucked-up shit they were able to rationalize and form a massive blind spot to whatever they couldn't. This is why they crossed certain lines with us: because they were comfortable enough to do so, believing that however ugly things might get in the short term, there would never be any *real* consequences in the end. Family is family, and you just have to deal. Then, after spending their lives perpetuating that cycle at their own expense, putting up with decades of their own parents' unrepentant toxicity, when their kids push back and refuse to do the same, they go completely apeshit. *Why can't you just grow up and, you know, let people fuck with you for the rest of your life? We all had to do it!*

Well, sorry, Mom and Dad, aunts and uncles. I'm sorry that you spent your lives putting up with a bunch of crazy bullshit you didn't have to. I'm sorry you predicated countless choices on a faulty premise. But it's not my cross to bear, and it's certainly not my kids', and this shit ends with me. But I digress.

My point being…I loved my grandparents, but they weren't saints. They were downright abusive at times, but my mom would die before ever admitting it. And now that my grandmother was dying, those rose-colored glasses were likely never coming off again. But I would know the truth. I would know how her high expectations and casual criticism had shaped my mother and created in her an insatiable hunger for validation and a near-phobia of mistakes and messes…things life just happens to be full of.

My grandmother had inspired not just the love and devotion of a daughter, but the awe and reverence of an acolyte. My mom hadn't aspired to *become* her mother—in many ways, they were very different women—but she'd aspired to her standard of excellence. My grandmother had been her heroine, her mentor, her sage…and now she was losing her. And even though I could see that dynamic was at least a little fucked up, I felt a compassion for my mother I don't think I'd ever felt before. And I thought that maybe I could move on. Maybe now, at this cataclysmic generational shift for all of us, it was time.

She died in the early morning, and I was sitting with her when she finally let go. Within an hour, family began to trickle in. While everyone gathered to comfort my grandfather and each other over bagels and coffee, Matt pulled me aside and asked me to join him in the hallway outside the apartment.

"You know the Beckmanns are going to come to the funeral, probably the shiva too," he said. It wasn't a warning. He already knew I'd assumed as much. He was just checking in. "However you want to handle this, I'll back you up."

I thanked him but assured him I'd be fine. And I mostly was. Knowing I'd be seeing any or all of that family was a trigger I would rather not have dealt with, but I was tired of fighting the quiet shade thrown my way every time I "forced" people to tiptoe around me on the matter of the Beckmanns. And I saw my grieving mother, who had lost so much: first Regina, then other friends through death, distance, or a falling out, and now my grandmother. Hadn't everyone been through enough?

I was tired of it all, tired of it hanging over me, of being resented and having this mess laid at my feet, so I decided it might be best to try and put it all behind me. I mean, wasn't that what I'd been trained to do my whole life?

Convinced there was no other choice, that it was my responsibility to fix everything before it imploded completely, I went home and wrote Jacob a letter, assuring him that I forgave him and that it was over; everything was behind us now, and we could all be okay. Every word of it was forced, but I was convinced it was a necessary one. Wouldn't everyone hate me if I didn't do this, didn't rise above?

When I saw Regina at the shiva, she came up to me and took my face in her hands. I stood there frozen, silently screaming "What the fuck?!" as this woman I didn't even like brushed my hair out of my eyes like some beloved auntie. I just pulled away, handed her the letter for Jacob, and avoided her until she left.

Months later, Jacob called me to thank me for what I'd written and ask if we could meet up at some point in the nearish future. I would have refused—I wasn't interested in anything he had to say, and he didn't exactly live around the corner—but I couldn't. Didn't I ask for this when I wrote him that letter? Didn't I have to do this for everyone?

I told Jacob that since our family would be vacationing in Rhode Island in a couple of months, I would carve out a few hours to see him. Paul went with me, partly out of solidarity and partly out of morbid curiosity about what Jacob could possibly have to say for himself. He gave us a brief tour of his place, which was dotted with pictures of him with his family, his friends, and the new baby he had with his fiancée, then suggested we all go for a walk.

After we'd exhausted all the chit-chat we could stomach, we stopped to sit on some rocks, and Jacob apologized to both of us, *really* apologized. And I believe he meant it. That didn't make it better, not to me and certainly not to Paul, who was deeply uncomfortable the whole time. He'd suffered at Jacob's hands too—not as extensively as I had, but one time is all it takes to leave a deep scar, and it had been more than once.

I was the first to accept Jacob's apology. Paul hadn't been conditioned as I had to smooth things over and swallow his pain. He did swallow a lot of pain, but he'd never felt that burden of diplomacy, and he wasn't gung ho about making nice. Though reluctant, he accepted Jacob's apology once I did. And then, just when we thought this scenario couldn't get any more bizarre, Jacob invited us to his wedding.

"It's in the fall, and I'd love to have your family there." He went on to talk about the rift between our parents, how unfortunate it had been for everyone, and how, if we went, our mom would go, and it might heal those ties. That was all I needed to hear to fall back into the role of diplomat, to accept everyone's harmony as my responsibility, no matter how much it hurt, no matter how many old wounds it tore open.

I ended up going to the wedding, along with Mom, Gene, and my brothers. Aunt Sally was there with her two younger sons. Matt and Emily were notably absent, having made perfectly clear to me beforehand that they wouldn't be going and couldn't fathom why I was. They knew how to take care of themselves, how to stand their ground. That resolve had never been ripped away from them the way it had been from me.

"Why?" Emily asked when I'd told her I was going. "What's the point? You don't owe them shit." I just nodded and shrugged it off, because… didn't I? Didn't I owe it to everyone?

At the reception, everyone was laughing and dancing. Paul and I were being appropriately social but a little more aloof than I think everyone wanted. My mom greeted Regina and offered her congratulations, which were accepted graciously but not warmly. Every attempt my mom made at reconciliation was coolly rebuffed, just shy enough of the cold shoulder to avoid making a scene, but anyone who knew better could see it. That bridge was burned, and Regina was over it.

The heartbreak in my mother's eyes made me simultaneously furious that she still wanted this reconciliation and sad for her that she'd been denied it. She had finally stood up for me, had lost everything for it, and would never get it back. I felt terrible and knew I had to do something, *anything,* to smooth things over. I found myself approaching Jacob on the dance floor, then slow-dancing with him very deliberately in front of everyone as if to say, "See? See? It's all good. It's fine. We can all be fine." But it didn't work. Regina never gave my mother another inch, and all I'd accomplished was a dance with my abuser.

As I swayed with Jacob on the dance floor, forcing myself to return his contented smile, it finally sank in. I felt something inside me turn and shift as I looked around at everyone smiling, all of them just so happy that we were all together, eating and laughing.

Just like brunch.

It stuck in me like a thorn until the whole illusion burst, and I could see everything. How dare they? How dare they look at me with contempt for pointing out that the emperor had no clothes? How dare they tell me black was white, up was down, that the true crime in all of this wasn't my abuse, but how I'd ruined everyone's good time by calling it out?

Fuck that and fuck this, I thought as the song faded out. I retreated to my seat at the edge of the room and never spoke another word to Jacob or Regina again.

"It was stupid to go," I said to Matt years later. "What was I even thinking? It's just crazy, how our moms had thrown me to the wolves my entire life. How could they do that?"

"Nikki," Matt said in a voice somewhere between love and pity, "You were always expendable. For the good of the family…you were expendable."

I knew at once that he was right. I *had* been expendable for years, decades, almost my entire life. I'd been brainwashed into believing the original sin had been mine, that I was the horrible, shameful child too selfish to just choke on my tears and let the dancing continue. Well, that was over.

Nothing I could do could heal the rift between Mom and Regina. Nothing could put things back the way they were. And for once, I was fine with that, because it wasn't up to me. It had never been up to me. It was neither my place nor my problem to fix what deserved to be broken, and I resolved right then and there that I had betrayed myself for the last time and would never take their sickness onto myself again.

CHAPTER 22

Down the Rabbit Hole

Casting off my family's bullshit was a huge moment for me, but I'd be lying if I said it was the happily ever after I'd hoped it would be. Life goes on, and sometimes the price of knowing the score is knowing the score. My family—my generation alone—was rife with anger issues, relationship problems, and histories of addiction, but I had been singled out as the cautionary tale, the lightning rod for everyone's disapproval.

It was easy enough to say fuck it, that I'd maintain ties with them on a case-by-case basis and not worry myself about the rest, but things are never that cut and dried. It still hurt, knowing how raw a deal I'd gotten and how okay with it everyone had seemed to be. It left a lot of ragged edges in my soul, an undercurrent of discontent roiling quietly beneath the surface while I went about my life, which was more than busy enough to distract me.

Val had come along at just the right time in my life, and I truly believe that sometimes people are meant to *get* together even if they aren't meant to *stay* together. For eleven years, Val and I could always be counted on to throw a great party or host a sleepover for the kids, but behind closed doors, things were far from perfect. The cracks would show from time to time, but we muddled through with a series of quick patches that were never going to hold.

The specifics are neither important nor very interesting. Suffice it to say some of it was Val, some of it was me, and much as we cared about each other and still do even today, our life together simply wasn't sustainable. There were miscommunications, resentments, fundamental disagreements, and on top of all that, Val had demons of her own she was wrestling with. They looked nothing like mine, but life is not the Heartbreak Olympics. Everyone has their struggles and their pain, and it's not a contest.

So, after a decade of ups and downs and giving it our best shot, we admitted it was over. I knew even then that it was for the best, but the thing about real growth is that it always hurts a little—sometimes a lot. Val and I agreed on a co-parenting strategy and remained friends, and any rancor between us died away relatively quickly. But I still felt like a failure.

There I was, a thirty-six-year-old mother of two, single again for the first time in a decade and relearning what that meant while keeping my life together. I went through a bit of a slump, but I wasn't alone. My circle of friends in Montclair was there to see me through, and Bella was never very far from my door or my heart, remaining a favorite aunt not only to Evie, but Dani as well. And for a while, things seemed like they'd be okay.

Maintaining my sobriety hadn't been an issue for me since I'd first returned to the mainland all those years ago. It feels a little obnoxious to say that, knowing what a daily struggle it is for millions of people, but that's my truth. Once I got back here with a life to rebuild and a kid to raise, I was feeling joy and connection, for the first time wanting to live my life rather than escape it.

This didn't mean that I was cured, of course. I was an addict, I am an addict, and I'll always be an addict. Addiction doesn't go away—you just have to find whatever method of starving it works for you. For me, that meant staying away from everything from hard drugs to any painkillers heavier than Advil, which is more challenging than it sounds. But as long as I stayed in that lane, I wasn't in any danger.

After my C-section, I was sent home with Dani and some painkillers, which I was reluctant to use. An addict's brain and body don't care who signs off on the prescription; a drug is still a drug, and I didn't want to have anything to do with them, but at my doctor's insistence, I compromised. I took the meds for a single day and set them aside after that. The pain leveled off more gradually than I might have liked, but I was okay and felt like I had really triumphed. I'd managed the pain on my own and soon healed, proud of myself for not falling back down the rabbit hole. Then, one day, I started to get migraines.

When a bad one hit, it became nearly impossible for me to get out of bed, but they only occurred a few times a year at most, so the problem was manageable. Who doesn't need to take a sick day here and there? My doctor prescribed Percocet, which I was understandably iffy about, but with a really bad migraine—it's hard to say no to anything that might make it go away, so I made a deal with myself. One pill per migraine, max.

In hindsight, it was reckless and even a little delusional to think that I could hold myself to something like that, but I somehow did. When a migraine hit, I'd refrain for as long as I could, then take one pill, and sleep the rest of the migraine off. When I woke up, I'd go right back to my life, making lunches and loading up my SUV for carpools, and that bottle would stay in the cabinet untouched for months. I had everything under control…kind of.

My unraveling started like it always starts. I broke my one-pill-per-migraine rule only when it was truly necessary, when I wouldn't be able to function without it. And I told myself it was necessary; I wasn't popping pills for the hell of it, for the rush. I had a life to maintain. I had kids to raise. I *needed* those pills just to tread water. It was some superbly crafted bullshit, and I bought right into it, playing this game with myself to justify just how much I was taking. I just kept telling myself I needed it. I had to remain functional for my kids. Of course I was doing it for my kids. Of course I was.

One day, I got slammed with a migraine that left me in the fetal position on my bathroom floor. The tile was cool on my face as the world fell away layer by layer. It was just me, floating in some void on a patch of tile. And then, one by one, sounds and smells started seeping back in… the subtle perfume of soap, the sound of kids playing outside…and when I rolled onto my back and opened my eyes, I was staring up at a bathroom ceiling. It was the middle of the day, and I hadn't bothered to turn on the light, and there was something about staring up at that ceiling, cool tile at my back, nothing illuminating the room but ambient daylight…

And I was suddenly flooded with fragments of some shattered memory that started drifting into place, fitting together until the cracks disappeared. And there the picture was: a day when I'd been pulled into a bathroom and silenced, brutalized as I heard the dulled laughter of my cousins beyond the window. I was back there, reliving every tight breath, every intrusion.

When it subsided and I realized I was in my own bathroom in Montclair, I picked myself up off the floor and stumbled out into the hall. As if my migraine weren't nauseating enough, the restored memory of what had happened to me that day clung to me like wet clothing, making me cringe and shiver. I couldn't think of anything else, and I lay in bed and cried, unable to sleep. I needed to make it stop and was willing to do just about anything to forget it again. Well, I had an easy out for that, one that would kill the physical pain of my migraine while it was at it, so why not? I needed this. I couldn't function if I couldn't get out of bed. And the pills helped me get out of bed…at first.

There was more at work than just the migraines. The memory that had resurfaced during that episode in the bathroom was only the first. Before I knew it, there was this kaleidoscope of fractured memories in my head…pieces that started drifting toward one another, knitting together. Dozens of fragmented pictures became clearer and clearer, filling in the gaps in my memory, things my young, forming mind had simply locked down so that I wouldn't have to deal with them. I'd known all along that I was abused, but to be confronted with just how much of it I'd forgotten, how much of it there actually was, sickened me and took its toll, each flashback re-triggering the trauma.

"Had you experienced any bouts of depression or anxiety before?" Barbara asked.

"Oh, yeah." I almost laughed. "Sometimes it comes and goes before I even know what's going on. Other times, it's a slow burn. By the time

I realize what's happening, I'm in too deep to do anything but just ride it out."

"And have any antidepressants helped at all?"

"I took Celexa for the really big depressions, the ones that pulled me down so deep I was practically catatonic. It took about three weeks to kick in, but once it did, I bounced back pretty quickly."

"And when this would happen, did you reach out to anyone?"

I nodded. "My mom, actually. She'd come over and feed the girls and check up on me."

"Did that help?"

"You'd think it would. I mean, it did help. It absolutely helped, but it also sort of made me feel worse."

It was bad enough for me to fall short as a mom, but for my own mom to swoop in, infantilize me, and show me how motherhood was "supposed to be done"—it did not feel good. I didn't want to give her the satisfaction of seeing me at my lowest and using it as evidence of my incompetence and failure as a mother, but I had no choice. I physically couldn't help it.

I told myself not to be ungrateful. A helping hand is a helping hand, and I needed the help. I just couldn't stand all the strings that came attached, and all the pain and self-loathing that came with it.

I woke up one morning with a high fever and what I thought was a migraine. I tried to take it in stride, but my body had other plans. My condition worsened so severely throughout the day that by the afternoon, I wound up in the emergency room with a splitting headache and a throat so sore and constricted I had trouble breathing. After several hours in the ER, I was diagnosed with a virus and discharged.

I went home to sleep it off but woke up the next day still burning up. I got up to splash a little cold water on my face but never made it to the bathroom. I passed out right there in the hallway. And it was not a long hallway. I was only out for a few seconds, maybe a minute, but once I came to, I knew I had to go back to the hospital.

When I turned up with a raging fever, barely able to move, they still didn't know what was wrong with me but could see I was too sick to send home. Only minutes after I was laid in a hospital bed, the pain and exhaustion knocked me right out.

I surfaced again to the sight of doctors all around me, calling my name. I was so weak and woozy I began to drift off again immediately, when a nurse grabbed my hand. A doctor shook me and told me over and over again not to close my eyes. I somehow managed to keep them open. After I was firmly conscious, the doctors said a few things that I couldn't quite make sense of and left. The nurse that had been holding my hand was still there beside me.

"Did I just…die?" I asked.

She patted my hand and tried to soothe me, but I asked again what had happened. She hesitated for a moment, then told me she had come by my room right at the tail end of what would have been my death rattle and called a code blue, saving my life.

"How did you know to check on me?"

The nurse shook her head, bewildered. "I didn't. I was making my rounds, came to the end of the hall. I usually turn right, and for some reason this time I turned left, and your room was the first one."

In the years since, I've tried not to think too hard about it, but it's never escaped me that if that nurse had made her usual right turn or had just been a few seconds later, I would have died. If that's not divine intervention, I don't know what is.

I spent five more days in the hospital with what eventually turned out to be strep and double pneumonia, which they should have caught when I'd come to the hospital the first time. It would also have been nice if they'd caught it before giving me a spinal tap on the theory that I might have meningitis. The spinal tap led to what's called a spinal headache, which is basically when the puncture site doesn't close up and starts leaking spinal fluid, which feels exactly as horrible as it sounds. It made the worst migraine I'd ever had feel like a touch of sinus pressure. The worst part is that there's not much anyone can do. You just have to wait two weeks for the hole to close up and the leak to stop. Wonderful.

I was discharged from the hospital sick, weak, and in pain, but alive. The doctors gave me more Percocet and told me to take it until the headache went away. Any resistance I might have had to the idea had been worn down to nothing.

I burned through one bottle of pills fast, then another. Before I knew it, I was taking them around the clock for two weeks, then three. I was hooked. My body wanted more. *I* wanted more.

I was so fucking furious that medical problems for which I could not avoid treatment had led me back to my vices. I had been so happy, so proud, to be clean. I didn't want any coke or crystal or anything like that. I didn't crave it. I wasn't looking for a way to get high. But then there I was, hooked again after all those years—this time on perfectly legal prescription opioids.

I'd gone seventeen years without a slip, never taking more than one pill to ease a migraine, and after just a few weeks, I was popping pills four to six times a day, every day. I knew I'd already lost control and that I was in danger. I'd stepped into this river before, and it had almost drowned me then. I wasn't going to give it another opportunity, so I found a nearby twelve-step meeting and headed over.

Most of the chairs were either occupied or had a purse or jacket on them to mark them as claimed by someone at the refreshment table grabbing some coffee or a donut. I didn't see a lot of options.

"Hey," a raspy, lowish voice called up to me. I looked over to see a tall, slender woman with an ash-blonde mullet sitting nearby. She patted the chair next to her. "This seat's free." I gave her a weak smile and sat down. "First time or first time in a while?"

"A long enough while it might as well be the first time. I'm Nikki," I said, holding out my hand.

"Hey, Nikki. I'm Cyndi." She shook my hand, and within seconds, people started sitting down so the meeting could begin.

CHAPTER 23

Breaking Down

"Seems like a good crowd," I said, standing on the curb with Cyndi as a few stragglers from the meeting passed us. "Though that one old-timer, the lady with the Bea Arthur hair…"

"Oh, Terri?" Cyndi nodded, taking a drag off her cigarette. "Yeah, she is one spicy Dorito."

"I was going to say a little intense."

"You could say that. I'd say that woman hopped a plane to Crazy and did not spring for a round-trip ticket."

We stood there, chatting for a while, Cyndi quick on the draw with one pithy one-liner after another. It was good to laugh, and she kept them coming. Laughs had been in short supply recently, so hanging out with Cyndi made a whole lot of sense—or at least appeared to. We became friends for a hot minute, then for reasons I can barely even make sense of now, we became more.

They call it thirteenth-stepping, getting involved romantically or even just sexually early on in your recovery, and it's never a good idea. I'm not going to bury the lede here. Cyndi was, on every level, a mistake. She was bad for me, she was bad for my kids, and I should have known better. A healed person would have known better. But I wasn't healed. Not enough, anyway.

I'm not going to wax poetic about how seductive she was or how I was blindsided by physical attraction, because I wasn't. Cyndi was not my type *at all,* but she was easygoing, funny, and most of all, persistent. Her humor and willingness to listen helped me see past the fact that she was a little odd and, at times, even a little off-putting. It was nice to have a friend who really got what I was going through. I loved my other friends dearly, but none of them had ever been down this road, one you really can't know unless you've walked it yourself, and I needed somebody who would get it.

I knew from the start that Cyndi was into me—the woman wasn't subtle—and it was a one-way street, but she wore me down. Trauma and abuse survivors often have issues with saying no even when we can see all the red flags. The girls weren't thrilled with Cyndi's sudden intrusion into their lives, but I figured they weren't going to be happy with my first post-divorce girlfriend, no matter who she was. I should have trusted their instincts.

Cyndi became a kind of floating radical added to the household. And when I say radical, I mean a real wild card. We had a big fight one night after she'd been acting particularly erratic and had admitted to finding my journal and flipping through it. She even started reciting things she'd read in it, just to hurt me.

"That's private. Those are my private thoughts! You can't just go reading—"

"Well, I did! And I can do it again. I'll read anything I want, anytime I want!"

I knew immediately this wasn't about jealousy or mistrust. She had no cause for either, and nothing she could have read in my journal would have given her any. This was about control, plain and simple, and it made my guts twist. The feeling of someone trying to control and exploit me was one I knew all too well.

At that moment, I knew I needed her to leave. I couldn't have Cyndi around me or my kids. I decided it was over and told her to get out. She was so angry that she went ahead and left, and I was somehow naïve enough to think that would be it, but she came back later that night, ringing the doorbell until I came to the door. I didn't need to open it to know it was her. I told her to leave, but every time I got halfway up the stairs, she rang the doorbell again. The third time, I told her that it was late, and my children were home, and if she didn't go away, I'd call the police. After that, the ringing stopped, so I finally made it upstairs and went to bed.

I couldn't even escape Cyndi in my dreams, where I heard her voice insisting she'd never leave. I opened my eyes to find her standing over me, staring down. I sat up, scrambling backward and smacking into the headboard.

"What the fuck?! How did you get in here?" I would later learn that she'd gone around back and forced open the sliding door.

"You can't just throw me away. I've been there for you. How could you be so selfish?" I didn't think I had been, but when she sat down on my bed, she looked so…vulnerable…and hurt…and I hated the idea of hurting anybody, especially those close to me. How could I? How could I be such a hypocrite? Still…

"You can't just freak out and expect everything to be cool."

She nodded. "I'm sorry about the diary thing. It was out of line."

"Yeah, it was. And a complete violation of my privacy." She just nodded. It still wasn't too late. I could still call the police and make her leave. It was the perfect reason and opportunity to sever ties with her permanently.

Instead, she moved in.

I told myself all the clichés women tell themselves when they latch onto the wrong person. *She's not always like this. Most of the time, she's fine. And what relationship doesn't have its problems?* These were just ours, and given time, they would just fade into the tapestry, part of the story of how we'd grown together and what we'd overcome. That's what love is, isn't it? Acceptance, forgiveness, and working things out together.

I swallowed that bullshit whole, and it's fair to say it disagreed with me, enough that what started as a simple upset stomach quickly became a recurring inconvenience. Pretty soon, it didn't take much to trigger a stomachache, and every one of them hit with a vengeance. Cyndi always had me on edge for one reason or another, if not with her caustic words and erratic behavior, then by pushing me to defend her to outsiders, that is to say anyone who said anything negative about her. Which was pretty much everyone.

I woke up one morning in such searing pain that I went straight to the emergency room. It was too much for me to stand any longer. I needed to know what the hell was wrong, because something had to be wrong. It had to be some kind of virus or an ulcer or *something.* Several tests and examinations later, the hospital determined that I did not, in fact, have an ulcer; I had *five* of them.

I was prescribed some pills to coat my stomach and allow the ulcers to heal, but it wasn't an issue that could resolve itself overnight. It would take weeks, at least. In the meantime, the only way I was going to be able to endure was to take something for the pain. But it was those Percocets again. All right, then. All I had to do was strictly adhere to the prescribed dosage, and I did for a while, but by the time the ulcers had healed, I'd already started playing it fast and loose with the pain meds. I ditched them while I still could, before I hit the point of no return into a full relapse.

About six months after *that,* I felt a stabbing pain in my abdomen. I found myself doubled over at least once a day, often for hours at a time. I suspected my ulcer problems had returned, but even at their worst, they'd never kept me up all night, vomiting. Back to the hospital I went, and we determined the cause of my pain: My gallbladder had to come out. With more surgery and more pain came a need for more painkillers, and with the pain seemingly constant for one reason or another and just part of my life now, so were the pills.

"It's my fucking house, Cyndi. This is my kids' home. I can't sell it."

"Well, I can't live in the same house you lived in with your ex!"

It was a bonkers proposition, and Cyndi was in no position to make demands. She'd only moved in because she'd lost her own apartment and had nowhere else to go. She'd been homeless and desperate, and now she had the nerve to insist I sell my home, *my daughters' home,* to pacify her ego? It was yet another red flag I just couldn't see, because I was already skidding, gripping the wheel tighter and tighter when I should have just bailed out. Cyndi had taken up so much space that who I was had become completely tangled up in her.

Val was already leaning toward selling the house, so we split the profits from the sale, and Cyndi and I got an apartment across town. Evie had graduated high school early, was already off at college, and could always crash at Val's place, so a second bedroom for Dani was all we needed. It was a new beginning, and new beginnings had always worked for me in the past—at least for a while.

The day before we were set to move into the new apartment, I was stricken with a sharp pain once again and ended up right back in the hospital. Tests confirmed that I had acute appendicitis that needed to be addressed immediately, so I missed moving day to have an appendectomy. The surgery solved the problem, and I recovered pretty quickly, but I was worn out. The past year had put my body through the wringer, and I was now working on a background hum of chronic exhaustion.

We say it all the time. "I'm exhausted." We mean we're tired, maybe very tired, but for most of us, it's nothing a few canceled plans and extra naps can't fix. There's "If I have to carpool to one more soccer practice, I'm going to need a nice, hot bath tonight," and then there's "My body is a shell of what it should be, and I feel like an old woman at forty-one." Take it from someone who's experienced both…they are *not* the same thing. I was falling apart, and with every surgery or medical issue, the pills were there, the devil on my shoulder tempting me to take just one more.

The incident with my journal wasn't the last time Cyndi invaded my privacy. She would read it again…and my texts and emails, anything to make sure I knew she had control over me. She didn't even bother denying it. She straight up used every morsel of information to manipulate me and to crush me by inches, declaring that not only *could* she violate me at any time, she *would*.

Everything she learned, she would throw back in my face to shame me at the perfect moment, usually during arguments, especially ones where I'd start to gain the upper hand. She would even casually repeat her discoveries around other people, as though they were common knowledge to be shared with anyone. And I was frozen. I couldn't leave. And the worse she got, the more I froze. Once again, my inability to protect myself with healthy boundaries had left me vulnerable to someone all too willing to exploit my weaknesses. She had two goals: to keep me in my place and to keep me in need of her.

My pills started vanishing even faster than I'd been going through them, and I realized Cyndi had been stealing them for her own recreation. When she came home one day with a bottle she'd obtained by some illegal means, I took a few of her pills to even the score. When both of our pills were all gone, she'd just steal my bank card to take money out for more, never even feeling the need to hide it. She was in control, and anything that was mine was really hers.

I wasn't innocent in this. I wanted the oxys just as much as she did and took my share, but there were times I *tried* to stop. I really did try, and every time I did, if I cut Cyndi off, she'd just find a way to steal from me again and bring more into the apartment.

I was struggling to hold on by my fingertips, to do whatever I could to pull myself up from the abyss I was dangling over. Cyndi faced no such struggle. She wasn't conflicted about anything, especially not using me to fund the style to which she'd become accustomed while I completely unraveled.

In the beginning, I had actually admired her grandiosity, her willingness to tell anyone off and move along completely unburdened. I didn't see her audacity for what it was. Hell, here was this woman who'd never had a kid of her own or even had to care for one, and she would sound off with such condescending certainty about what children needed and how they should be raised…like she knew the first fucking thing. As if she wasn't practically a child herself, with the emotional immaturity she displayed, always needing to be the center of attention, only concerned with her needs, her wants, her addiction.

At this point, I was high on opiates most of the time, and all Cyndi had to do was wait until I was floating to get the juiciest info out of me, stories about my trauma, practically a how-to guide on manipulating me.

She learned exactly which strings to pull until I ended up isolated and scared, powerless before her and unwilling to leave her. The abuse even turned physical on occasion, easy for Cyndi, being almost a foot taller and twice my strength, but it was the psychological torment that did the most damage.

That's not to say the pills weren't wrecking me.

I eventually decided enough was enough. I braced myself for a detox and stopped taking the pills, but Cyndi didn't and wouldn't, and as long as I was with her, it would only be a matter of time before I backslid into my disease. I realized her opioid addiction was more than just her disease; it was a weapon in her arsenal. Her pill hookups got me what I needed, but they also kept me weak, confused, and completely off my game.

I had kept on smiling to hide that everything was falling apart, and I could have reached out for help, but it was classic sunk cost fallacy: I'd invested so much in this relationship and the choices I'd made because of it, the thought of admitting how wrong I'd been was just too humiliating. I was afraid that even if I did reach out, who would even be left to help me? Cyndi had been working straight from the abuser's playbook, isolating me from family and friends—any support system that might intervene on my behalf. I'd fallen back into opioid addiction with her, while she stole from me and disappeared for days on drug binges, until my savings from the sale of the house was completely depleted.

It certainly took me long enough, but I finally realized that Cyndi did not give a single fuck about me and definitely not my kids. I was living in Hell, feeling deader and deader inside every day. The shame of failing to protect my kids from an unhealthy and unstable home was the slap in the face I needed to finally wake me up.

I was barely sober, white-knuckling it to save myself, but more to save Dani, and though Evie was no longer living with me, I was still her mother and my presence was no longer a place of safety. My own parents having failed to protect me all those years ago, I could see no greater failure in myself.

No…it was done, and I had to get out.

Cyndi, of course, refused to accept my decision. It was too much of a net loss for her. She wasn't about to let her meal ticket go, and I

Hanging out in Florida, fresh out of rehab, c. 1992.

My halfway house apartment in Florida, complete with a rescue dog (because we all needed a little rescuing) and super-classy furniture. Of course, the picture wouldn't be complete without the Gameboy and pack of menthols.

The road trip back to Rockland with Mark. We stopped off to spend the night at the house of an old Bennigan's friend, reminisced, smoked, and laughed our asses off.

Back in Rockland during the limbo between Florida and Hawaii, fresh and ready for my new life.

One of many beachside mornings. Our mopeds were just out of frame. The sign behind me was…prophetic.

A night out on the town with Deb just before everything went to hell. Johnny snapped a pic of us.

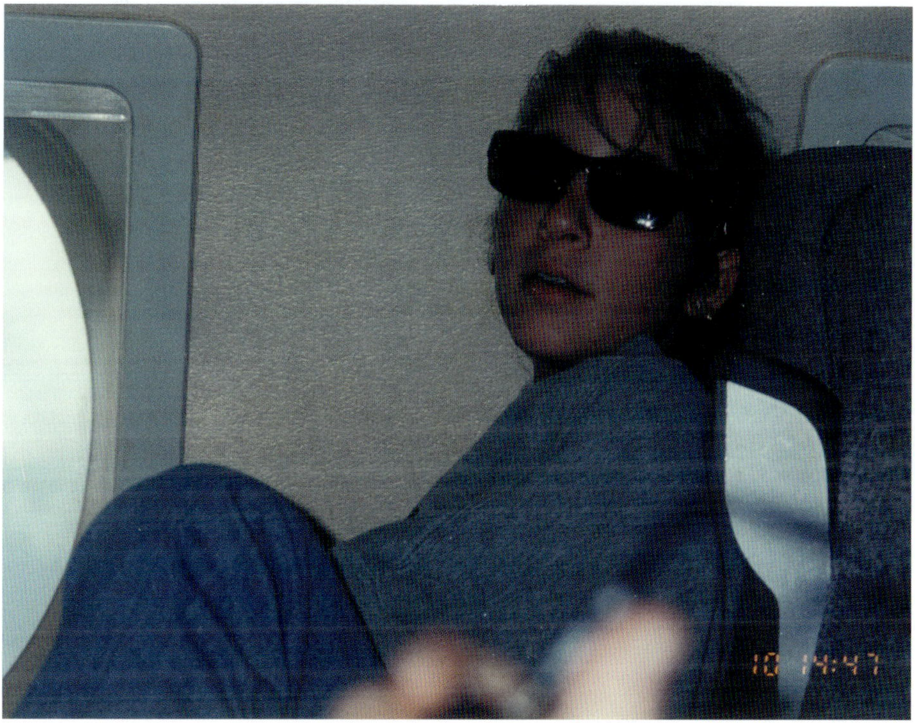

Coming down on the flight back from Maui after several days of tripping and shenanigans.

Do you have any idea how much coke I was on in this picture? Because I sure don't. But I was prepared: the water, the nasal spray, the mirror, and the straw behind that mug. There are no pictures after this, folks. It was all downhill from here.

realized that trying to end this neatly by going through channels was never going to work.

I found an apartment for me and Dani, signed the lease, and moved us out as soon as Cyndi disappeared on her next binge. My new place was the converted third floor of a large house on a central street in Montclair. There was only one bathroom, and I could live without having to go up two flights of stairs, but it did the trick and quickly became home.

There were a few loose ends to tie up, whether I liked it or not, and it meant eventually seeing Cyndi one last time. It wasn't until that final encounter that she fully realized I wasn't going to change my mind, that her last chance to manipulate me was behind her. Any sweet talk she might have used to lure me back in was futile, so the mask just dropped.

"You don't look so good," I told her. And she didn't. If she wasn't high at that particular moment, she was coming down, and it showed.

"Yeah, well, you know how it is."

"Not anymore," I said.

With nothing left to sink her claws into, she just scoffed and started off, turning back around for one last volley. "I tried to keep you sick. So you would never leave me." It was meant to hurt me, but she'd already hurt me so much worse so many times. An admission of her abuse barely even registered and didn't even merit a comeback.

Cyndi wandered right out of my life, never to be seen or heard from again, and not for a single moment have I missed her.

CHAPTER 24

Breaking Open

Rebuilding my life from scratch was a daunting task, and while I was making progress, there was still so much ahead of me. Before my relapse, I'd fit so well into the upscale life of a Montclair mom, and now I was back at square one, living on food stamps and Medicaid. It was humbling, to say the least.

I tried my best to get back into my old lifestyle, and while I was living much more humbly than I had before, I managed to cover the basics. I got Dani to her extracurriculars, made sure she got her homework done (not that she needed much of a fire lit on that front; both my girls were better students than I'd ever cared to be), and checked in with the other parents when there was something worth checking in about. I even became social again, when I had the time, energy, and spare cash to do so.

Unfortunately, it didn't make my occasional depressive episodes disappear. The shame and guilt over how I'd stumbled in the past few years weighed me down, and predictably, I did what I'd always done when confronted with pain: I ran from it. I stuffed it down and busied myself with the details of my day-to-day until I could no longer ignore it, then, once confronted with it again, I'd feel even worse. This cycle kept repeating over and over, a little less of me coming up for air every time.

I spent two years like that, in survival mode, until I couldn't pretend any longer that I was doing fine. I wasn't fine. I had been completely worn down physically and mentally. I was tired of hurting, but I was even more tired of running, which never spared me in the end and was just as exhausting. My life had been hijacked by my trauma and my issues for forty-five years, and it was time. I needed help.

My available options and my medical coverage overlapped at a low-income mental health clinic. And that's how I found myself sitting across from Barbara in a no-frills office with stock seating and fluorescent lights, surrounded by people who dedicated their lives to healing those who had nothing to give. And no, I wasn't sitting on a comfy couch decked out with pillows, but that doesn't matter. I wasn't there for the scented candles. I was there to get better.

It took Barbara the first few months just to burrow past my flippant accounts of my childhood, things I'd always dismissed as normal family crap. Barbara impressed upon me that they were anything but normal. They were well outside the healthy range of familial quirks and conflicts, and the gaslighting used to normalize them and turn the blame for the discord in my family around on me was just another trauma added to the pile.

I'd been through hell in my life—several kinds of hell. I'd been raped, terrorized, pressured into smiling through it, shamed when I couldn't, and then further shamed for coping in whatever ways remained. Worst of all, I'd been manipulated into taking the blame for all of it.

"So, tell me," Barbara said softly, "was there ever a time growing up that you felt safe?"

What a weird question, I thought. Of course there had been. There had to have been. But as I thought about it, peeling away year after year, going further and further back, I kept coming up short. When was the last time I'd felt truly safe?

"There was this one time I was at a friend's house. I don't even remember her name. I was pretty small—five, maybe six—and I was walking through the living room and saw her mom sitting in a chair. And I don't know what possessed me, but I walked over to her, climbed into her lap, and put my head down on her chest. She held me tight in both arms, and I was just frozen there. I didn't want it to end." I shook my head. "Which is just…what was wrong with me, just climbing into some stranger's lap?"

"Nothing," Barbara said. "Love and safety are basic human needs, and with everything that was happening to you, how were you supposed to look to your parents for safety? You were drowning, you saw a lifeline, and you reached for it. You did nothing wrong."

I still had my doubts, convinced there had to be something I could have done differently, been smarter about. There had to be some way this was, underneath all the excuses, my fault. Whatever it was, it was always my fault. Always.

"I still don't see how that explains fucking my life up at every turn."

"Every adult in your life had either hurt you, left you, or failed you. It was too much."

"So, what, that was just the green light to do all kinds of drugs?"

"Nikki…thank God you did drugs. Thank God. Because you know what? The pain would have destroyed and probably killed you. Those drugs saved your life."

Well…that was certainly a fresh perspective. I could see what she meant, though. I'd been burned raw. Every time I'd been ignored or silenced, every time I'd been made to believe it was my fault, it was like my family had thrown acid on me, then demanded to know why I was burning. They poured fucking acid on me, and the drugs had been the balm that soothed my burns.

I'd carried so much shame for so many things: for being abused, for being the family fuckup, for being a junkie and a whore and a criminal… but mostly for building a good life only to burn it all down. I'd let my girls down so fucking hard. Could they ever forgive me? For that matter, did I have any right to expect them to?

Barbara was right. All the pain I'd been carrying around my whole life would have killed me, either by way of suicide or enough self-destruction to yield the same result. The drugs had numbed the pain here and there, but only temporarily and just enough to keep me going. They would also have killed me eventually, but they had been killing me a lot slower. If it was just death by narcotics versus death by pain, what other option had ever really existed?

The more trauma Barbara and I unearthed, the more the picture came into focus, the harder I found it to concentrate on anything, and sleep became next to impossible. It came in short stretches, only a few hours at a time, when it came at all. I would go days sometimes without so much as a nap, and I spent all that time haunted by every negative feeling my progress in therapy had been stirring up, my ability to cope already eroded by my exhaustion.

Without sleep to partition one day from the next, they all started to bleed together. Was it Monday? Thursday? Saturday? Did it even matter? Every memory brought with it more pain, and without any coke, meth, or pills to kill it this time around, all I could do was feel it. It was healthier in theory, but with a lifetime's worth of repressed distress hitting me all at once, I felt like I could barely stand some days. I couldn't tell if I was more exhausted physically or emotionally, and I wasn't sure what the difference even was anymore.

I walked into Barbara's office one day, completely depleted. Memories were returning more frequently, full-on flashbacks as well sometimes, and between the horror of recalling my experiences and resurgent pain of occasionally reliving them, I was growing overwhelmed.

"Nikki, we have to slow down," Barbara said before I could even make small talk. "It's all coming at you too fast. We need to give you time to process all this." So, we did, but it only put a delay on the inevitable. Once that train had left the station, it just kept picking up speed.

The chilly March air still had that bite of early spring, and everything smelled like rain and grass. I took it all in, fresh, damp, and cold…and I felt nothing. Absolutely nothing.

I was weaving in and out of awareness. Not consciousness, just awareness, and at one point I surfaced to find myself at the train tracks in Montclair. There were a few people around, but I wasn't paying any more attention to them than they were to me. We were just all there, existing in that space at that moment. I looked at them and wondered what it must be like to walk around without all the pain. Not a complete absence of it, obviously; I wasn't so deep inside my own head to think that I was the only person in the world with problems. Everyone goes through things, has their ongoing struggles and issues, their own open-ended stories, and I knew that. But to not go through every moment of every day under the weight of your memories, to not have them constantly welling back up, scalding your insides…what was that like?

How much longer can I keep doing this? How much longer? I'm so tired.

I realized then that my arrival at the train tracks had not been random wandering. Even while I was checked out, some part of me had led me there. It was so overpowering, so absolute; through everything, this was what I wanted deep down. Maybe there was a reason for that. I'd done my best, and maybe it was just time to call it a wash and do myself a favor—do *everyone* the favor—of calling the game and removing myself from the field of play before I could fuck it all up again.

Drugs hadn't worked. Having two children hadn't worked. Building a perfect suburban life hadn't worked. Nothing I had done to outrun my pain had ever worked in the long term. It always caught up to me eventually, and now it had once again, so what really was left? The last time I'd felt this way, holding a gun to my own head as I looked into that shattered mirror, I couldn't go through with it…but I was pretty sure I could now. I thought of Paul standing on the stairs that day with a belt around his neck, all of ten years old and saying with full sincerity, "I don't want to be alive anymore." And what I couldn't understand then, I finally did.

One well-timed step forward was all it would take. It was a relief almost. I could hear the train's horn in the distance, and then…

My head jerked down at my phone ringing in my pocket. I pulled it out to see an incoming call from Dani.

"Mom, are you coming to get me?"

"Uh…" That's right. I'd said I'd drive her to an appointment. "Yeah, of course. I'll be right there."

I stepped away from the tracks, then held there for a minute, collecting myself before I drove home to pick Dani up. I put on a smile and powered through her appointment, not even a single hint on my face of what I'd almost done. Once I was home and settled, I left Barbara a voicemail. We had an appointment later that day, but I couldn't chance waiting that long. When she called me back, "I'm trying to not kill myself," was all I could mumble into the phone.

She paused for a moment, then said, "I have some time now. Why don't you just come in?" I was too depressed to see what difference a few hours would make, but I headed over.

Barbara sat with me in her office for as long as it took. At one point, her supervisor joined us, and we talked for some time, enough for them to properly assess the situation and insist I go to the hospital.

"No, I'm fine. I'm not going to go to the hospital. I'll be okay."

Undeterred, Barbara said, "Nikki, you've done a really good job of staying alive, but I'm going to help you now," and then she called Crisis Support Services. Seeing me onto that ambulance would have fulfilled her professional obligation, but she got right in and rode with me. "We'll go together," she told me, and even then, I still doubted, but she kept her word.

When we arrived at the emergency room (the medical ER, which is the obligatory first stop), Barbara never left my side. She made sure I was treated with the care and respect I needed, patiently explaining every step of the process and why it was necessary. It was a courtesy I wouldn't have been afforded without her there.

It's shameful how different the psych ER is from its medical counterpart: bare cement walls, bright lights, even the air was harsher—cold and stale. There are reasons, of course, why the rooms have to be spare and a little sterile. This is psych; the safety of the patients and the staff has to be taken into account, and you can't have anything around that might be repurposed as a weapon, but there has to be a way to ensure that without the place being so cold and scary. The comfort of some warmer tones and softer lighting would not be a hazard, is all I'm saying. And cement walls? Come on. Explain to me how some Sheetrock is a danger to anyone.

I was ushered into a small, sterile room, given paper scrubs to change into and a cup to pee in for a drug test, which I'm proud to report came back 100 percent clean. I'd been sober for some time, and the urinalysis proved it.

I sat on the end of the bed for what felt like forever, Barbara a few feet away in a metal chair. She'd already spent much of the day with me but showed no signs of restlessness. She just sat there, and we talked for hours about everything. Once I started, I couldn't stop, aside from sporadic moments of silence where I simply hurt too much and words failed.

Whenever I seemed to be falling deeper and deeper into that dark well, Barbara pulled me back to the present by turning the conversation to idle small talk. It worked, and I realized as I opened up to her that I'd been holding her at arm's length for months. Even with all the stories I'd told and details I'd given, I hadn't really touched on what had been lying behind it all—the shame, pain, and humiliation. I couldn't admit that I needed real help, but now? Well…

Doctors and nurses had wandered in and out the entire time, checking up on me and jotting down their observations, but in the midst of all these people, there was only one I could trust. The conversation reached a lull, and the room was quiet for a long beat, and then out of nowhere, I murmured, "I don't want you to leave."

"I know," Barbara whispered back. It was so sincere. She wasn't placating or pitying me. She was just so fully *present* with me. In that moment, she'd done what no one else had, what I'd needed all along.

She'd met me in my pain.

There we'd been, in the thick of all my darkness, and she hadn't turned away once. She didn't even flinch.

About an hour later, as she was leaving, she turned back at the door and paused. I could tell she wanted to say something, but there was nothing left to say. It didn't matter, though. Whatever she was thinking, whatever she was feeling, it was all over her face. Just seeing that she cared, *truly* cared, changed something in me. It was subtle but immediate. I wanted to thank her, but I couldn't speak either. Even then I understood how much boundaries mattered, and she'd been riding the line with me all day. She had to take care of herself, and now that she knew I was safe, I had to take the next steps on my own.

My first morning in the psych ward, I awoke to the sound of someone screaming down the hall. When I opened the door to my room, I could finally make out some words. A woman was ranting at the nurses. She was old, old enough that the onset of dementia didn't seem unnatural. Unfortunate, but not unnatural.

"The fuck?" I whispered. A fellow patient strolling past glanced at me, then back at the struggling woman, as if it was the first time he'd noticed the commotion.

"That's just Helen. You'll tune her out after a while," he said, then moved right on. Tune her out? I couldn't imagine how that would be possible. Did I really belong here in a place where the rantings of an unhinged old lady were the kind of thing you just overlooked after a while? Then I remembered that I'd nearly killed myself less than twenty-four hours ago, and perhaps I wasn't in the best position to be judging anyone's mental health.

I saw Helen later in the day room, a common area where the patients spent most of our time, mumbling to herself. She approached me, not even looking at me and seeming like she was about to sweep right past when she held out her hand. Not knowing what else to do, I took it and walked the halls with her for what turned out to be hours. She tried to open doors leading to other areas of the hospital as we passed, but being a lockdown unit, they didn't budge. After long enough, she got frustrated and wandered away from me.

Well, I thought, *that was weird.* And it was. And yet, I took more walks around the ward with Helen, and she'd always try to escape, every time as disappointed as the first.

"How about you sneak around and open the door for me?" she asked me once with a crafty smile, briefly lucid and very aware of what she was saying. I can't say I wasn't tempted to try, but I knew it was fruitless and wouldn't be for the best even if there was a chance of success. But somewhere just beneath whatever good sense I had, I kind of wished she'd find a way to pull one over on the staff and sneak out, if only because it would be hilarious and because she wanted it so badly.

Helen had no idea she was in a lockdown unit or even that she was trying to escape. She just wanted to go where she wanted to go and was frustrated that she couldn't. I knew she had dementia, but it never came up in conversation. Why would it? So, I'd just walk with her and talk as if she were lucid, and we'd laugh. I guess for all that the dementia was ravaging her mind, our walks had struck some kind of chord, because she recognized me well enough to come over to the tables in the day room when I was hanging with other patients and talk to us.

Aside from Helen, I mostly kept to myself that first day or two. It wasn't the first time I'd been penned up in a psychiatric facility with a bunch of strangers, but the sort of community you build in rehab…it didn't come as easily to me now. I'd been a teenager then, impressionable and groping for the kind of meaning and connection that I now had. I wasn't really in a place, emotionally speaking, to be forging new friendships. At least I didn't think so.

On my second day, I saw a nurse pushing a cart of meal trays down the hall and recognized her as one of the bunch Helen had been screaming at the day before.

"Need a hand with those…" I eyed her security badge. "Melinda?"

I don't know why I offered. I was probably just desperate for something to do. Melinda must have picked up on that, and she'd been around the block enough times to know that any ulterior motive I may have had was harmless.

"Uhh…sure. Thanks," she said. I followed her into the day room and helped pass the trays out.

"So…Helen. She's got spunk for her age."

"For any age. Every day she tries to get out. Lord only knows where she thinks she's going."

I liked Melinda and got along with the other nurses almost as well. I'm sure it helped that I was often there to lend a hand whenever theirs were full. I handed out meals and distributed handouts for group therapy sessions. I hadn't really set out to become an unofficial adjunct to the nursing staff, but it gave me a distraction. If I could be of use, I couldn't be that far gone, could I?

"There's a music appreciation group this afternoon," Melinda told me one morning. I cringed as subtly as I could and came up with a few flimsy excuses not to join in, but Melinda poked a hole in every one of them, so an hour or so later, there I was in the day room, grabbing an instrument and attempting to play it.

As I looked around the room, I was struck by the complete absurdity of it all. You know your life has taken a sharp left turn when you find yourself shaking a tambourine during a psych patient sing-along while some woman in a shawl plays "I Will Always Love You" on an acoustic guitar.

I finally started getting to know the other patients, not just observe them from afar. We were all suffering, trying to cope. We came together in groups, at mealtimes, playing cards, shuffling through the halls, and we would laugh. Even when there was nothing to really laugh about, we could end up belly-laughing hard enough to rip a hole right through our paper scrubs.

In particular, I think of Louis, the guy I'd met my first day who'd told me who Helen was. Louis was around my age, maybe a little older, and I never learned exactly why he was in the psych unit, but I remember his sadness and the tiny spark of joy that shined through his regret when he talked about his kids.

"As dads go, I haven't been…they deserve better," he told me one day over a game of Go Fish. "And it might be too late, maybe it is, but if there's a chance…" He trailed off, his eyes roaming all over the room. "I hate this place. I feel like I've been here too long, but…it's my kids. Whatever it takes, right?"

I couldn't disagree.

In the end, my stay in the psych unit lasted a week. The day before I left, I learned that Helen was being transferred to another facility. There was no way I was letting her slip out without a little fanfare. As it turned out, she was better regarded by our fellow patients than I had realized. A bunch of us stood there at the exit as the orderlies wheeled her out on a stretcher. Melinda unlocked the automatic doors, the same ones Helen had tried to escape through so many times. The orderlies wheeled her past us, and we clapped and cheered, "Helen, they opened for you! You made it! You're getting out!" She had the biggest damn grin on her face. She was free!

That night, Melinda came into my room. "I'm off tomorrow," she said, "so I won't be there when you check out. Thought I'd come and say goodbye now." Then she came in for a hug. I hugged her back.

"You going to run this place without me?" I asked, knowing full well helping Melinda had been far more to my benefit than hers. And she knew it too.

"I'll manage," she said, then sighed, gave me a tight squeeze, and whispered, "I wish you could see what the rest of us see." She patted my back, then let me go and looked right at me. "You're going to be okay," she said. Then she smiled and left.

I'd moved past my suicidal thoughts. I wanted to live, in part for myself but mostly for my daughters. I know we're supposed to put our own life-jackets on first, but self-preservation wasn't my top priority. My girls, one of them in high school, the other fresh out of college, needed their mom, and I owed it to them to be there, but I didn't know how to get there. I didn't know how I could fix everything I'd broken.

As a mother, all I'd wanted was to protect my own children from experiencing their own pain and trauma, including whatever dysfunction my family had been passing from parent to child, especially mother to daughter, generation after generation. I'd wanted so badly for it to end with me, and it hadn't. Despite all I'd done right, I hadn't healed myself, and the pain of all my psychic wounds had oozed out onto my kids.

I was now faced with the toughest choice yet. Would I continue to ignore my wounds like I had my whole life, like my mother had, or would I face my darkness and stare it down? Given some thought, the choice turned out not to be that tough after all.

As soon as I left the hospital, I resumed my sessions with Barbara, willing if not quite ready to dive in and accept whatever harsh truths awaited me. I knew she'd be honest. I could rely on her for that, and if there was anyone who could confirm I was as crazy as I'd been told I was my whole life, she could do it gently, kindly.

"Crazy?" she said when I asked her. "You're not crazy, Nikki. You have PTSD."

CHAPTER 25

Breaking Good

I flinched, confused.

"PTSD? As in…"

"Post-traumatic stress disorder."

I eyed her suspiciously, not quite buying it. I wasn't a combat veteran. I hadn't been buried alive in a collapsed building. *Those* were traumas. I'd just had some really bad luck, a few sad stories. I tried to tell Barbara as much, but she was unfazed.

"There are all kinds of trauma, Nikki, and your mind and body don't know the difference. You didn't literally grow up in a war zone, but neurologically, you might as well have."

She broke it all down for me: how the initial traumas had been compounded by how they'd been handled in the aftermath. Being forced repeatedly to socialize with Jacob and his family so the three sisters could hurry back to their family picnics and acoustic strumming as though nothing had happened had erased me by inches. For years, *decades*, I'd been force-fed a steady diet of everyone else's willful ignorance of the rot festering inside me. They were all content, so any problem was mine and mine alone. Why couldn't I just accept their reality, the happiness and grooviness and wholesome good times? Why couldn't I just go with that flow, go along with the narrative everyone else had agreed upon?

My wounds reopened every time I was confronted with those people and had to witness my mother's affection for them. Every time, I was reminded that I was an acceptable sacrifice to keep the good times rolling. Sure, they had addressed the issue, but only in the most cursory, self-serving ways—just enough to reassure themselves they'd done their due diligence and could put it out of their minds…except, of course, when I so thoughtlessly reminded them.

And my dad? He'd had no hand in any of that, but only on account of his glaring absence, and how at home could I have ever really felt in his house, where he lived with the woman he'd taken back even after she'd terrorized and attacked me? Which, while we're talking about trauma… holy fucking shit…

I stepped back and looked at my life, forty-something years of hanging on by the skin of my teeth even when I was surrounded by organic groceries and top-grade water pressure, always just one fuck-up away from ending up back at square one. How had I ever made it *this* far?

"I never had a chance," I said softly.

"No…but you do now. Nikki, I really want you to hear me right now." Barbara leaned in and waited until she had my eyes. "There is no other way your life was going to go. You experienced *a lot* of trauma as a child. Too much. Your whole life has been a response to that trauma, and everything you've done since then, every skewed instinct you've followed, every bad turn you've taken…you were set up to fail. There's nothing to be ashamed of. You're not to blame." Barbara paused to let it all sink it, then said, "You're going to get better, but it's going to take work. And it's going to take time."

I looked at her and nodded. I wanted a chance, just one more chance to get it right. I wanted it more than I'd ever wanted anything.

My breakthrough in Barbara's office had been cathartic, but it didn't solve everything. It had only been the first step of a long, involved journey. I'd beaten the rug, kicking up a cloud of crap I was now choking on. Talk about a game of bad carpet.

Over the following months, a picture slowly began to form. It was like this Rubik's Cube of images sorting itself out, a solid picture always just a twist or two away but never quite complete. In the chaos of it, though, I saw just enough to start putting it all together. Suddenly, several seemingly isolated incidents began forming a pattern of something I was only now learning the name of: gaslighting.

What my mother had begun in my childhood, blaming me for destroying my family's peace, had continued into my adulthood with all the concerns about the welfare of my children, how well they were fed and bathed, my overall fitness as a mother. Then and now, my self-esteem and mental health had been sacrificed to maintain her delusion that she'd been this selfless, all-sacrificing mother who'd never made any mistakes beyond the pettiest, most trivial offenses. And it had been killing me inside.

That session in Barbara's office had chipped enough of the wall away to let a trickle of water through, but now the dam had burst, and that trickle was a raging current. What exactly had happened to me? How had it happened? Had I really been gang-raped as a child over and over? Had my family really thrown me to the wolves, leaving me to tend to the rotting cancer of neglect and self-blame for my own abuse? Had I really been strung out, selling my body for my next meal or next high, always hungry and scared? Had that been me?

As my past became clearer in the months that followed, I began to not just remember but *relive* those moments I'd so carefully hidden behind that wall. And every time I did, more and more details returned, and with them a fresh swell of shame, fear, panic…and grief. Grief for the innocent girl I never really got to be, grief for a life that had been stolen from me, crawled beneath my skin and kept me awake at night to the point beyond exhaustion.

I was certain I was going nuts, and I asked Barbara time and again if I was crazy. After a brief reminder that she didn't care for that word, she would assure me that no, I was quite sane: in pain and at times struggling to cope…but sane.

At one point, I asked her what she saw when she looked at me. Even after everything she'd done for me, how clearly she'd shown she cared, I still assumed she looked at me and saw some fucked-up failure, ruined beyond any hope.

She took a moment to look at me and take in the view. I didn't expect her to give it that much thought, but after a long pause, she nodded to me, eyes fixed on mine.

In a low, steady voice, she said, "I look at you and think, 'How are you alive? How did you make it? How did you learn to function in society? How did you learn how to establish and maintain friendships? Relationships? How did you learn to love your children? How?' You shouldn't be able to do any of that." She nodded, eyes distant for a moment as she thought about it. "Most people who have been through the things you have don't survive physically *or* mentally, but you did. That's what I think when I look at you."

My dad had been married and divorced three times, the last time over thirty years ago. For someone who'd jumped into marriage so eagerly and often, he was horribly suited to it. Marriage requires too much compromise, too much obligation, for someone practically allergic to responsibility…or rather, accountability. Some people really need to just do their own thing without ever having to answer to anyone, and that's a personality as good as any other but not one well-suited to partnership or, if we're going to be honest, fatherhood.

For most of my adult life, my dad has never lived more than thirty minutes away in good traffic and he's got my number, so we catch up on the phone sometimes, grab lunch, shoot the shit. The conversation is pretty limited but at least it's familiar.

"So, your mother calls me, saying, 'We need to do something about the kids and this and this and that.' And I'm thinking, 'We? There's been no *we* since 1981. They're adults! You've got a problem, it's your problem! You talk to them.' I don't know what she…" He grunted on the other end of the line. "I tell you, she's just…she's just so controlling! You know, it's no wonder you kids've…"

He didn't finish, and for some reason—why this time and no other, I couldn't tell you—I didn't let it go.

"Why we've what?"

"You know…you've all had a rough time. You've been through a lot. You've got your issues. You know."

"What, and you think you had nothing to do with that?"

"Whaddya talking about?" he demanded, his voice jumping an octave, as though he'd never heard anything so ridiculous.

"Dad…if Mom was so off the wall, who was supposed to shield us from that or at least step in from time to time to take the edge off? Okay, you got divorced. Parents get divorced. Dads move out. It happens. But it's like Paul and I left Christine's house that night, and you just let us go, and that was it. I went months, a year or more, without ever even seeing you. So, yes, Mom was kind of nuts and yes, it took its toll, but if you were so concerned for our welfare, where were you in that picture?"

Much to my surprise, I wasn't yelling. I wasn't even angry enough to yell; I was simply done mincing words. He tried to offer some explanation, some flimsy excuse about how Paul and I had been teenagers and hadn't wanted to spend time with him, but he knew it was bullshit and knew I knew it, and the conversation died pretty quickly after that.

I got a text from him a few days later, asking if he could come by. I was running errands all day, but he insisted he didn't have any plans and didn't mind riding shotgun if I didn't mind having him. We spent most of the day in silence, listening to music. "Hotel California" came on at one point, and knowing my dad's abiding love for the Eagles, I couldn't help but smile as he sang off-key.

Whatever his faults, the man had always been uncomplicated. What you saw was what you got: a simple guy who just wanted to chill and sing along to his favorite band. So, he did, and I let him, sometimes even joining in, and we continued on like that until, after several hours of semi-awkward silence, he finally spoke up.

"You know, I…I had to get out of there. It was just so weird, that whole scene. Regina, Harvey, all those people. It was a cult. I didn't know about…you know…the other stuff. I just knew I couldn't stand them."

I must have been gripping the wheel pretty hard. My hands hurt when I let go. "So, you figured…what? Just peace out? Leave us in all that?"

"I thought they were weird, not dangerous. And your mother was a pain in my ass, but she kept a clean house, she put food on the table—she got shit done. You were surrounded by teachers and therapists, people who are supposed to be good with kids." He shook his head, unable to even look at me, and I could see something heavy in his eyes. "I left. And it was selfish. I'm not saying it wasn't, but…I thought you'd be okay. I really did. And I was wrong." He still couldn't look at me. "I'm sorry."

It didn't change the fact that we *hadn't* been safe, that if not for this gross miscalculation, we might have been spared many of the physical and psychological horrors we'd suffered. It didn't change anything that had happened, but I could at least understand. Thinking you're doing right by your kids and being dead wrong…that I got.

He apologized again, and I accepted it and thanked him for everything he'd said. I think that day I forgave him. Maybe not completely—I don't know if that will ever be possible—but enough to move past it. Just hearing him acknowledge how badly his choices had hurt me, taking some accountability for them…it didn't make that wound disappear, but it allowed it to finally close and scar.

It turns out accountability was all I'd ever really wanted: to have my pain acknowledged and my trauma recognized for what it was. I'd spent so much of my life fighting to have my experiences not be minimized or dismissed or even denied altogether, but I hadn't realized how much of an empty place it would fill to just have them acknowledged without being sped through or glossed over.

I was never going to have the close, trusting relationship with my dad you can only establish in your formative years, but we could now have something honest, if a little offbeat. I could work with that. I was never going to get a do-over, and neither were my parents, but true, sincere accountability could go a long way toward healing whatever we could.

It made me wonder what else might be possible, but I wasn't ready to broach that topic with my mother just yet. I doubted she was ready either, so I decided it could wait.

When has my life ever gone according to plan?

"I just wasn't comfortable with the situation," Mom said offhand as she buzzed around her condo, tending to three different things at once, a quality that has always mystified me. Most mothers have no choice but to multitask, but I've never seen anyone do it so effortlessly.

The "situation" she was referring to was a social engagement hosted by company she didn't care for. She hadn't felt welcome and had decided to skip the event, fully expecting Gene to fall in line. When he didn't, she didn't take it well.

"Can you believe he went?" she said, bustling about.

"I mean, given the occasion, I don't really blame him."

She stared at me, mouth agape. It was that "shove the knife in a little deeper" look that there's just no arguing with. She pursed her lips and poised herself in a way I recognized all too well. She was about to lay a "teaching moment" on me to explain something I'd *clearly* failed to understand, rocking my world and making me reconsider my whole perspective. That was the fantasy, anyway. It never quite worked out that way for her.

"Let me ask you something, then. How would you feel if someone you loved didn't protect you?"

The question hit me like a truck, and my brain just jammed while I found the words to respond.

"Are you serious?" There wasn't even any attitude in it the first time I asked. "Are you serious with this? You're actually asking me that? *Me?*"

It took her a second, but the point hit home. She scoffed as if I couldn't have said anything more absurd. "That was different."

"You're damn right it was different. You were *my mother.* And however you feel right now, it does not compare!"

She went back to putzing around the place, scowling at how sharp a turn the conversation had taken in such an unexpected and unwanted direction. I could see her struggling with it, hearing me but really wishing she hadn't.

"I didn't know! And when I did, I put a stop to it. I did the best I could!"

"The best you could? Making me be *anywhere near* the guy who violated me over and over again? That was the best you could?!"

"I thought you were okay with it!"

"Okay with what? I was a child!"

"You accepted his apology!"

"Because you fucking made me! Why would that even occur to you? How did you not want to put a million fucking miles between us forever?!"

She frowned. "It was a complicated situation."

"No. It was hard for you because Regina was your best friend and losing her would have broken your heart, and I get that. But how was it even a question?" I took a deep breath to try and release whatever negative energy I could. It didn't work.

My mom shook her head, summoning all the patience she had. My God…she was actually *frustrated* with me, with this petty grudge I was holding.

"Are you ever going to forgive me for this? Ever?" she asked.

I wanted to so badly, but something kept me from granting her that last bit of grace. And then I realized what it was.

"I probably would have a long time ago if you could just own up to it. No excuses. No rewriting history so that you can live with it. Just own it."

More silence, then she went back into worker-bee mode, and I had nothing left to say. Then, in a casual voice, as if the last two minutes hadn't happened, she said, "I cut up some watermelon. Do you want to take some home?"

No, Mom. I don't want your fucking watermelon.

I turned to her, ready to spew some venom, and then I saw her face. There was no animosity there, no guilt, no tension. It was as if the conversation had never happened.

I shook my head and headed for the door. I had one foot over the threshold when she caught up to me. "What do you want me to do?" she asked.

"I don't know. I need some space." She looked so hurt, so wounded, like she knew what I was saying but still couldn't quite grasp why I was saying it. "I've got some healing to do. Do you understand what I'm saying?"

"I'm trying," she said, and it broke my heart, because I think, as much as she could, she *was* trying…but she still didn't get it. It opposed her entire way of thinking. She'd spent her whole life running from her mistakes and her pain, indignantly refusing to "focus on the negative," but what she really wanted was to deny it even existed, to scrub it from the picture so that picture could remain bright and wholesome and good. The pain was too ugly, too messy, too…well, painful. The saddest part of it all is that if she'd only faced the pain, been brave enough to walk straight into it instead of trying to ignore it, she would have found everything she was looking for on the other side. Everything.

Pain is like grief. There's no way around it; the only way through it…is *through* it. You can delay it, of course, but that doesn't make it go away. It just dams up the stream, and should that dam break, you can be washed away.

My mother was willing to take that chance for the rest of her life. I wasn't. I couldn't. I had to face the truth about myself, however much it hurt, and it was not fun. It was incredibly not fun, but I got my answers and the first glimmer of hope and inner peace by finally understanding the difference between fault and responsibility.

All the thoughts and patterns baked into me, that had steered me toward all those bad decisions, were not my fault. But I'd still made those choices and done those things, and now that I knew better, healing my trauma and whatever damage I'd left in my wake…that was my responsibility. And whether or not I'd ever receive the accountability and willingness to change I needed from my parents, I could at least give it to my children.

I spoke to Evie and Dani individually. Healing isn't a one-size-fits-all kind of deal. Every relationship is different and requires different things, but the important part was the same. I told them both I loved them more than anything, but it didn't mean I never fucked up, and I'd fucked up big time. I'd done my best, but sometimes my best wasn't good enough, and for the things I'd said, done, or hadn't done that had hurt them, I was sorry.

They both tried to brush it off and assure me it was okay, but it wasn't okay, and I wasn't about to let either of them comfort me at their own expense. Neither conversation could be finished in one day. Even with the best intentions, it would be impossible to cover everything. You leave things out that don't occur to you until later, and you don't always get things right with one try. Touch-ups and reminders would be necessary, but we could at least begin.

I asked them if they were hurting. If so, how and why, and what did they need from me to make it right? They took it easy on me at first—remarkable considering the green light I'd given them to sound off, no holds barred—but I insisted they not worry about my feelings. Whatever they needed to say, I needed to hear, however hard it might be, and I needed them to know I was hearing it.

I'd love to tell you that we lived happily ever after, that one conversation set everything right, but that's just not reality. We solved a few problems, we're still working on a few more, and new ones always spring up. That's just life. But I'm okay with that, and I think, for the most part, so are they.

And as for myself, I still had plenty of my own healing to do, plenty to process, in whatever form that took.

I went no-contact with my mother for nearly two years. We didn't speak, we didn't text, and I passed on family gatherings just to avoid getting backed into a conversation I wasn't ready to have. Then, taking all the risks and probabilities into account, I decided to attend a cousin's wedding, knowing she would likely approach me, which, of course, she did.

She started with how much she missed me, segueing quickly into how hurt she was, blaming me for why we weren't close. Years ago, I would have been furious, taken the bait, and gone off on her, playing the part in her script of the irrational, unreasonable child. Not this time.

I led her off to the side to sit down and talk, telling her plainly that the reason we weren't close was because she'd hurt me, and every time I'd tried to work it out, she either doubled down on her innocence or tossed me an empty apology, which she'd walk back once I'd made it comfortable enough for her to push my boundaries again. I'd played the game her way over and over since I was a child and simply would not be doing it anymore.

I got nothing out of playing her game, but I was getting quite a bit out of therapy, of processing my trauma and my feelings. I'd processed much of it through writing it all down, and on the advice of a few people close to me, I'd realized that sharing my story, everything I'd been through and learned, might be healing not only for me but maybe others as well. I didn't expect her to be happy or supportive of this, and she wasn't, but it was the last we spoke of the matter for a long time. I agreed to some light communication to be taken at a pace I was comfortable with, and she still overstepped but noticeably less than she otherwise would have. She was at least trying to respect my wishes.

Then, after several months, Paul and Michael informed me that Mom had been asking questions, pumping them for information about the book. They defended me and my right to tell my story while trying to assure her that neither the writing of the book nor the book itself was about hurting her. In fact, it wasn't about her at all.

I didn't owe her any explanations and was certain that she wouldn't be happy with any offered, but could I just let her twist indefinitely, wondering for months, maybe years, what my book would reveal about her deepest shame and starkest failures? I certainly didn't owe her any peace of mind, but could I leave her like that? No.

I sat quietly in my living room for a good, long while before I picked up the phone and called my mother. After an awkward minute of beating around the bush, I cut to the point.

"I need to be seen, Mom. I deserve to be seen and heard," I said. "You and Dad, Aunt Sally, Nonny, the fucking Beckmanns, everyone that abused me…you all hurt me *so terribly*, and no one seemed to notice. I was in so much pain, and none of you cared until it inconvenienced you. I struggled with it all on my own, and you guys did that.

"And I know you and Dad think this is all just revenge, that I'm just trying to hurt you back, but that's not why I'm doing this. I don't want to hurt you. I don't want to hurt anyone, and I'm struggling with the fact that it probably will. I just hope you can understand that this is about healing me, not hurting you."

She was quiet for a long time, then at last she said, "If this is what you have to do to heal and be okay…then do it. I won't do anything to get in the way. I won't try to stop you."

"Okay. Thanks," I said, surprised. Then, before I hung up…

"I really thought…" I braced for one last excuse, one last dodge, and then after a long pause, she whispered, "I'm sorry."

It didn't change the past. Nothing ever can. But for once, my mom wasn't trying to make it okay, wasn't hyping some silver lining to my violation and trauma, and wasn't making any excuses. And that was enough.

This book obviously isn't the answer to all my problems, the one-and-done elixir that healed me from the inside out, but it was a good start. It got the ball rolling—a few, actually. And that was the most important thing: to heal myself not just for my own sake but so that I could become the person I needed to be to do the work I had left to do.

There were patterns, behaviors, and anxieties I'd passed right on to my girls despite my best efforts. There were choices I'd made that had hurt and scarred them. And they had to live with that damage. However…

It wasn't too late to halt that process in its tracks, stop the infection from spreading any further, and possibly even reverse it. Together, we could heal. We could heal each other and purge the poison. The damage could never be undone, but now there's hope that if we love each other right, if we trust and do right by each other, we can break the cycle, and their children might never know it.

Wouldn't that be something?

I spent so long beating myself up, feeling that even at my best, my kindest, my most generous, there was something inherently wrong with me, something dark that could never be good. I'd never understood that everything screwed up about me was a result of what had been done to me. I hadn't been born wrong, I'd been *done* wrong, most often by the people I trusted, and this is where it had led me. But now, whether or not the fault had been mine, the responsibility to change the entire architecture of my life was mine. Breaking unhealthy patterns and making healthy choices…that was up to me. With a sizable amount of dread, I realized what the first step on that journey was, and it was only the first on one long fucking road.

But I could breathe a little. I could feel some small relief because I finally got it. I understood that I wasn't a bad seed or defective or any of that. Knowing that, I could start the process of healing. So, Barbara and I started from there, pulling apart, breaking down, and picking up all of the broken pieces of who I was in order to painstakingly put them back together, and I realized that all of it—the missteps, the relapses, the hospitals, the depression—had brought me to the point where I could either repeat the cycle all over again or do the fucking work. I chose the work.

And I put it all down. The fighting, the pain, the solo journey down my lonely road. I put it all down, and I let go.

I'd always been a runner, and in my running, I'd needed plenty of courage to survive, but it turned out the bravest thing I could have ever done was to stop running and stand in my pain, to let it burn through me. Only then could I be healed and whole. And I'm not done, not by a long shot. I'm doing the work, and it's going to take time.

When you've been through trauma, when it's ruled you for so long, there comes a breaking and a breaking open. One takes everything from you, the other takes everything you've got. Believe me, I know.

I've made a lot of mistakes in my life and caused a lot of damage, and I'm still making it up to my kids. And I'm still making it up to myself. It's taken me a lot of patience and determination (and even more therapy) to get me this far.

Redemption is rarely a straight line. You choose poorly, you backslide, you make fresh new mistakes while fixing the old ones. It's a process, one that doesn't work if you keep running from your demons, and what a runner I was. But you have to eventually stop, turn around, and stare those demons down. And if you can do that with enough honesty and a halfway decent sense of humor, you've got a shot.

As of the writing of this book, my relationship with my parents is, shall we say, a work in progress, as is the rest of my life. I live in a two-bedroom apartment with an uneven floor on the third story of someone else's house. Quite a step down from owning my own home, but I love my little "treehouse." It's cozy and Zen, and the view through the trees of the neighborhood below is damn near Rockwellian. The community I've cultivated is filled with kind, loving, and loyal friends. My checking account is…sufficient. Most of the time.

As for my depression and anxiety? I handle them pretty well, all things considered. It helps having two funny, whip-smart daughters to keep me grounded. We may not be the picture-perfect family I tried so hard to make us when they were little, but there's love there, we know how to hard laugh until it hurts, and our car karaoke game is on point. And when the painful stuff comes up, we talk about it.

My life overall is more or less held together with dental floss and Scotch tape, but I make it work. I'm still striving to be the best version of myself I can be, and though it's difficult at times to be proud of that, I manage. I just take a breath, look in the mirror until I can see that lost, damaged girl…and I cut that bitch a break. Because she deserves it.

We all do.

ACKNOWLEDGMENTS

Committing your life story to paper is no easy task for a number of logistic and personal reasons, and there are so many people without whose love, advice, and encouragement this book would not have been possible.

First and foremost, I have to thank my agent, Richard Abate, who believed in me and my story from the jump and didn't rest until he found it the perfect home. You promised you'd be with me all the way, and here we are. My heartfelt thanks to Gretchen Young at Regalo Press for taking a chance on an unknown, and to my amazing team at Regalo, Madeline Sturgeon, Caitlin Burdette, Kate Harris, Rachel Paul, Clayton Ferrell, and Mary Cantor. I must also sing the praises of Ashleigh Renard, social media and marketing specialist extraordinaire, for her valuable expertise.

Thanks to my dear friend Amy Friedman, who has championed not just this project but me personally from day one, and to Larry Smith, whose guidance in crafting my book proposal has proven invaluable. That proposal would not have been what it was without the statistical research of Conor Dugan and the astute editorial eye of Lisa Romeo.

Thanks to Melissa Schaffer and Elissa Siegel for many encouraging porch talks and for getting the ball rolling when I didn't know where to begin, and to Geoff Shandler, who took time out of his busy schedule to read my proposal and open all the doors for me he could. For reading every word of every draft and offering endless encouragement and constructive criticism, Mary Kalazan. Jessica Henry, Madelana Ferrara, and Evelyn Gonzalez for your absolutely priceless feedback. Special shout out to the Lazarus Sisters, Jenny, Robbie, and Lisa, and to Marty Finkelstein, for all your support.

To my Bennigan's crew, you made me who I am today, and I love you all with all my heart. Those were the times to remember. To my "four top," Crescent Maaz, Jacquie Ruderman, and Jill Raleigh, for catching me and being my soft landing always. To Beth Egyed for getting me to write the first line. Gette Zacharias, for carrying me when I couldn't take another step. Kathleen Fitzgerald, for keeping it real always and for yours and Dan's limitless generosity. Pamela Saffer, for her endless talks and home-cooked meals. Martha Holmes, whose warmth and wit kept me rolling on the floor even through the toughest of times. To Dan and Sharon Castelli, my first friends after my dive into suburban motherhood, thank you for your brilliant artistry and your friendship. And Katie Rogers, who is always there, no judgments, no explanations.

Extra-special thanks to Val for being the best co-parent an ex could ask for, and to Bella for being my ride or die since '94.

I can't give enough credit to my therapist, Barbara Brownsword. There are no words to describe how you've shown up for me time and again. Thank you for meeting me in my pain and never flinching. In every conceivable way, I wouldn't be here without you.

Last but by no means least, my deepest thanks to my brother Michael for the crash course in narrative structure, helping me organize a mountain of anecdotes into the story of my life, and for always, *always* picking up the phone.

ABOUT THE AUTHOR

Author photo by David Plakke Media NYC 2025

Nikki Mammano grew up in the greater New York metro area and spent her early twenties in Hawaii before moving back to the Northeast, earning her BA in Communications from Ramapo College, and settling in Montclair, New Jersey to raise her daughters.